IMAGES of America

WESTON COUNTY

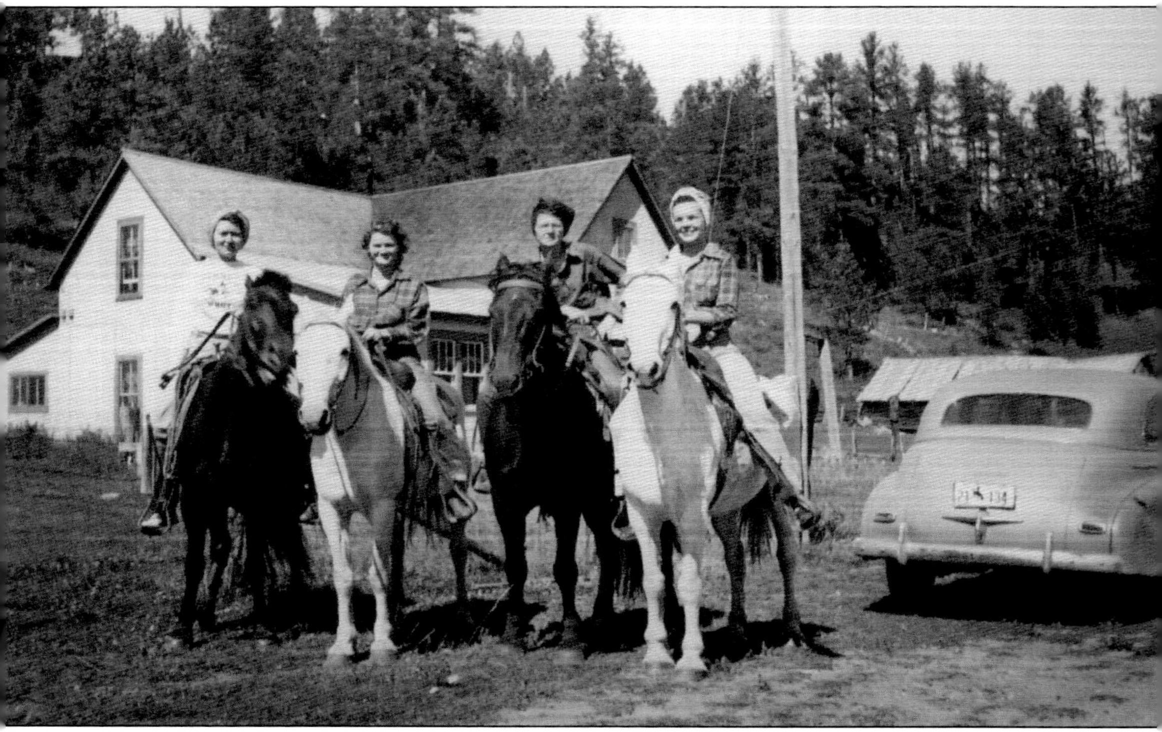

ON THE COVER: WESTON COUNTY COWGIRLS. From left to right, Ruth Christensen, Mae Darlington Christensen, Elsie Christensen, and Marguerite Butterfield are shown on the day before Ruth left for St. Louis. (Courtesy of Earl and Mae Christensen.)

IMAGES
of America

WESTON COUNTY

Shelly Ritthaler and Mike Jording

ARCADIA
PUBLISHING

ISBN 978-0-7385-9544-3

Published by Arcadia Publishing
Charleston, South Carolina

Printed in the United States of America

Library of Congress Control Number: 2011944361

For all general information, please contact Arcadia Publishing:
Telephone 843-853-2070
Fax 843-853-0044
E-mail sales@arcadiapublishing.com
For customer service and orders:
Toll-Free 1-888-313-2665

Visit us on the Internet at www.arcadiapublishing.com

Contents

Acknowledgments

In part, the content of this book, including both the images and the text, reflects a history of Weston County that has been previously documented in other volumes of research and publications. The authors acknowledge that, while some of the images and stories have been previously published, others have not.

The authors wish to acknowledge those persons who have contributed historic images or text for publication. They include Alice Schuette, Barbara Barritt, Bobbi Jo Stith, Shirley Demerrit, Jim Dixon, Dave Paulley, and the families of Earl and Mae Christensen, Tom and Judy Mitich, Al and Edel Smith, William Townsend, and Leo Perino.

Museums and their staffs have contributed significantly to this project. The Anna Miller Museum in Newcastle, the Red Onion Museum in Upton, and the West Texas Trail Museum in Moorcroft assisted the authors in photograph collection and scanning, text content, and the opportunity to use images of museum displays. Also thanks to Wyoming State Archives, Department of State Parks and Cultural Resources, for the use of images from their photographic collection.

Additionally, technical photographic and scanning expertise from Anthony Wilkening has allowed this project to be completed professionally.

The authors also wish to acknowledge the Weston County Historical Society for accepting the responsibility to work on this project for the betterment of Weston County history and the preservation of the history of some of Weston County's families and businesses.

The authors would also like to recognize the First State Bank of Newcastle for its financial contribution to allow the project to have funds to pay for technical equipment and services.

Last of all, the authors wish to acknowledge the support and assistance of our families. The interest in Wyoming history instilled in us by our parents, the encouragement and patience of our spouses and children, and the financial help from our families has allowed this project to be completed.

Unless otherwise indicated, the images in this volume appear courtesy of an agreement between Alice Schuette, project director of the publication of *Weston County, Wyoming: The First 100 Years*, and the Weston County Historical Society. That agreement has produced an electronic file of 650 photographs of Weston County.

Other specific images in this volume appear courtesy of Alice Schuette (AS); the Anna Miller Museum (AMM); *Dance Halls of Weston County* (DH), by Mike Jording; the Oelkers Collection (OC); Earl and Mae Christensen (EMC); and the Wyoming Annual Narrative Report Weston County Extension Work in Agriculture and Home Economics (WCEW).

INTRODUCTION

In many ways, Weston County is similar to surrounding counties in Wyoming and South Dakota. Its history predates man's arrival by nearly 70 million years and records the presence of large bodies of water, sea-based animals, and dinosaurs. The plains of Wyoming, once very rich in aquatic life, now bear the remains of the past residents. Weston County residents live in the richness of this past, but few appreciate the significance and value of the million-year artifacts. While paleontologists and historians agree on the presence of earlier inhabitants, sometimes there is controversy dating their existence.

Like other areas of Wyoming, the Dakotas, and surrounding states, the area's first human inhabitants were perhaps in this region 6,000 years ago. Cultural information from rock art and arrowheads gives evidence of the first human inhabitants. Lives focused on the natural landscape, and the nomadic Native Americans spent their time as hunters and food gatherers. Native Americans' lives were intertwined with the laws of nature. Valuable evidence of their existence is left across the area in the form of petroglyphs and pictographs, stone circles, and the tools and weapons of the people. These cultural artifacts are the interest of anthropologists and archaeologists.

The last of the Native Americans to live freely in the region were the Sioux and Arapaho in the 1800s. The first white men to come to the area were explorers searching for adventure and an experience that could not be had in a more civilized setting. People searching for a better life and the riches that nature might provide followed them. First, a discovery of gold in the Black Hills sparked a wave of people to Weston County and the surrounding hills. Trails and roads were followed by railroads, which brought even more people to explore and live in the Black Hills and the surrounding areas.

Then, coal and oil became mining interests that supported another wave of people searching for a better life. Independent and hardworking people came to Weston County to stake their claims to jobs or mineral interests that could make them rich. The story of a young man's venture into the mining business was repeated over and over. After he proved to be successful in his work, his family or friends from the East Coast or overseas joined him.

The vast lands also supported livestock interests, which encouraged people to go out into unknown, and often dangerous, lands. Large cattle barons occupied the lands early on, and cattle roamed freely over the large expanses of grasslands. As smaller entrepreneurs moved to the area to raise cattle, sheep, or horses, conflicts arose between the cattle barons and squatters, as the smaller landowners were called. The story repeated itself over much of Wyoming and the West.

The federal government encouraged settlement of the new lands, even though it had promised some of the lands to Native Americans through treaties. Agreements were made between the white man and Native Americans. However, the appetite of the white man for new land vastly overshadowed the abilities of the Native Americans to keep the white man from coming. In the end, large numbers of people came to occupy the regions of Northeastern Wyoming, and the Native Americans were removed to reservations in Wyoming, South Dakota, and other states.

By the late 1800s and early 1900s, people were homesteading the lands of the West, and Weston County was not left out of the grab for free land and the potential for a better life. Men came alone or with their families; sometimes, women would venture to the new lands alone. They left the confines of a more civilized life and set their sites on establishing a life on the plains or forested lands of the new territory or state. It was often a land that seemed barren and harsh compared to what they left. However, many left hardships in the East and were ready for the challenges bestowed upon them by the competition for survival. The lives of those early residents reflect those strengths and values that helped the people succeed in the difficult years of early homesteading. Many did succeed and became permanent residents of Weston County. Others found the toils of life in Weston County too challenging and moved on, leaving traces of their passage. For some of those who left, their paths in life have led them back to Weston County for another trial at life in the rural county.

Those persons and families who stayed or returned became the leaders of their communities. Upton, Osage, and Newcastle supported schools and churches, businesses, and trades, and people moved to each of the Weston County communities. Some communities all but disappeared after their residents died or moved on. Cambria thrived for 40 years, and Clareton, Thornton, Morrissey, and Soda Butte supported rural communities. While some people chose to live in communities, other people chose to remain on ranches or farms and live a more agricultural life. However, many of those people built businesses to serve others and to improve the living conditions of the time. They built roads, constructed buildings, hired entertainment or made it themselves, and built schools and churches, all to add value to their lives. People flourished, and population numbers indicate that Weston County was a popular location to live.

Generations of people and the businesses they represent have left their marks. Visitors have come and gone, like Walter P. Jenney, Deloss Tubbs, and Theodore Roosevelt. Names like J.C. Spencer, Peter Kinney, and Frank Mondell were prominent in Newcastle's early history. George Upton and John Nefsy were prominent names in Upton and Osage, but their importance, like those early-day people of Newcastle, exists only in history today. Those people and the buildings they built vanished as new people moved into Weston County. Generations of new people attained prominence. There were Gladys and Roscoe Michaels and Bill and Virginia Klodt of Newcastle, Kathrine "Kitty" O'Connell Moats of Osage, and William and Emma Oelkers of Upton. But they, too, passed on, leaving family histories or stories in history books. Interesting names like Podlaszewski, Trosello, Bozanich, Pedulla, Hansen, and Jonasson dot Weston County history and give significance to the immigrant families from Europe. In this book, Weston County's history is portrayed through its people and places, buildings and families, and cities and communities.

Historians and genealogists find great pleasure in recording, researching, and preserving the lives of those Weston County people, businesses, and buildings. We hope that you enjoy this window into Weston County's history.

One

The Gateway to the Black Hills

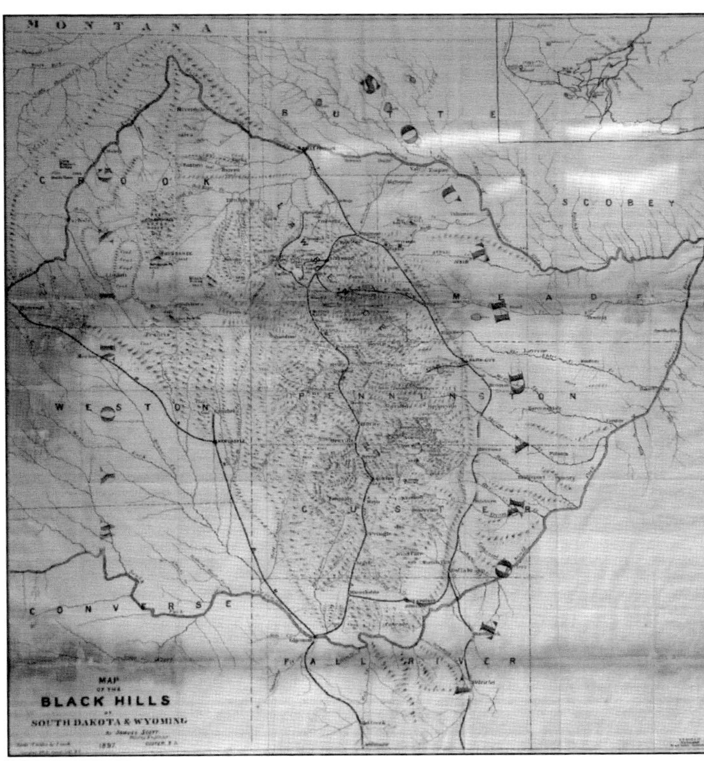

Map of Weston County. In Northeastern Wyoming, Weston County is tucked next to the South Dakota border in the foothills of the Black Hills. Over time, Weston County has been described as the following three things: a gateway to the Black Hills, a byway for many people and industries going from one place to another, and lastly, a home to those who built houses and businesses and made a way of life.

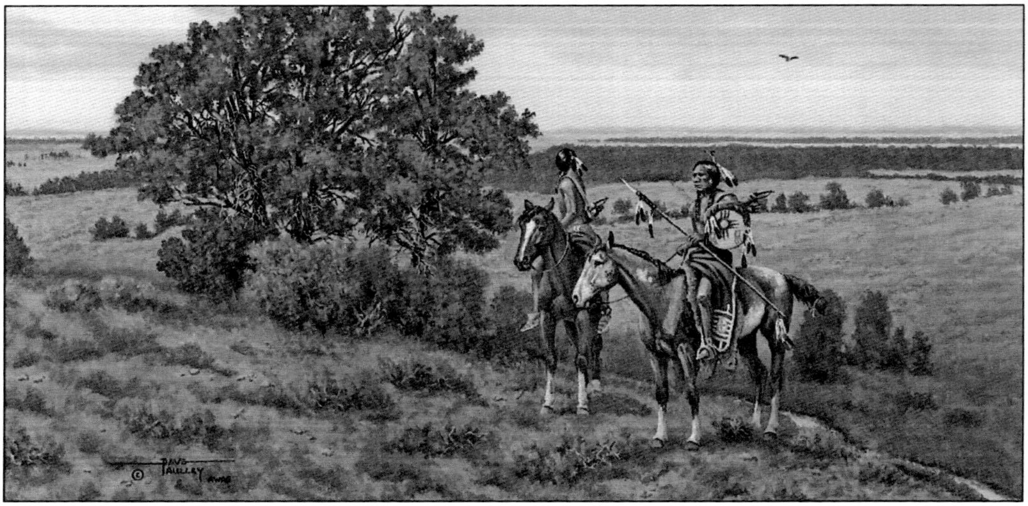

On Lookout. In the beginning, different tribes of Native Americans called the lands of Weston County home. In the early 1800s, the Sioux and Arapaho tribes gained control of the Black Hills and the surrounding hunting grounds, which included the future Weston County. But trappers, traders, missionaries, explorers, and gold-seekers caught wind of rumored gold in the hills. All of them increasingly and illegally infiltrated the area. (Painting by Dave Paulley.)

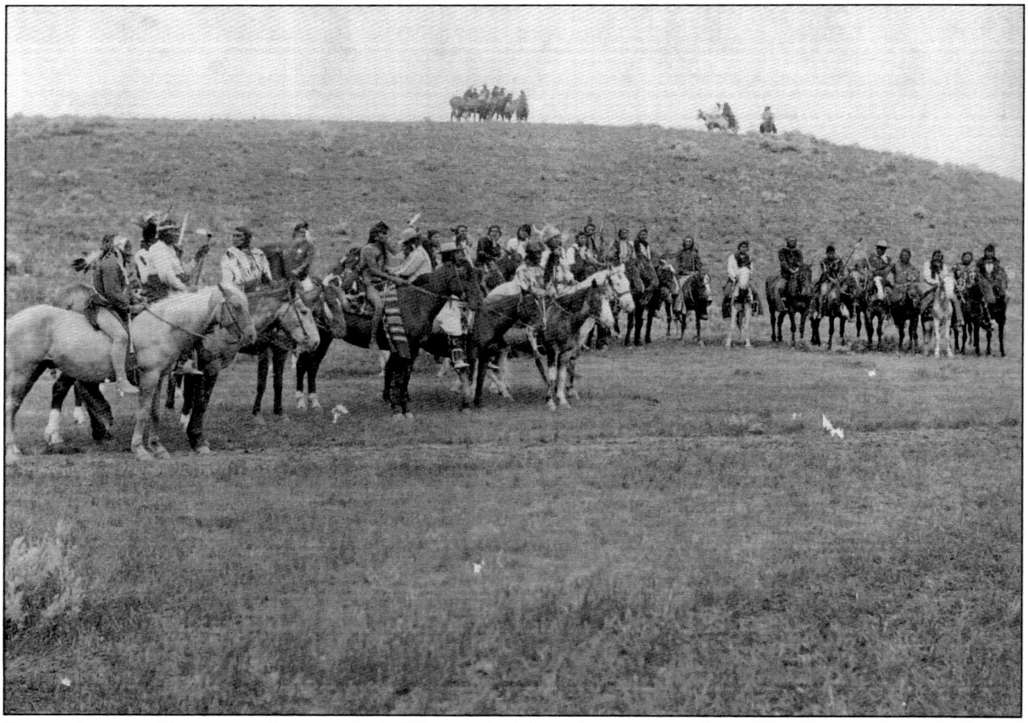

Sioux Indian Hunting Party. In 1857, Lt. G.K. Harding set out from Fort Laramie to map and explore the Black Hills. He was also looking for proof to support the rumors about there being gold in the Black Hills. Harding met a hostile hunting party of Sioux Indians. They threatened him to the point that he and his men left the hills and returned to Fort Laramie.

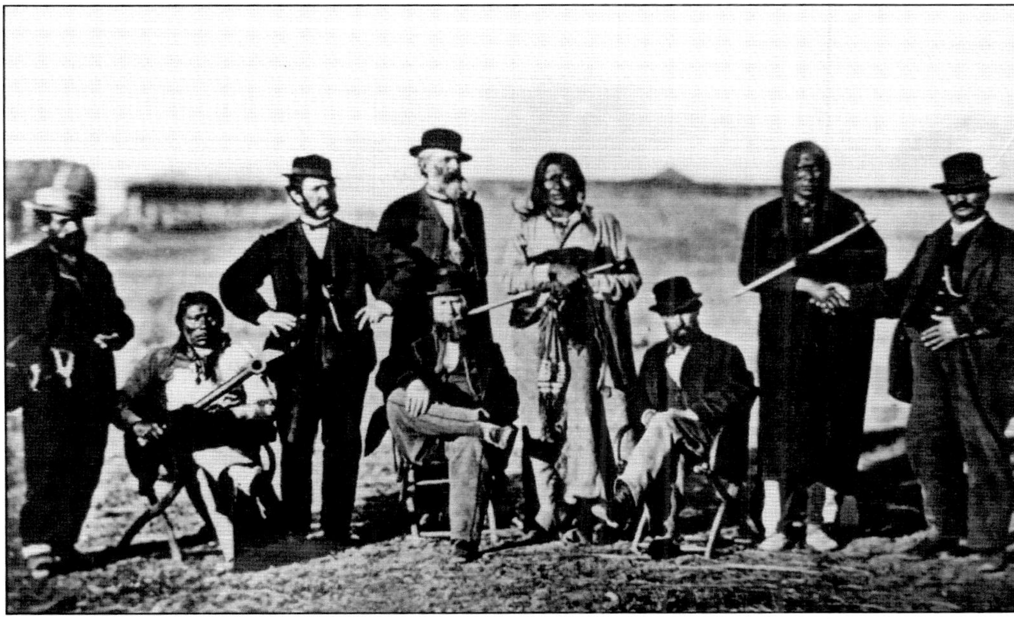

TREATY SIGNING AT FORT LARAMIE. By the 1860s, continued intrusions created explosive tensions between the white people and the Indian people. In April 1868, the most famous of all Indian treaties was signed at Fort Laramie. It gave the Black Hills to the Sioux and Arapaho Indian Nations. The government told all others to keep out. The land that is now Weston County was relinquished as Indian territory for hunting grounds. Shown are treaty commissioners at Fort Laramie in 1868.

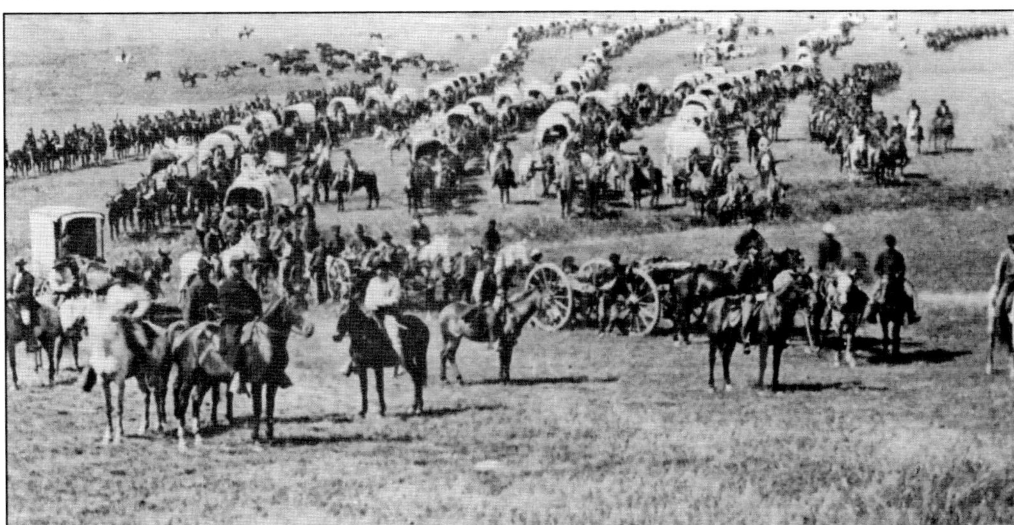

BLACK HILLS EXPEDITION PARTY OF 1874. The beautiful land of the Black Hills was a magnet that beckoned anyone seeking opportunities. The federal government sent explorers to the hills, and in 1874, an expedition led by Lt. Col. George Armstrong Custer came to the hills and Weston County. When the soldiers found gold in the Black Hills, rumors turned into undisputed truth. This impacted the lives of the Native Americans ever since. Shown is the Black Hills expedition of 1874. (Courtesy of Wyoming State Archives, Department of State Parks and Cultural Resources.)

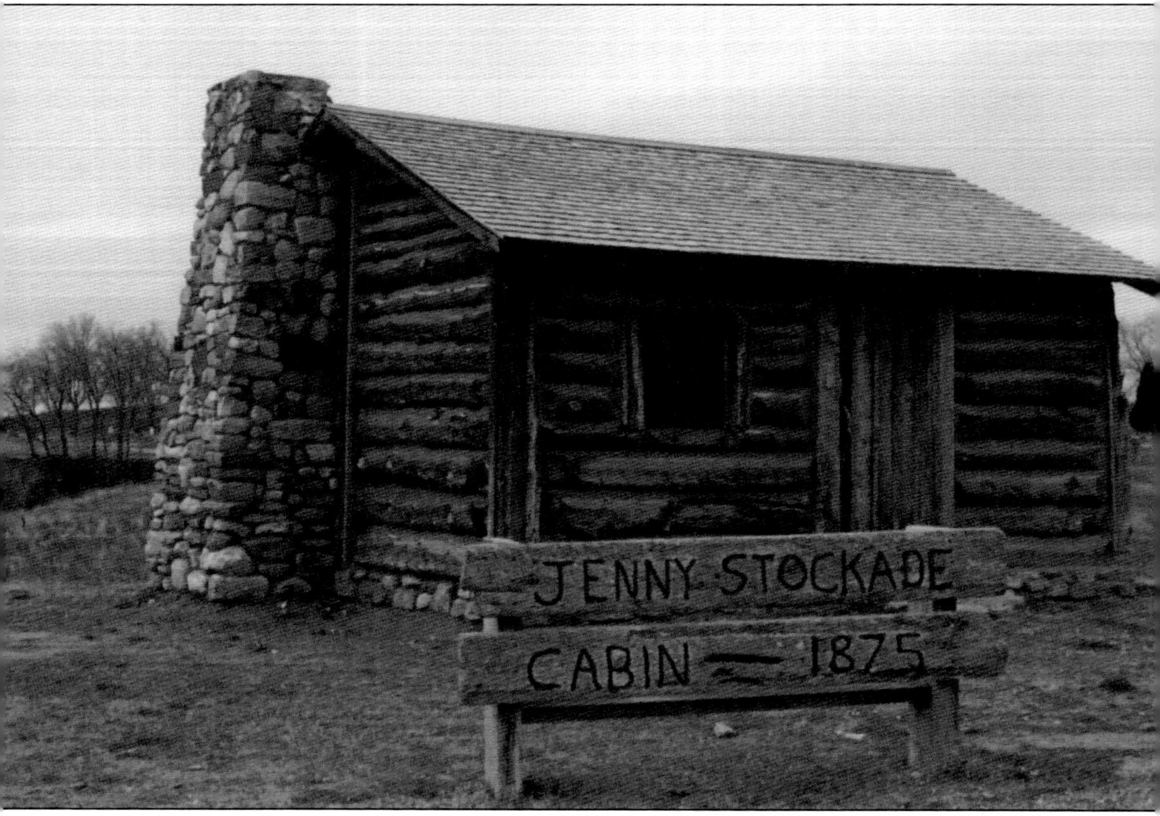

Jenney Stockade. In 1875, under orders from the secretary of the interior, Walter P. Jenney left Fort Laramie with a huge entourage. Their job was to map the Black Hills region and verify claims of gold. When they arrived at Beaver Creek, what is now known as Stockade Beaver Creek in Weston County, they made camp and began construction on a stockade. When it was finished, the Jenney party completed its explorations. Jenney found hundreds of trespassing miners and prospectors. The army had tried to keep them out, but it was an exercise in futility. Jenney's final report to the commissioner of Indian affairs was that, although there were already miners in the hills, "the yield of gold is small and the richness of the gravel has been greatly exaggerated. The prospect, at present, is not such as to warrant extensive operations in mining."

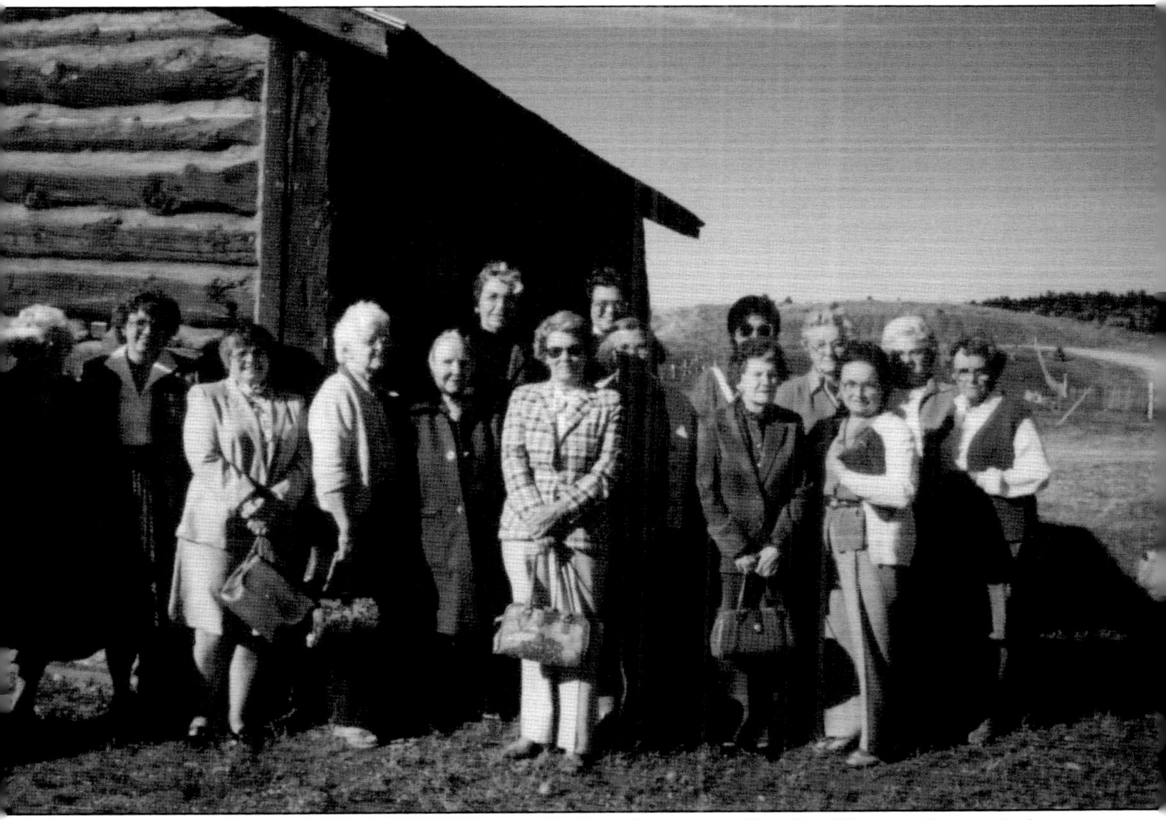

Weston County's First Building. This stockade cabin is unofficially Weston County's first building. Built under the supervision of Walter Jenney, this cabin served as a stockade, stage station hostelry, ranch house, storehouse, barn, office for the Newcastle Chamber of Commerce, and finally as a historical building in its lifetime. The Twentieth Century Club saved the Jenney Stockade cabin from destruction in 1928 and 1980. In 1928, the Newcastle Twentieth Century Club encouraged other groups, such as the Inyan Kara Chapters of Daughters of the American Revolution, to participate in the restoration project. It has been restored and is now located at the Anna Miller Museum in Newcastle, Wyoming. The picture shows members of the 1980 Twentieth Century Club at Jenney Stockade Museum; from left to right are (first row) Vera Cooper, Elma Brown, Lucille Dumbrill, Pat Lane, Marian Cleworth, Helen Oliver, Doris Voss, Janice Whitley, Ruth Graham, and Ann Marten; (second row) Liz Field, Bethel Smith, Ruth Spence, Erma Thoeming, Doris Engle, and Mabel Brown.

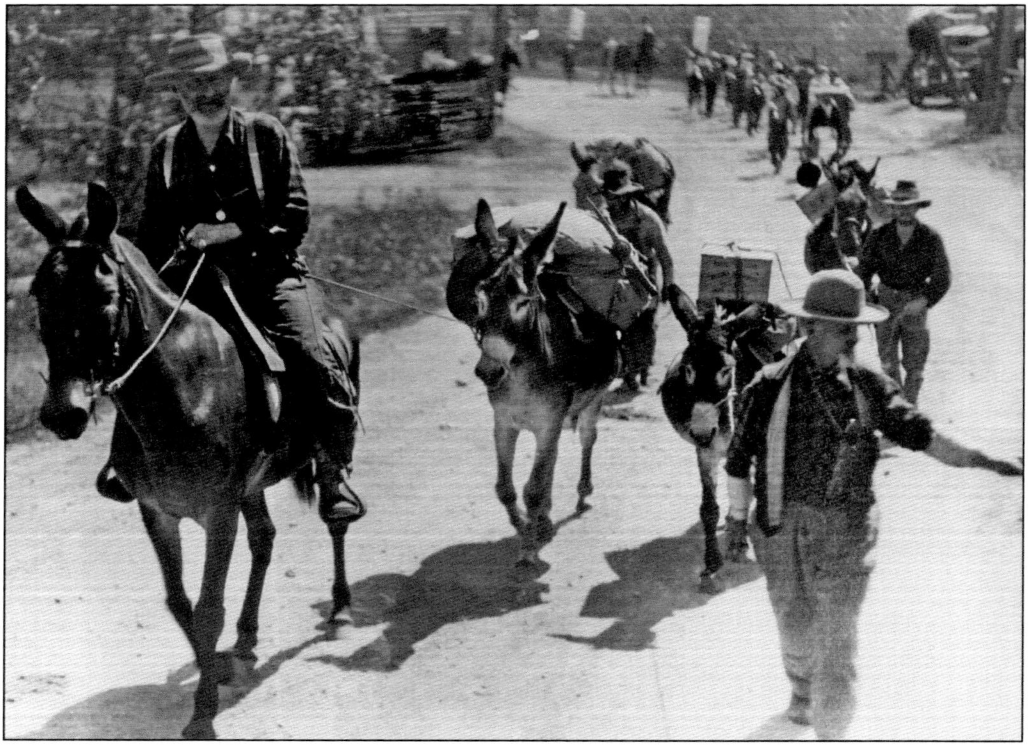

Gold in the Hills. Jenney's negative report should have dispelled rumors of "gold in 'them' hills," but it fell on deaf ears. At that time, the nation was experiencing an economic depression. For a poor and depressed people, the smallest hope of a way out can lead to great expectations. The Black Hills were seen as a means to return prosperity to a depressed country. The government was under increased pressure to secure the Black Hills from the Indian nations. Newspaper headlines intensified the pressure. This resulted in several negations, skirmishes, and battles with the Indians. Shown are prospectors in Deadwood, South Dakota.

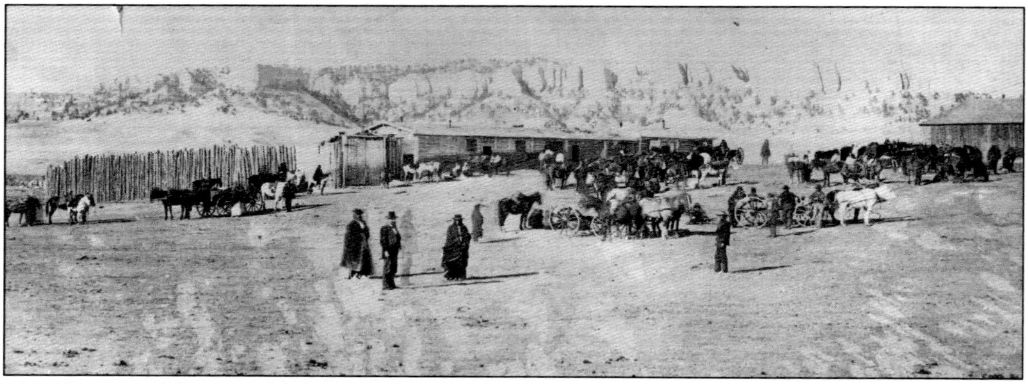

1876 Treaty. After horrible battles, the white man and Native Americans were ready to negotiate. A meeting was held at the Red Cloud Agency in September 1876. The Indian chiefs made moving protest speeches, but in the end, they had no choice—the Indians relinquished all lands, which included present-day Weston County, on October 27, 1876. The Black Hills and surrounding lands were officially opened for settlement. Shown is the Red Cloud Agency trading post in January 1876.

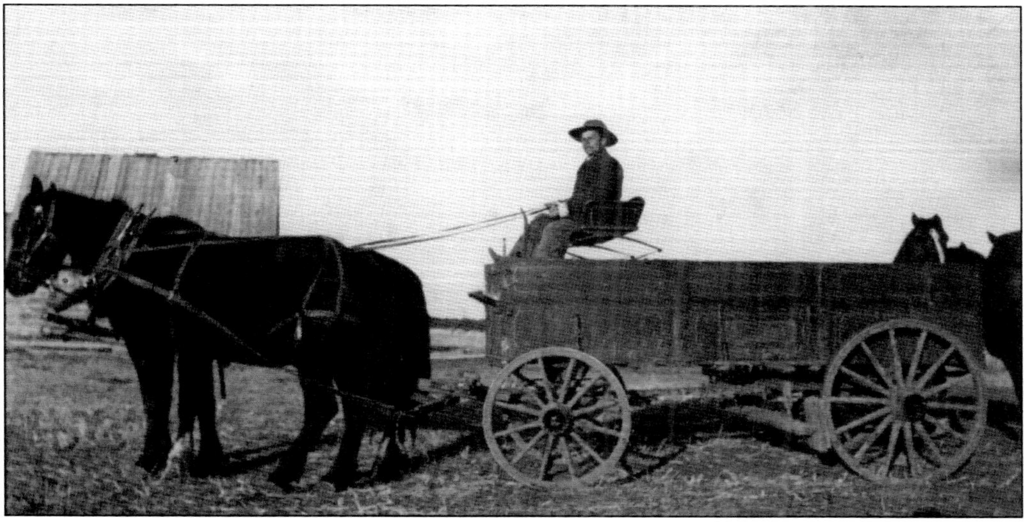

FREIGHT WAGON. Stoian Ristoff is shown with his Moline Wagon.

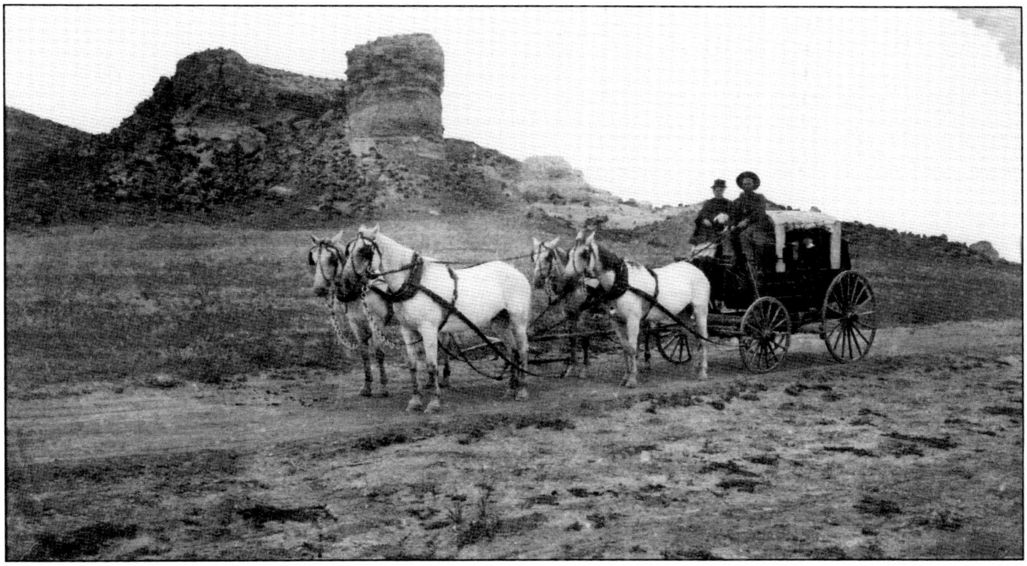

CHEYENNE-DEADWOOD STAGE. Two things, the transcontinental railroad and the treaty being negotiated at the Red Cloud Agency, officially made Weston County a gateway to the Black Hills. It was a foregone conclusion that the Indians would be removed from the hills. Opportunists poured into Cheyenne waiting for the official opening of the hills. To get to the Black Hills, travelers might take a stage, ride with a freighter or bull team, ride a horse, or walk. All these methods took a path directly through the future Weston County. It was said that once the rush was on, a "pilgrim–gold miner" left Cheyenne for the Black Hills every four minutes. A stage trip was not a romantic ride, and passengers were subject to wind, rain, and snow. It did not matter. They were going to the Black Hills goldfields as soon as possible. Shown is the Point of Rocks Stagecoach north of Chugwater, driven by George Lathrop. (Courtesy of Wyoming State Archives, Department of State Parks and Cultural Resources.)

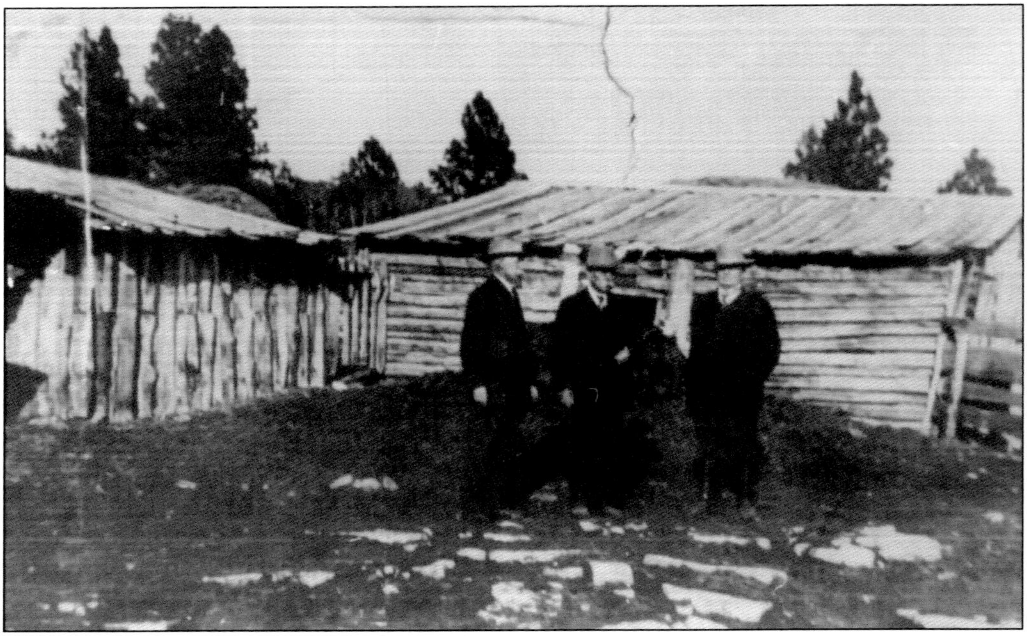

Canyon Springs Stage Station. When gold mining went into full swing, gold poured out of the Black Hills. The byway through Weston County soon became a golden pathway. One of the treasure coaches was successfully robbed in Weston County at the Canyon Springs Stage Station on September 29, 1878. This picture was taken on September 14, 1919, at the station. From left to right are Capt. A.M. Willard, Jesse Brown, and Scott Davis.

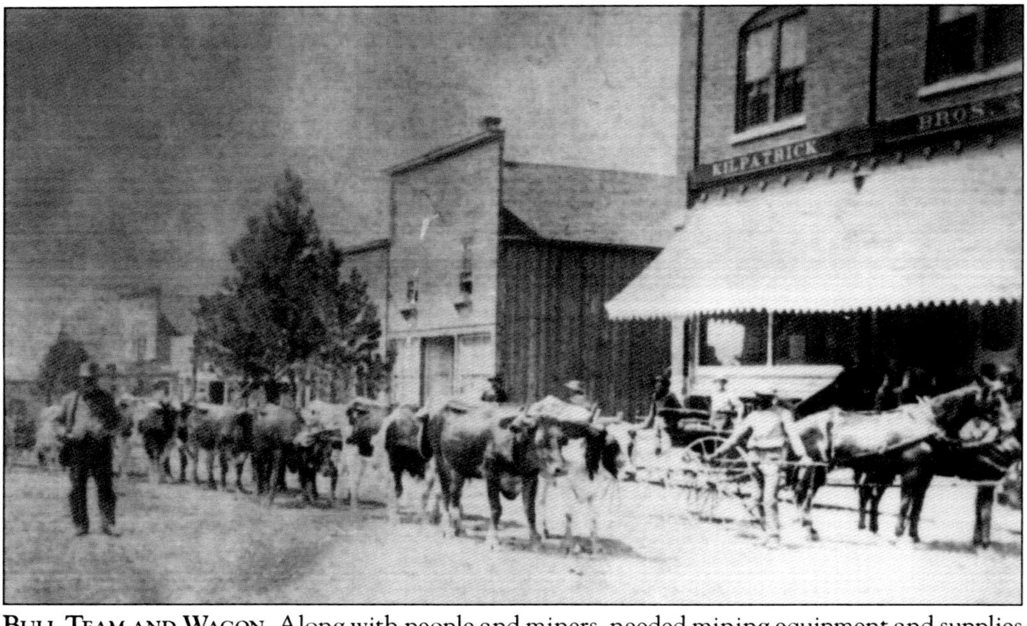

Bull Team and Wagon. Along with people and miners, needed mining equipment and supplies were hauled on great bull teams driven by bull whackers through this area. Bull teams and wagons, like these parked on the streets of Newcastle in 1900, were the means for getting everything necessary for mining to the Black Hills.

Two

THE BYWAY

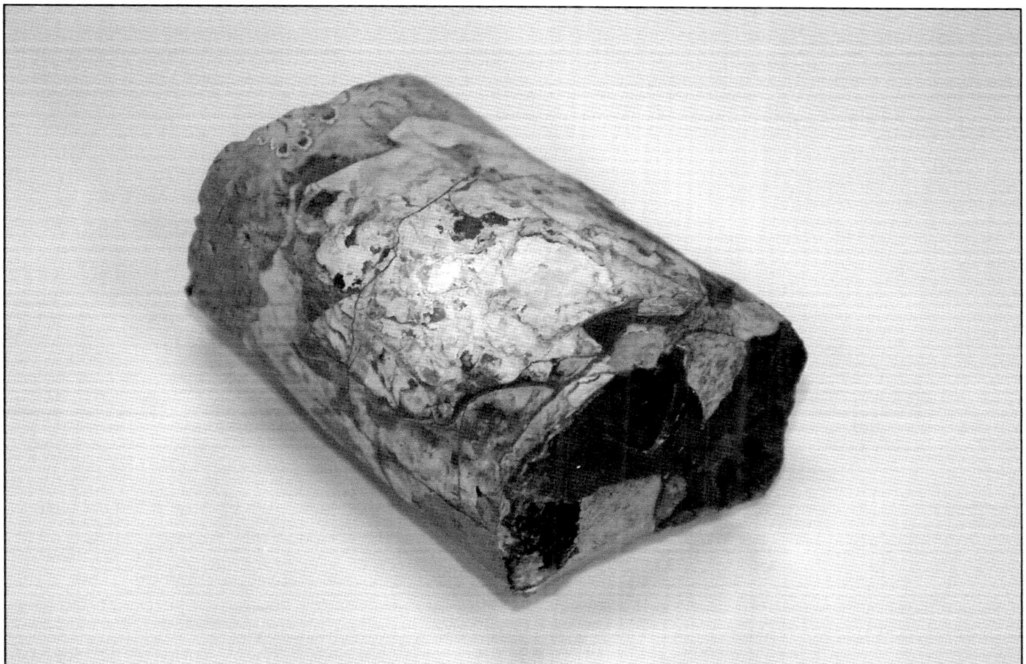

FOSSILIZED SHELLS. Long before gold passed through Weston County, riches of another kind were deposited below the soil's surface during the Cretaceous Period, a period that lasted 80 million years and was characterized by large bodies of water. A record of that first history can be traced by the fossils found in the region. Bachulites, ammonites, crinoids, and dinosaurs all left signs of a watery creature–filled prehistory that led to Weston County's mineral-rich land.

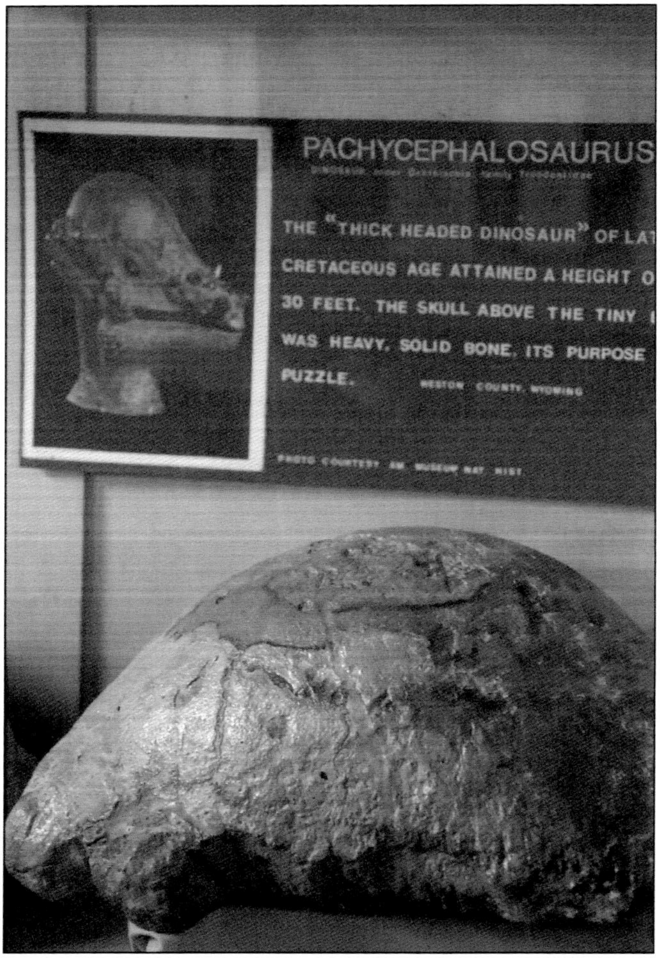

PACHYCEPHALOSAURUS SKULLCAP. In 1928, Mike Marchant found the skullcap of a pachycephalosaurus, also known as "thick-headed lizard," near Newcastle. The dinosaur from the late Cretaceous Period attained a height of 30 feet. Charles W. Gilmore named *Pachycephalosaurus wyomingensis*, the type and currently only valid species of pachycephalosaurus, in 1931. A cast of the cap is on display at the Anna Miller Museum in Newcastle.

DUCK-BILLED DINOSAUR, GLENN AND PHYLLIS HANSON SITE. The hadrosaur, a herbivore of the Cretaceous Period, is known as the duck-billed dinosaur due to the similarity of its head to that of modern ducks. Toward the end of the Cretaceous Period, dinosaurs became extinct, new plant forms appeared, and sedimentary deposits were laid down under the bodies of water in the area. It was from these deposits that the great reserves of coal, oil, and natural gas developed.

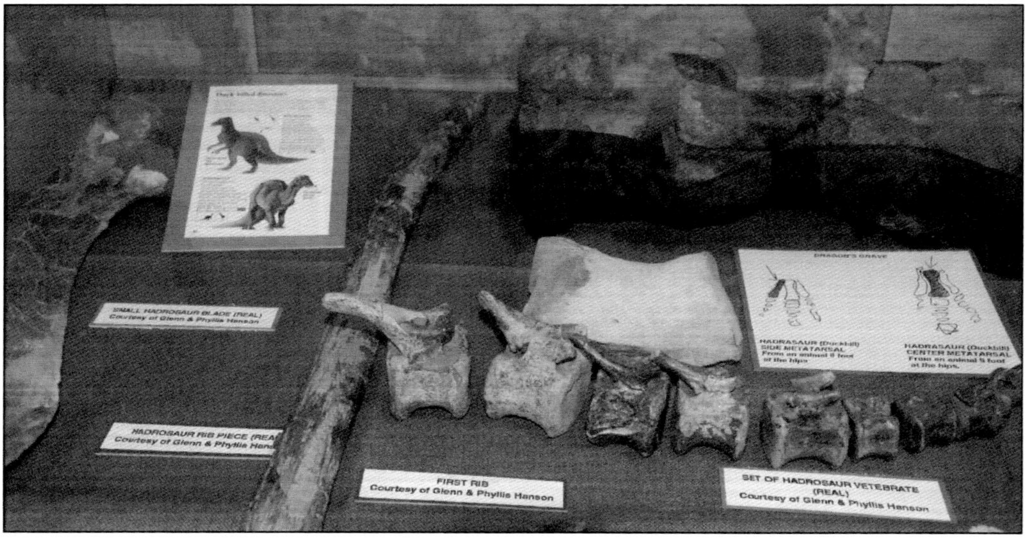

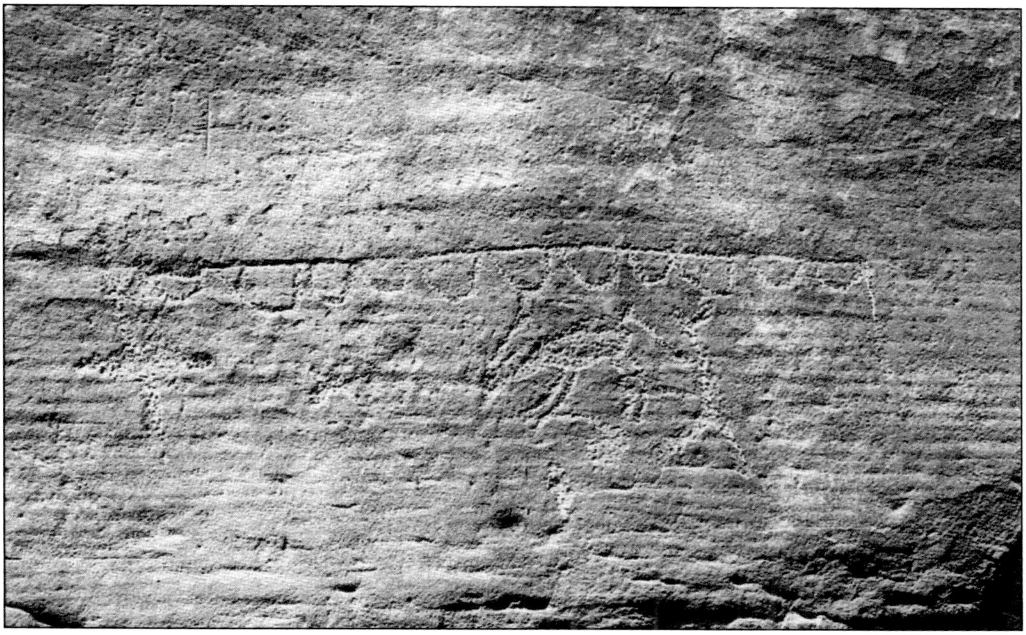

Petroglyphs. Some of Weston County's earliest people attempted to leave written records of their lives in the region. In three separate county locations, petroglyphs have been found. This ancient art is carved into the stone walls of a cliff or cave. It tells people today that an ancient people walked and hunted in this land at one time. Whoopup Canyon petroglyphs span 9,000 years, and the oldest are more than 12,000 years old. The petroglyphs show game-driving scenes and depict deer, antelope, bison, mountain sheep, elk, dogs, and humans. The loop line appears to represent a brush fence or game trap wall. Another hunting scene shows a hunter clubbing an antelope that is caught in a net that was propped up with poles. No one knows exactly what the unique many legged figure on the lower left represents. The Bureau of Land Management manages the site by providing guided tours. (Both, Courtesy of Alice Tretabas.)

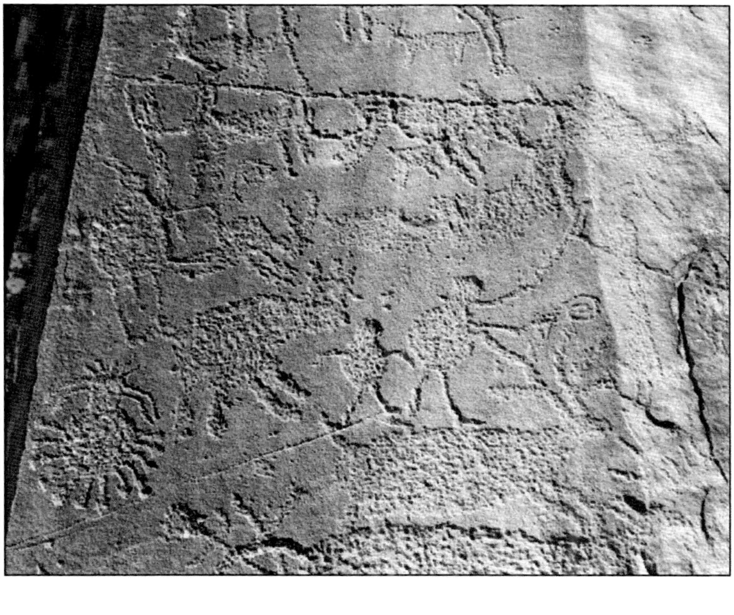

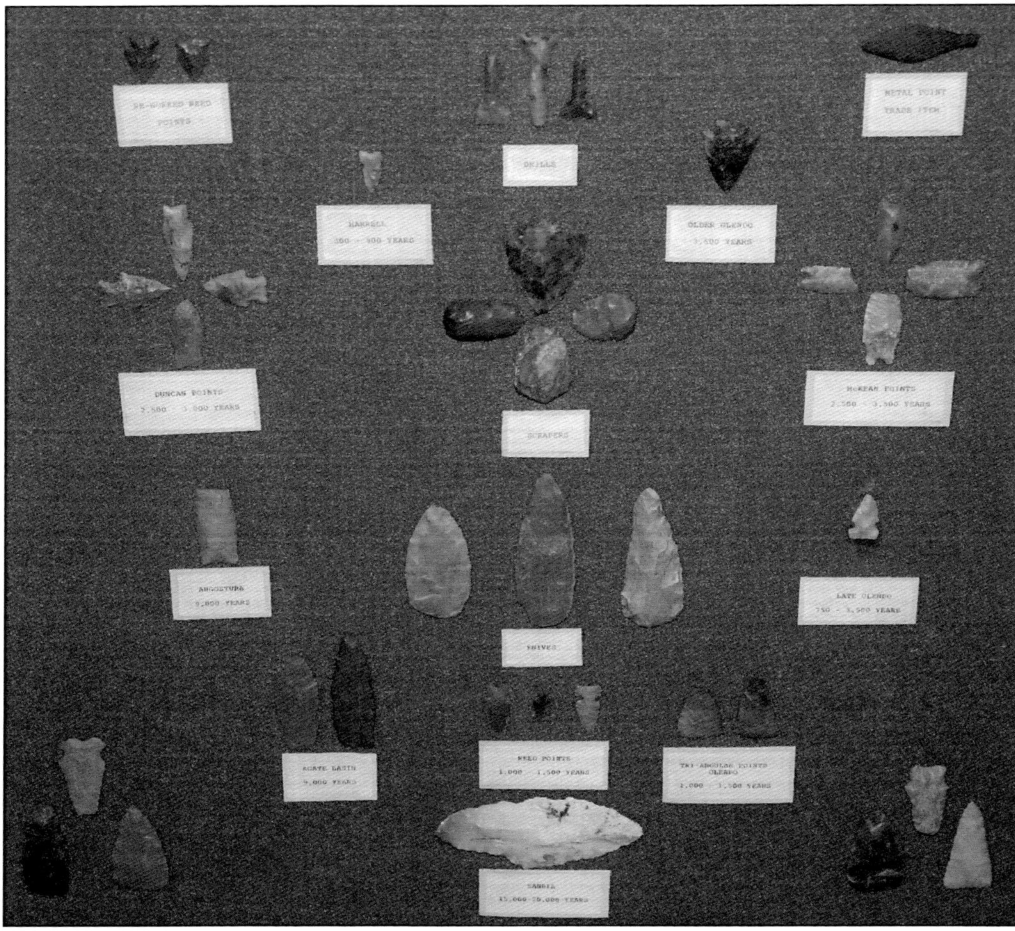

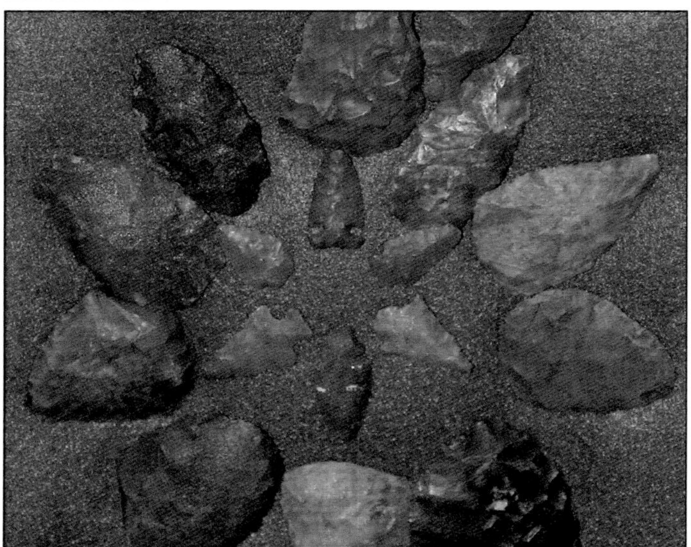

Arrowheads. Little is known of the earliest people who lived in the land of Weston County. Arrowheads found everywhere in the county tell of a past hunting culture. Arrowheads have been dated as old as 6,000 years and tell of an ancient people who sojourned here. Photographed are drills, scrapers, and knives.

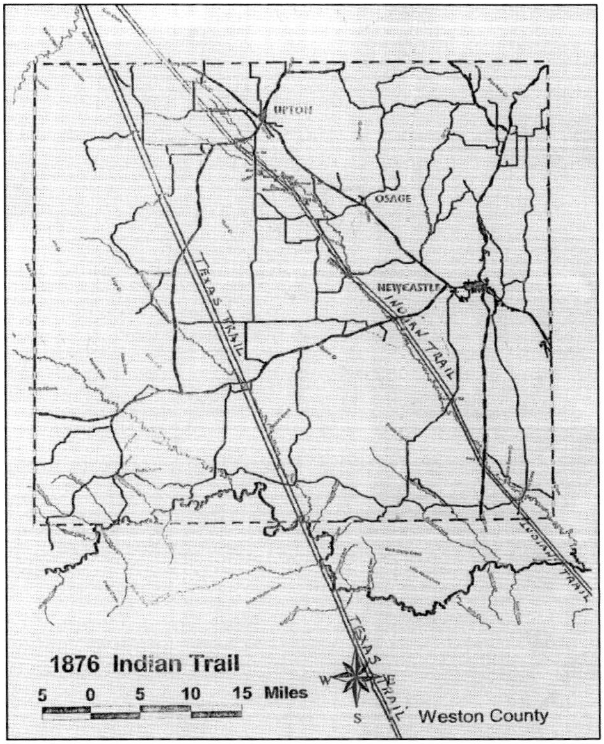

Indian Trail. Running directly through Weston County is a visible trail that dates back perhaps thousands of years. The travois markings and hoofprint-worn trail etch a path through Weston County visible to this day. The trail runs in a direct path from Fort Robinson in Nebraska into the Little Big Horn Country in Montana. (Courtesy of the Don Gose papers at the Red Onion Museum.)

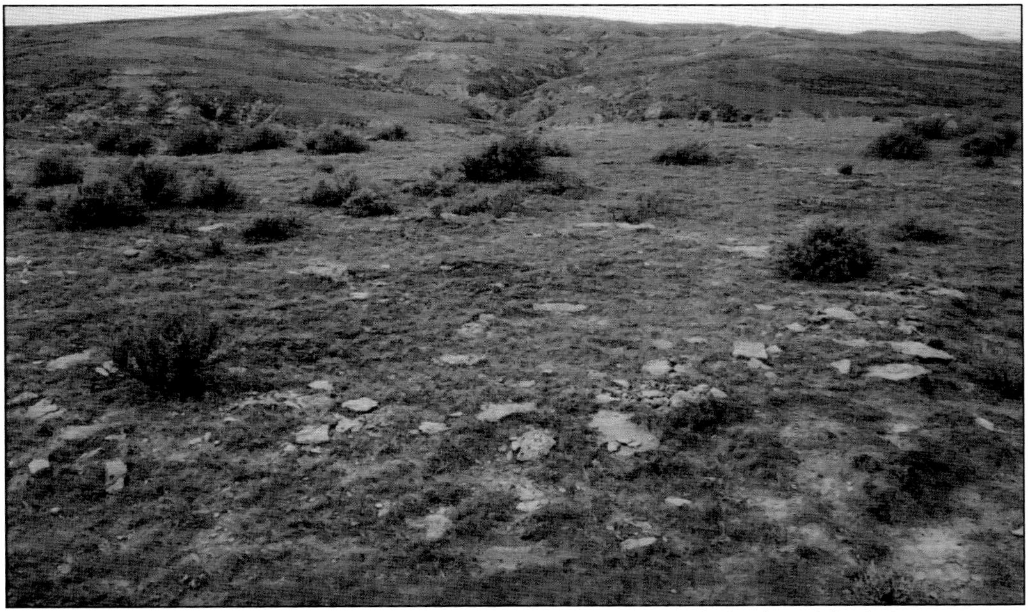

Teepee Ring. The ancient Indian trail took countless Indian people back and forth from summer hunting grounds to winter habitat and sacred grounds. Throughout Weston County along high windswept ridges are stone rings known as teepee rings. The final use of the trail took place in 1876, when the Indians traveled to the Little Big Horn in Montana, where they fought Lt. Col. George A. Custer and the US Army. (Courtesy of the Don Gose papers at the Red Onion Museum.)

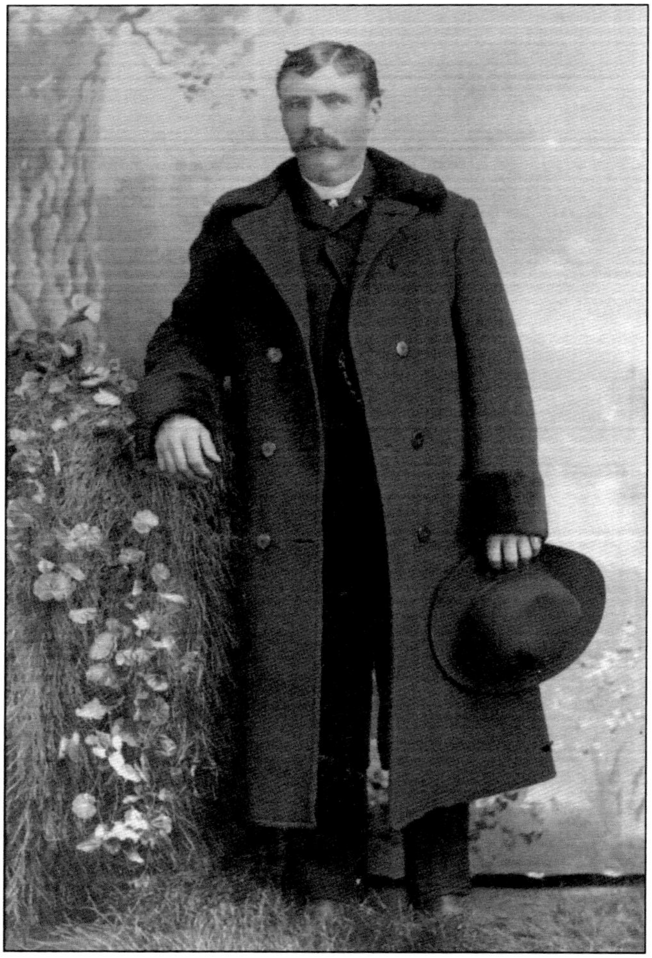

Billy Miller. In October 1903, several bands of Indians left the Pine Ridge Indian Reservation looking for food and were hunting illegally in Weston County. Weston County sheriff Billy Miller (pictured) and a posse apprehended the Indians. Sheriff Miller and Louis Falkenberg, a deputy, were fatally shot. This conflict is thought to be one of the last battles fought between white people and Native Americans in Wyoming.

Oelkers Open-Range Roundup. When the Indians were removed from Weston County, vast tracts of land became public domain and were open to cattle grazing and homesteading. Here, the Oelkers gather cattle on the open range. As far as one could see, there was land, open and free from fences, posts, and wires. Little did these cowboys know they were lucky to see and enjoy this land as no one else ever would. (OC.)

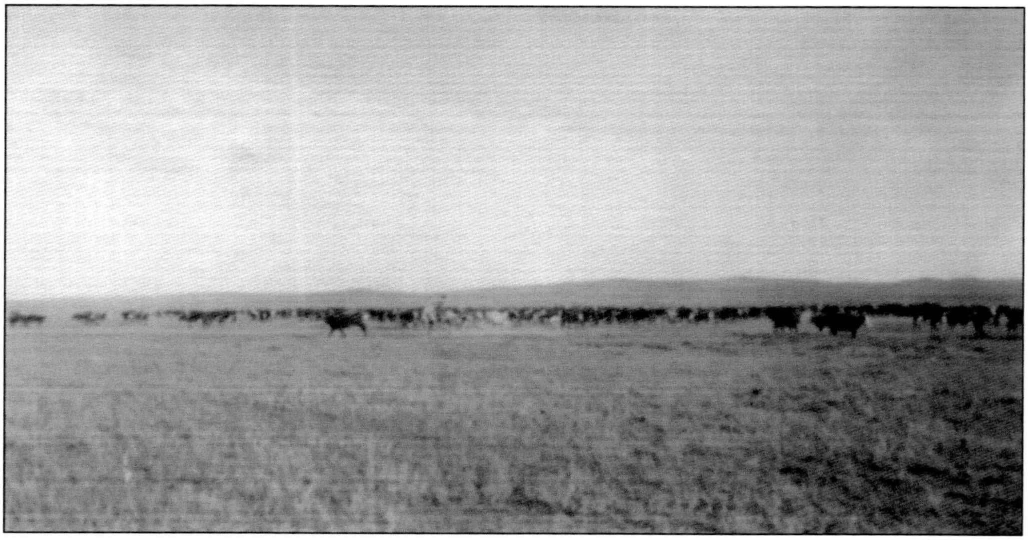

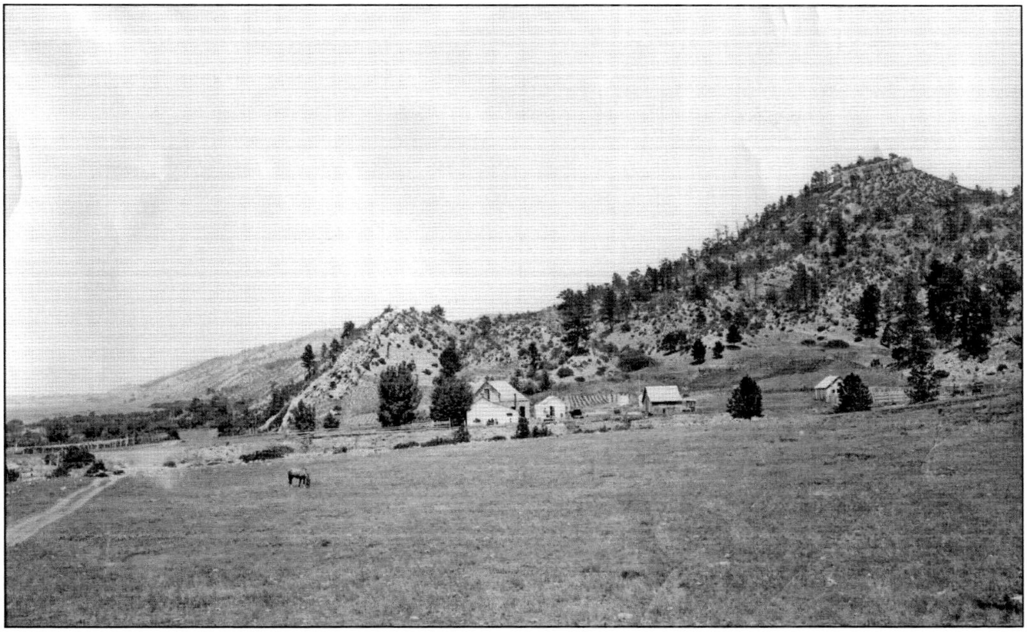

W.H. Fawcett Ranch. William Henry Fawcett was born in 1838 in Galena, Illinois. In 1877, after several grocery jobs, he drove a freight wagon to the Black Hills of Dakota Territory. In 1883, he acquired a homestead and water rights on Stockade Beaver Creek in Crook County, Wyoming Territory. At the age of 52, he married Mary Alice Brown in 1890. Although they spent their early years in a cabin, he moved his family into a newly constructed Victorian home in 1904.

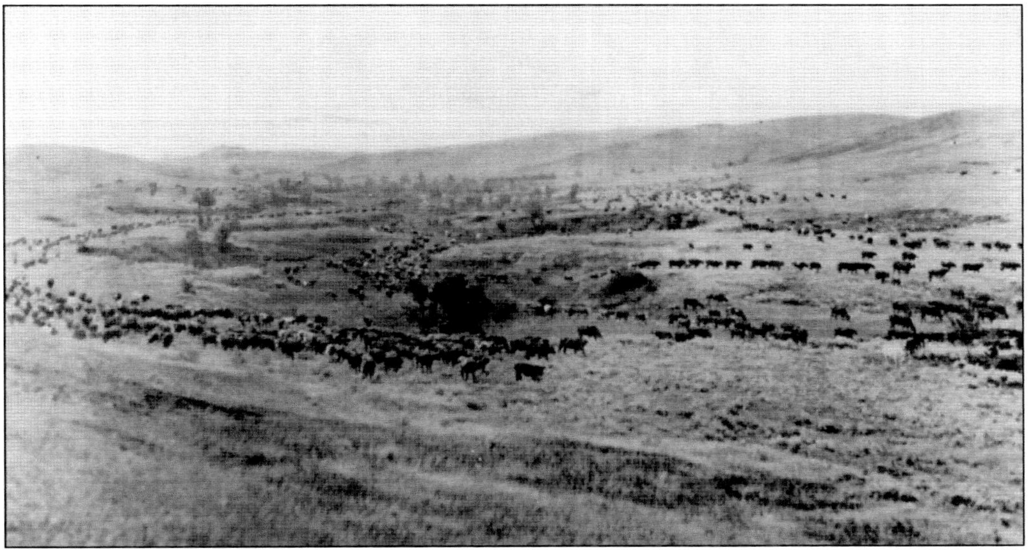

Texas Trail. From 1868 to 1887, cattle moved northward from Texas to Montana along the famous Texas Trail, a widely used trail that ran directly through Weston County. Most of the cattle were Texas longhorns, purebred Durhams, polls, reds, and roans. Hereford cattle were later imported from England by English investors and stockmen. Pictured is L.A. Huffman's *Throwing Rangers to the Round-Up* in Big Dry near Miles City, Montana. (Photograph used with permission from West Texas Trail Museum in Moorcroft, Wyoming.)

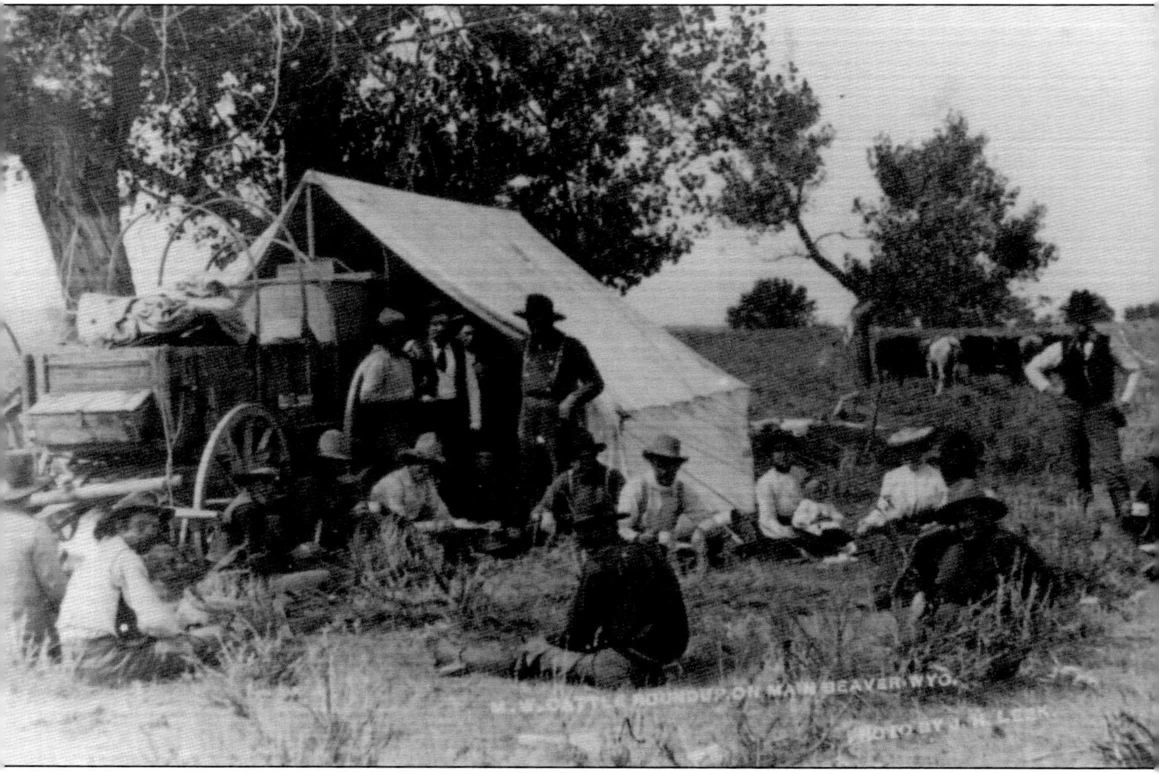

M.W. Roundup on Main Beaver. By the late 1870s, cattle covered the rich Weston grazing lands. Cowboys, wagons, rustlers, and roundups were a big part of early life in the county. Pictured is the M.W. roundup on Main Beaver Creek. Lee Carr, the father of Myrtle Strickling, is sitting in the center foreground eating his dinner. Carr came to the area around 1886 and began working for the Union Cattle Company on its Beaver Creek ranch (the S&G). In 1892, he and Sam Bunker went to Johnson County, Wyoming, where they witnessed the events of the Johnson County War. After trailing cattle for the 777 outfit into North Dakota for two years, he returned to Wyoming and eventually purchased a ranch on Main Beaver Creek. The man on the extreme right is I.C. Jeffries. The second man from left looking at the camera is Pug Lindsey. (Photograph by J.H. Leek.)

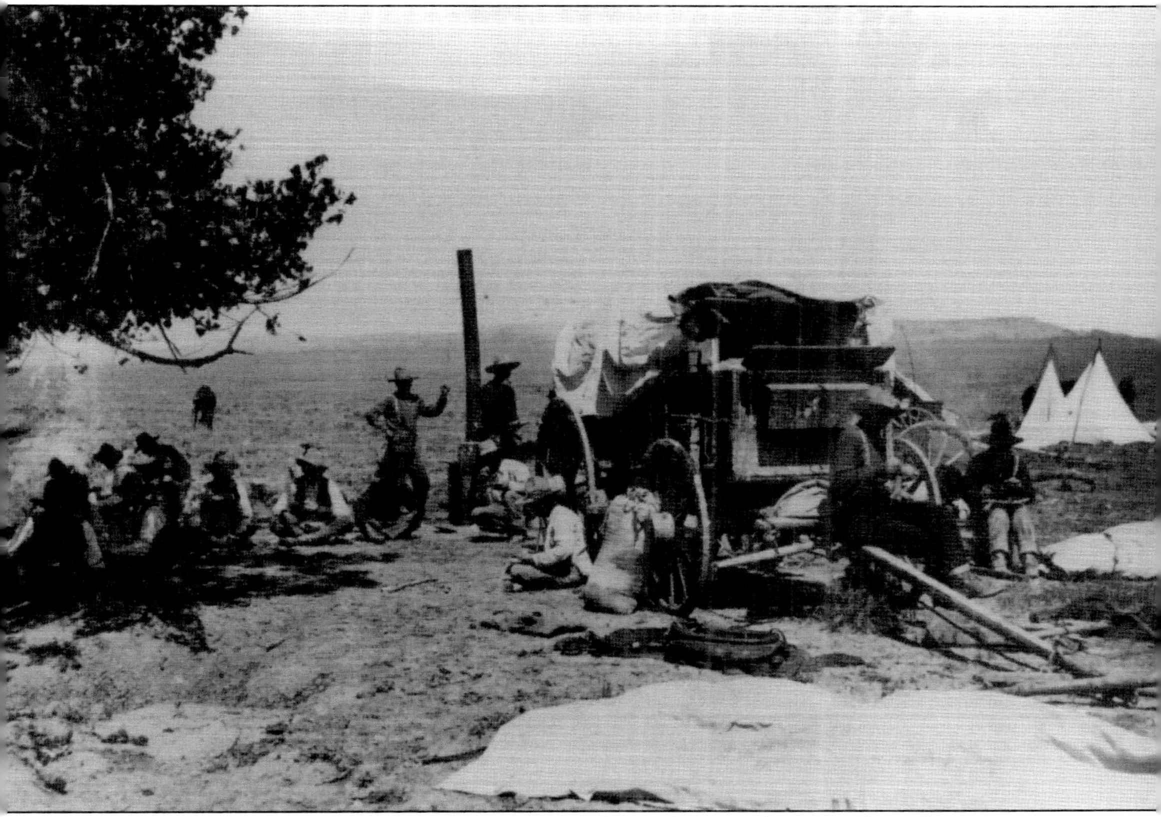

Roundup Wagon. Probably the most important job on the roundup was that of mess wagon boss, the cook. The mess wagon was a rolling restaurant that carried some 1,500 pounds of food, plates, cooking utensils, and doctoring supplies, as the cook served as doctor and first aid station as well. This roundup wagon belonged to the M.W. Ranch. There were storage places for food and a fold-down table that was used as a workspace for the cook. Breakfast was served at 3:00 in the morning. Dinner could be served anywhere from 10:00 to 2:00. At dinnertime, the cowboys would change horses and go out on another circle. Supper was at 4:00. After supper, the day herders went to bed, and the night herders took over. Mont Quest, wearing the black hat, is seated to the right of the man on the wagon tongue.

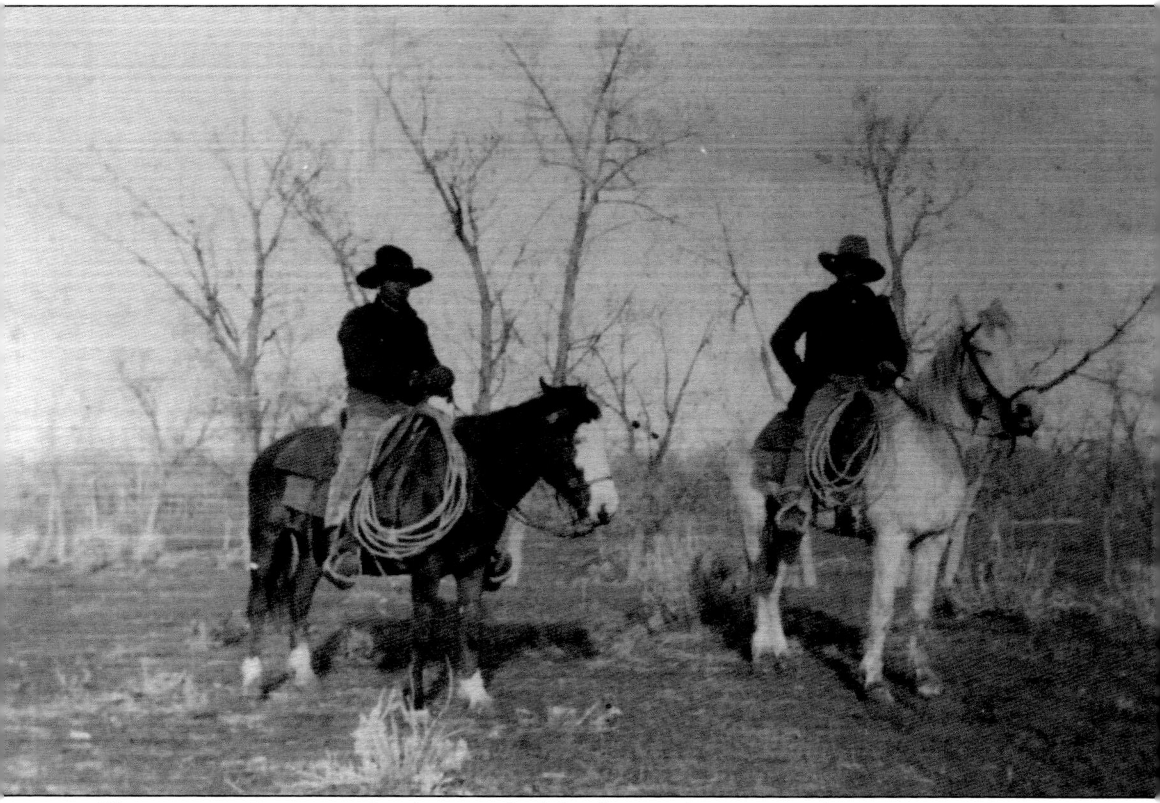

Horses and Cowboys. Cowboys worked for the ranch owners and were sent to the roundups as representatives. The cowboy was one of the most romantic and idealized figures in American history. It was his job to look after his boss's cattle and interests as well as work the cattle during the roundup. His equipment included a slicker for protection against the rain, high-heeled riding boots to keep his feet from slipping in his stirrups, a broad-brimmed hat for protection from the sun, chaps, a saddle, and his rope. However, the romantic life of the cowboy on the open range came to a screeching halt in the winter of 1886–1887. The ranges were overgrazed, and snow and wind blasted the ranges. Thousands of cattle died, and cattlemen lost as much as 75 percent of their herds that winter. Devastating financial losses ended open-range cattle grazing in Weston County as well as the West. Cowboys Frank Smith (left) and Mont Quest rode for M.W. roundup wagon in southern Weston County.

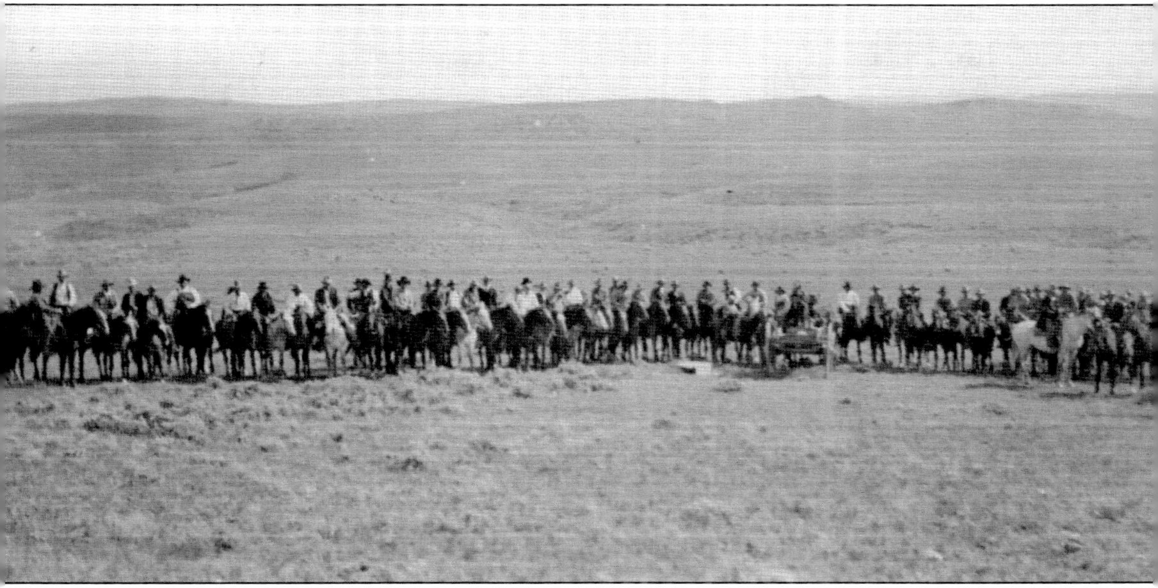

Last Open-Range Roundup. There were prosperous years for the open-range cattle business. The grass was free, and the markets were good. Miners in Colorado and the Black Hills, soldiers in the forts, the government providing beef for the Indians on the reservations as part of their treaty obligations, and strong Eastern markets all created a high demand for beef. These factors drew more investor interest in the business, which meant more cattle was brought to the ranges. After a few years, the ranges were overstocked and overgrazed. The stage was set for disaster, and it came in the winter of 1886–1887. The winter was bad, and heavy snows covered the ground and turned to ice. The Union Cattle Company lost 93,000 head of cattle. Other cattlemen lost as much as 75 percent of their herds. Cowboys from the Oelkers and Watt crews are gathered and ready for an open-range roundup in western Weston County. This was one of the last roundups on the open range. (OC.)

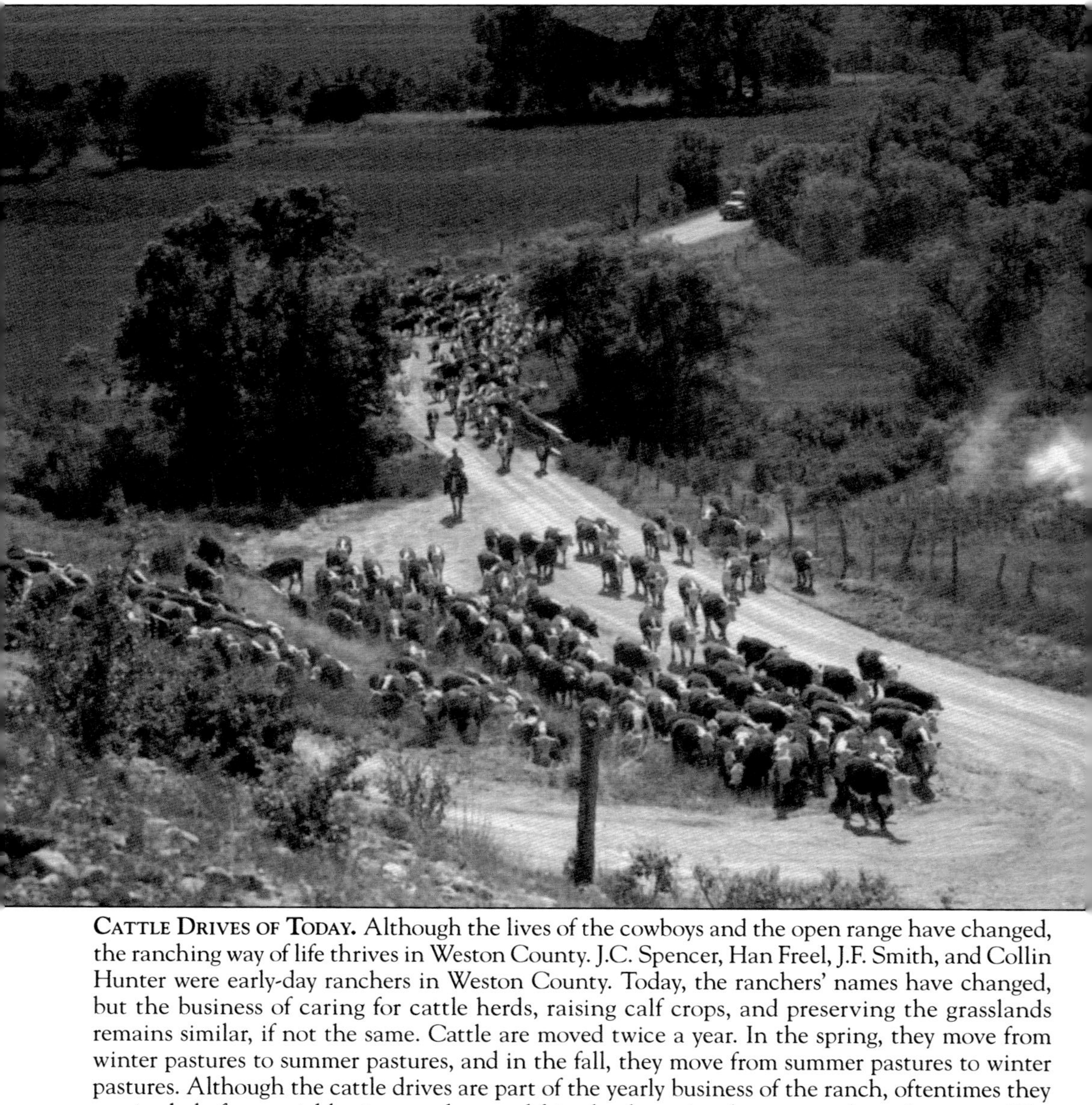

Cattle Drives of Today. Although the lives of the cowboys and the open range have changed, the ranching way of life thrives in Weston County. J.C. Spencer, Han Freel, J.F. Smith, and Collin Hunter were early-day ranchers in Weston County. Today, the ranchers' names have changed, but the business of caring for cattle herds, raising calf crops, and preserving the grasslands remains similar, if not the same. Cattle are moved twice a year. In the spring, they move from winter pastures to summer pastures, and in the fall, they move from summer pastures to winter pastures. Although the cattle drives are part of the yearly business of the ranch, oftentimes they receive help from neighboring ranchers and friends who enjoy the two- or three-day event. The picture shows M.W. Ranch cowboys driving cattle in the early 1950s from Beaver Creek to the Limestone. (AMM.)

Three

Homestead to Home

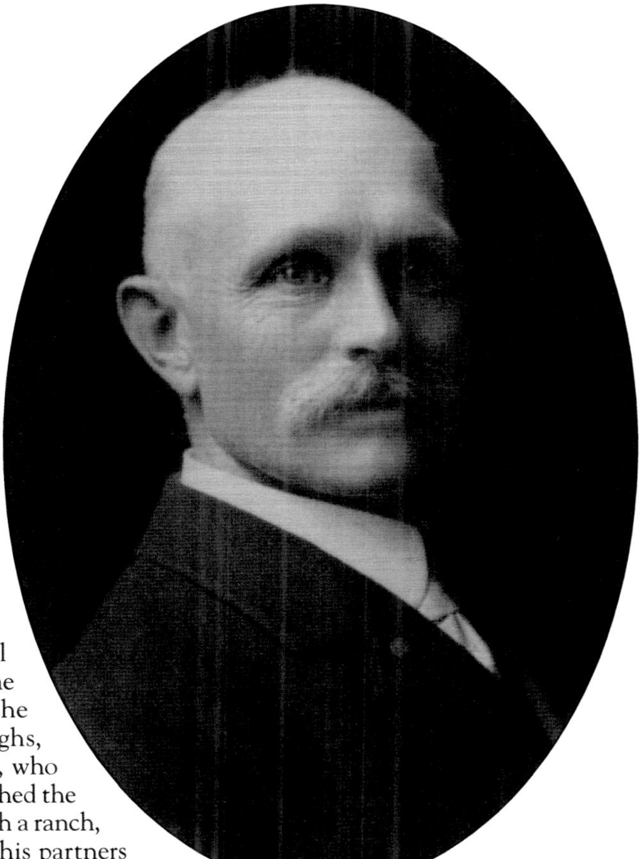

J.C. Spencer. Sojourners to Weston County got a peek at the beautiful country. Soon, it was seen as a home and a productive place. One of the stage station agents, a Mr. Burroughs, described the land to J.C. Spencer, who came to Weston County and established the LAK Ranch. Not only did he establish a ranch, he also built a home. Spencer and his partners stocked the ranch with Texas cattle.

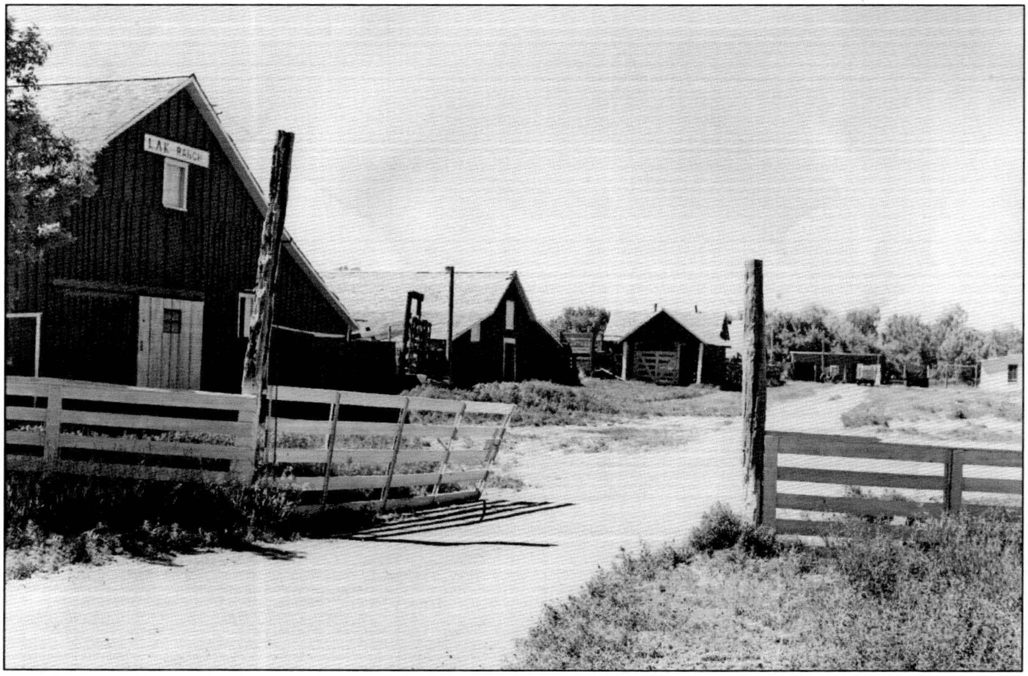

LAK RANCH. After the devastating winter of 1886–1887, Spencer became the sole owner of the LAK Ranch. Although the ranch changed hands over the years, it remains a successful operating cattle ranch and home today. Spencer was correct in believing that the land in Weston County, with its fertile creek bottoms, prairies of buffalo and wild wheat grass, and rolling plains, was excellent ranching country. (AMM.)

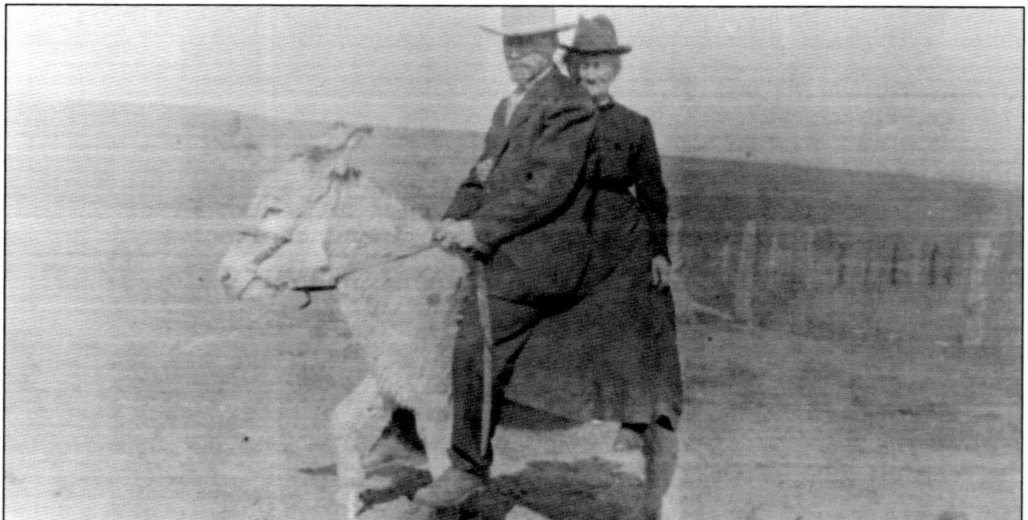

HENRY AND HARRIET WARE. In 1900, Harriet and Henry Ware, accompanied by their 10 children, three horses, and a dog, followed the old Texas Trail in a covered wagon over 400 miles to make their new home in Weston County. Their homestead on Buffalo Creek lay on the route used by the Sioux and Crow Indian tribes for their annual migrations between South Dakota and Montana.

Robert and Rosa Cowger. Robert H. Cowger and Rosa E. Stothard were married on April 12, 1904, in Kansas. Robert came to Wyoming in 1910 and homesteaded 20 miles west of Newcastle on Mush Creek in 1911. Rosa and the four children came to Wyoming in April 1912. Robert farmed and raised cattle, and Rosa gardened and sold produce to the people in the Osage oil field, about 10 miles north of the ranch.

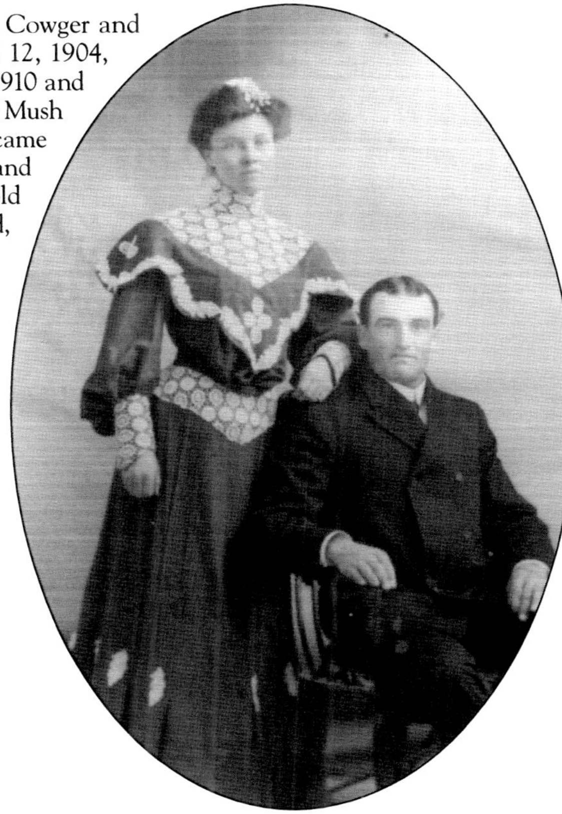

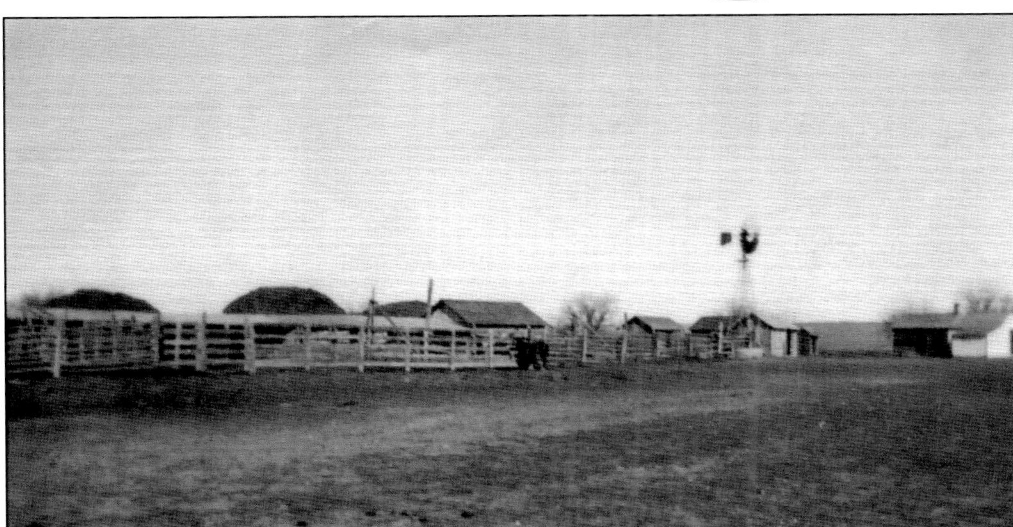

Frank Watt Ranch. Frank Watt was born in 1871 and filed on his homestead on Buffalo Creek in 1898. His first improvement on the ranch was a small one-room building that he shared with his horse. He married Catherine Oelkers in 1902. Frank spent his entire life on the ranch raising Hereford cattle. Frank's Triangle T Ranch, with its barn, corrals, and windmill, was representative of the new cattle-ranching industry. (OC.)

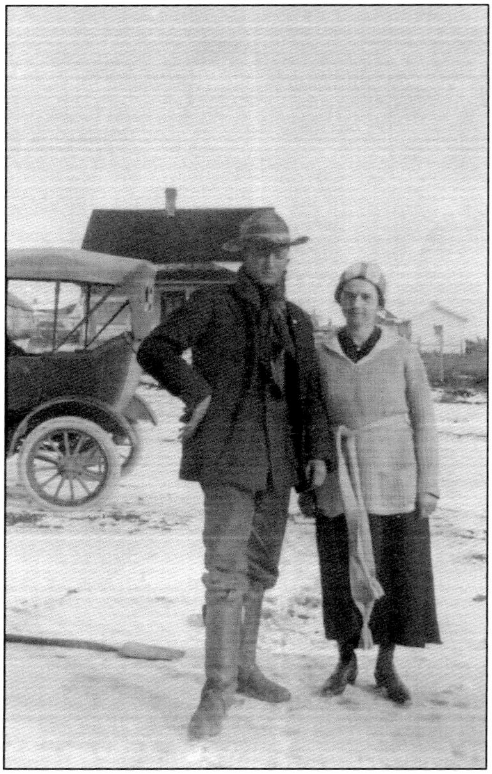

William and Emma Oelkers. It was common for those who came and established themselves in Weston County to encourage other family members to come join them. Frank and Katie Oelkers Watt convinced family members William and Emma Oelkers (pictured at left) to come to this country, too. They, like many others, traveled here and set up homesteads and ranches.

Salt Wagon. In the early days, agricultural work utilized animals to carry the heaviest part of the workload, but as time changed, ranchers and farmers changed to steam-engine tractors and machinery, then to gas-powered equipment and vehicles. William Oelkers loads salt for his ranch on a wagon pulled by a bull team. (OC.)

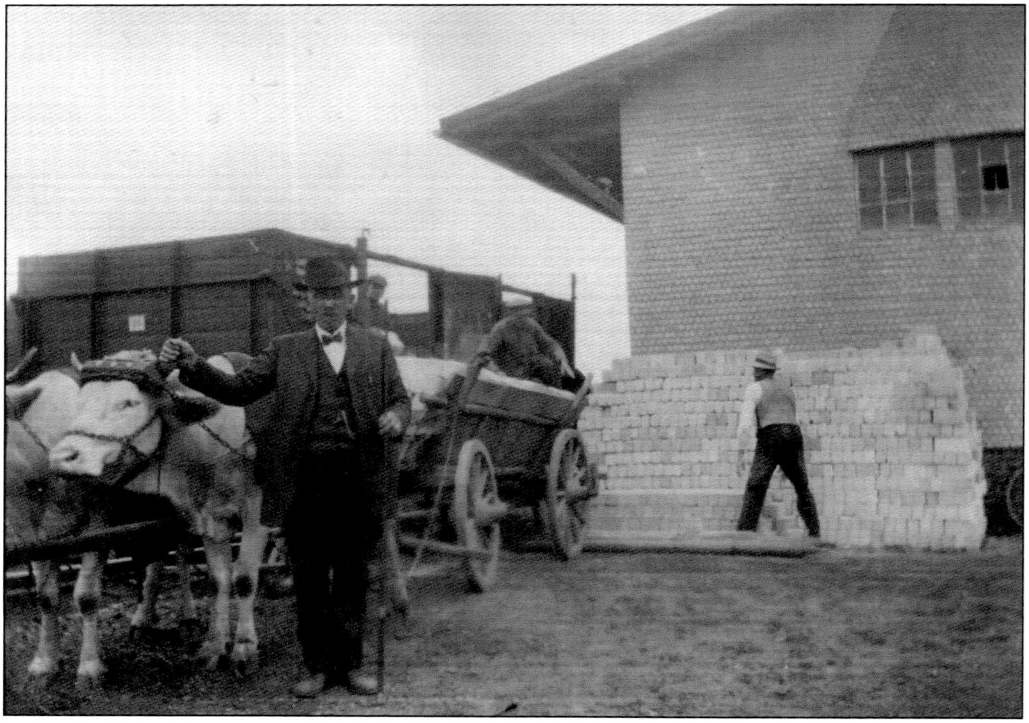

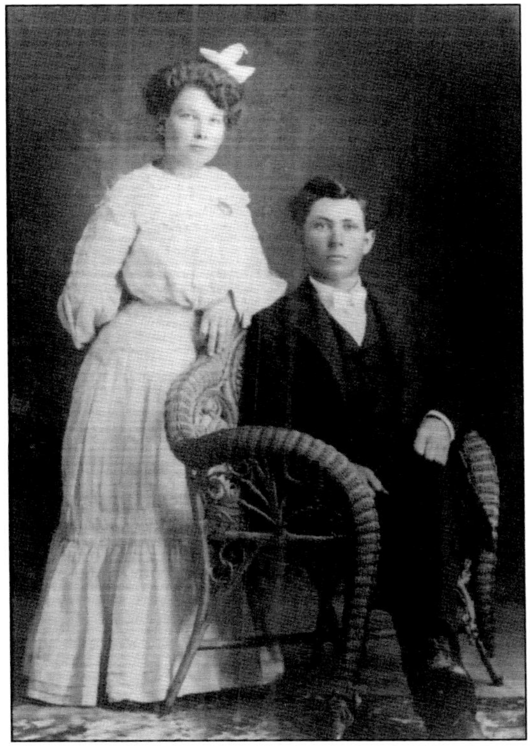

NOAH AND GRACE CLINEBELL. Noah Lee Clinebell and Grace Hansen married on March 4, 1904, and came to Newcastle by train in 1919. While Noah went to work at a ranch in South Dakota, the family became ill with influenza. Grace and her newborn son, Howard Lee, died in early 1920. Noah filed on a homestead 25 miles south of Newcastle on the Morrissey Road over Big Beaver Creek in 1921.

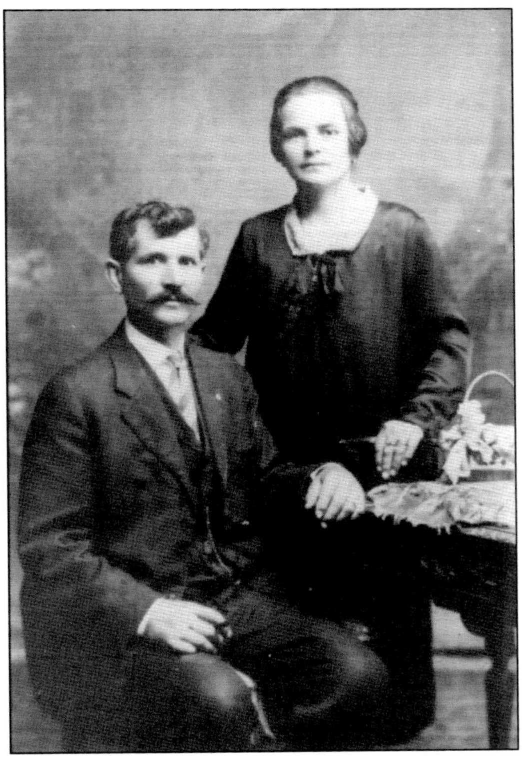

DOMENIK AND GIOVANNA TROSSELLO. In 1885, Domenik was born in Silva, Italy, about 40 miles from Torino, and he came to the United States in 1901. He came to Cambria, where he worked until the coal mine closed in 1928. He returned to Italy and married Giovanna Martinetti, who was born in Silva in 1899. He worked for the railroad and as a janitor, and Giovanna worked at the Sewing Room during the Depression.

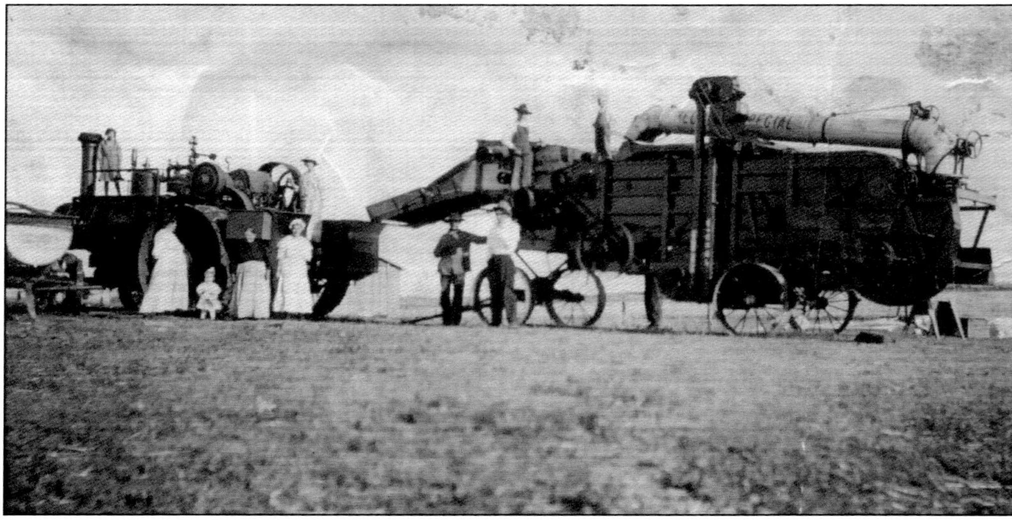

CHARLES MILLER AND HIS THRESHING MACHINE. In 1872, Charles Miller was born Walentz Podlaszewski in Eastern Poland. In 1896, he filed on a homestead on the Canyon Springs Prairie, and he later enlarged his holdings. In 1915, he purchased an 85-horsepower twin-cylinder steam engine and a 36-inch cylinder threshing machine. The Red River Special separator was the most modern and largest in Northeastern Wyoming. His Nichols and Shepard steam engine was used for 26 years.

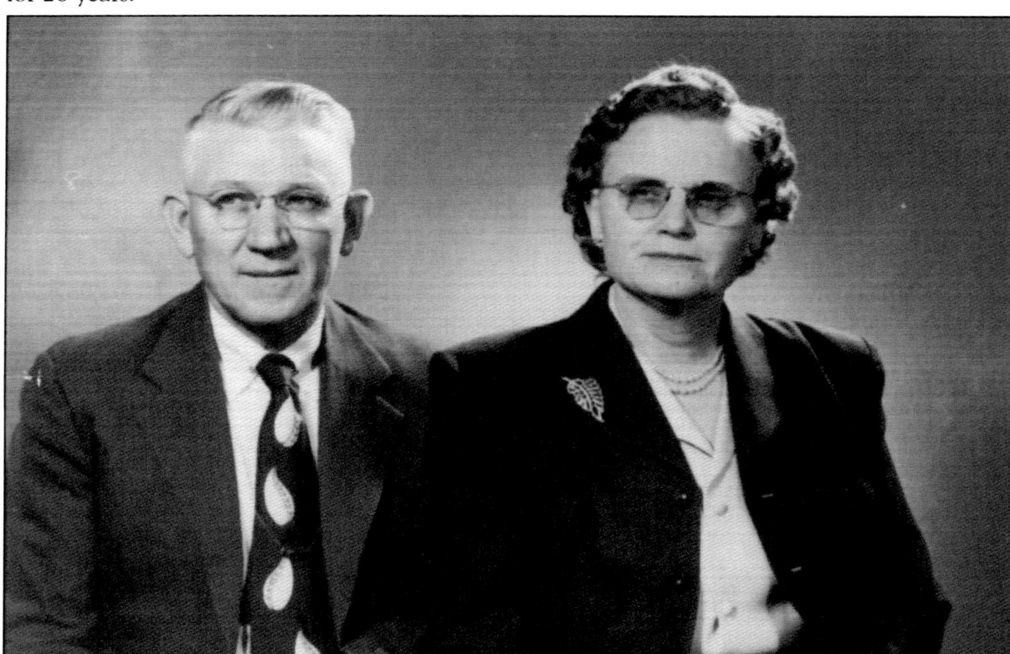

JAY AND ANNA MOYER. In 1918, Jay homesteaded in the Morrissey community of Weston County. In October 1919, he married Anna Sytsma of Brady, Nebraska. They proved up on the homestead, and their son, Clarence, attended the Morrissey School for 10 years. Jay was deputy sheriff and brand inspector for the county for many years, and Anna was a cook at the high school and Lion's Club.

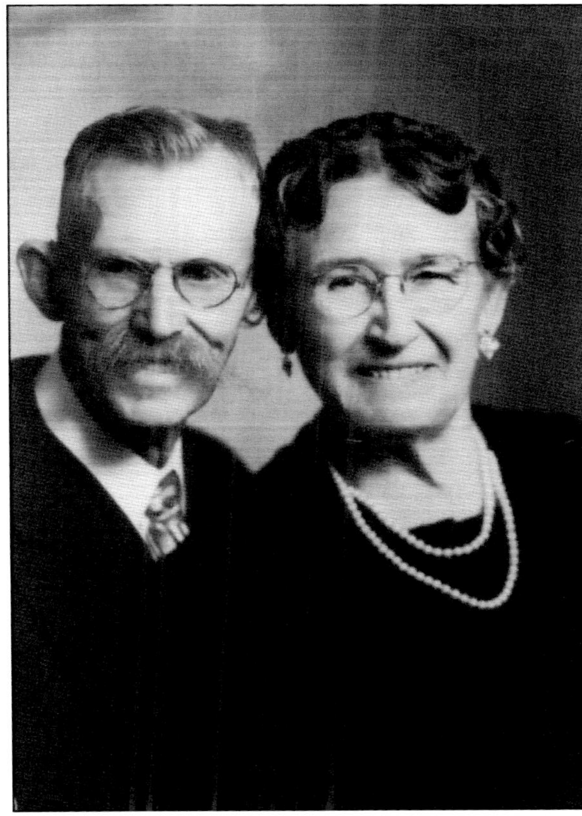

Lytle and Nellie Brook. In 1864, Lytle was born in Indiana, and in 1871, Nellie Rentfro was born in Illinois. They were married in 1888, and they came by freight train to Moorcroft, Wyoming, in 1914. They homesteaded the Wildcat area southwest of Newcastle in 1915. Their home was about 40 miles from Newcastle, and they made the trip twice a year by team and wagon.

John H. Lane. In 1898, John was born at the family ranch in Nebraska. He had a unique interest in correspondence study courses and completed 16 violin lessons in 1912. He completed 11th grade in 1917 and then worked the family ranch until he contracted tuberculosis. He chose a drier climate and took up a homestead northwest of Upton on Iron Creek. He operated Lane Motor and Machine Service and Upton Equipment Company.

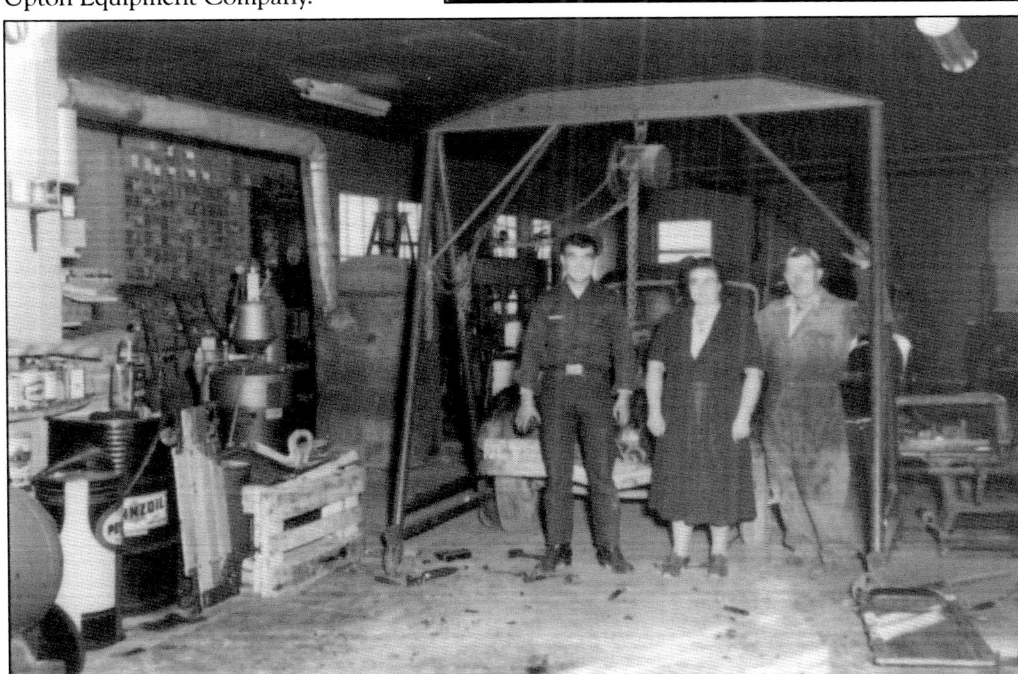

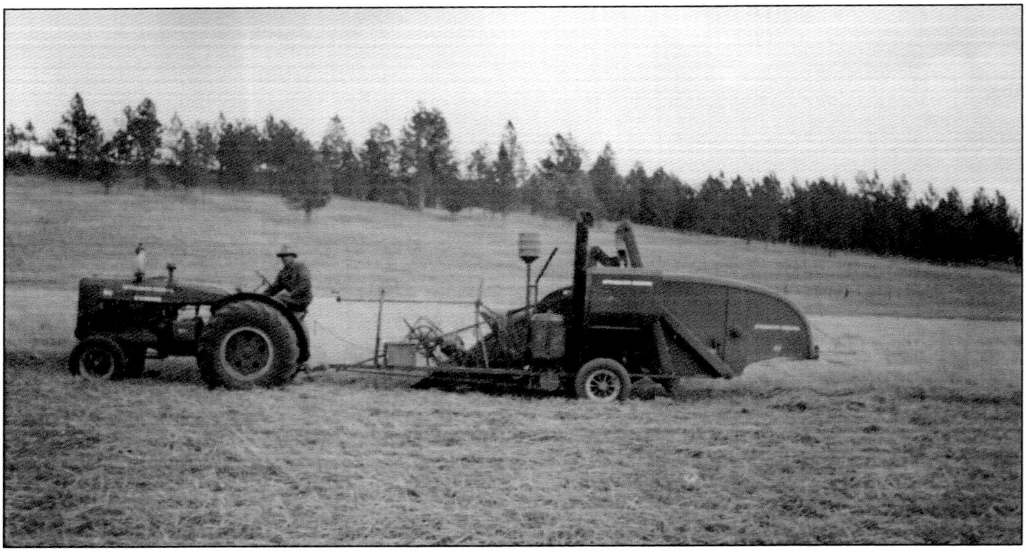

GAS-ENGINE TRACTOR. Earl Christensen was born in 1919 and continued the Weston County ranching and farming tradition of his father, John C. Christensen, and his paternal grandfather, Peter G. Christensen. In 1942, Earl paired a McCormick Deering gas-engine tractor and combine, which replaced the steam tractor. (EMC.)

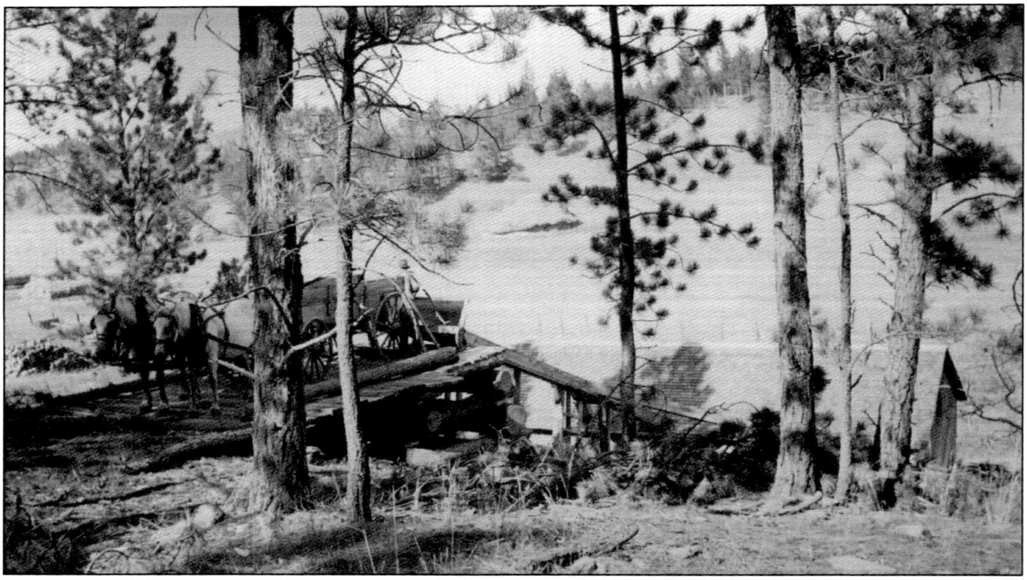

SKIDDING WHEAT. After Earl Christensen combined his grain with a gas-engine tractor, it was loaded onto a wagon pulled by a team of horses. The grain was then unloaded onto a skidder and slid down into a wooden granary. The horse-drawn wagon and the gas engine made a good team. Even today's ranchers and farmers use equipment and livestock that have served Weston County agriculture well during several eras. (EMC.)

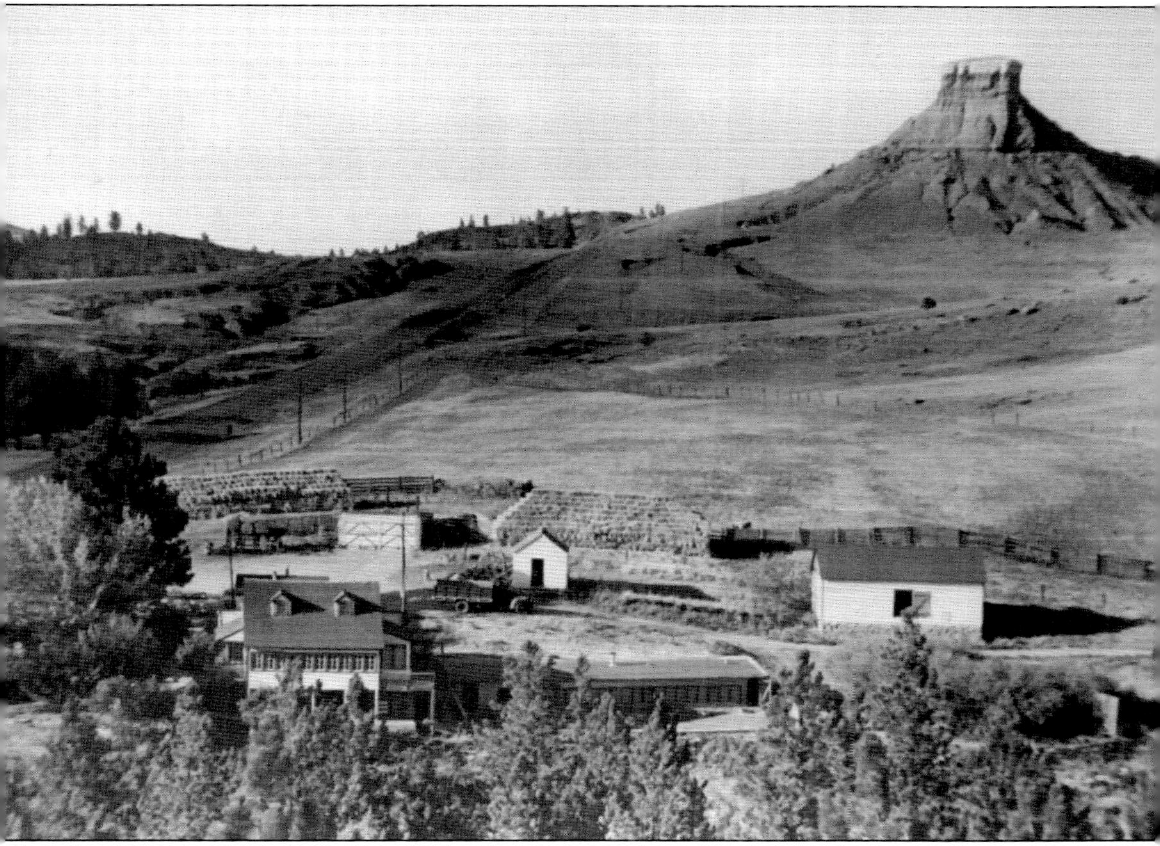

Ranch at Red Butte. Nick Mitich emigrated from Temska, Serbia, in April 1914, moved to Cambria, Wyoming, to work in the coal mines in 1915, and married Ella Miller (Anjella Podlaszewski) on Christmas Day, 1917. He worked coal mines until his lungs became affected by "black damp" and eventually realized a dream of owning his own farm. He was successful and enlarged his ranch, purchasing properties owned by Bob Rainey. He then owned the entire north end of Mount Pisgah. He remodeled the Rainey house, and his family made their home at the ranch about 13 miles north of Newcastle near the base of Red Butte, a geologic marker in Weston County. During the winter of 1915–1916, he organized an authentic *tamburitza*, a Serbian orchestra, with his friend Radovan Bocichevich. Ella enrolled at the Pine Grove School at the age of six, but she could not speak English. Polish was the language of her home. However, she graduated with honors from the Catholic high school in Alliance, Nebraska. Nick and Ella operated the Roundhouse Dance Hall from the mid-1940s to the mid-1950s.

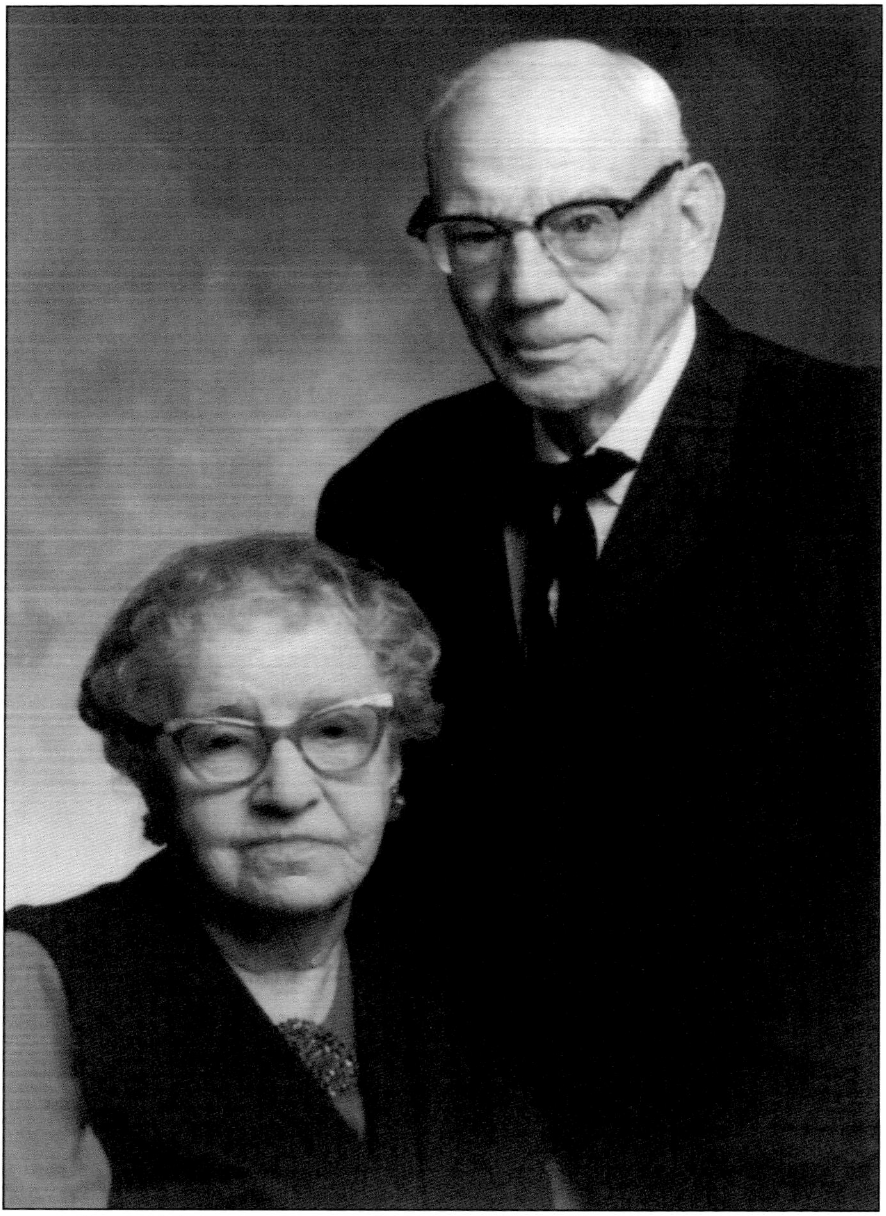

ROSCOE AND GLADYS MICHAELS. In 1910, Roscoe Michaels came to Weston County and filed on a homestead on Fiddler Creek, near Upton, Wyoming. Gladys Wade was born in 1889 in Iowa and moved with her family by railroad immigrant cars to Weston County in 1910. They filed on homesteads about 17 miles southwest of Newcastle. Roscoe courted Gladys on horseback, and they were married in 1920. Roscoe and Gladys made their home on the J.J. Klodt Ranch, where Roscoe was ranch foreman. They were successful cattle ranchers, leased their Mush Creek land for the drilling of oil wells in the 1940s, and even had the Dodge Plymouth agency in Newcastle. Having had no children of their own, the Michaelses were civic minded and responsible for the development of Michaels Senior Citizen Center. Their lives, like those of many who made their early homes in Weston County, bridge from homestead years to the present day.

Four

RAILROADS AND CAMBRIA

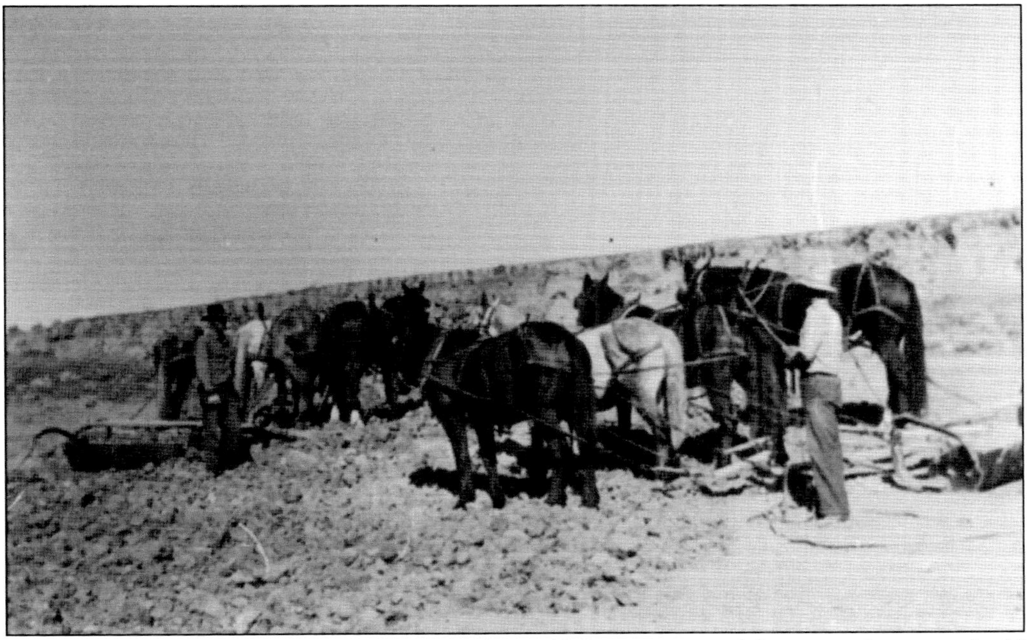

FRESNOS AND RAILROADS. Francis Cowger and Harold Cummings used fresnos and teams to build a dam. The same building method as well as equipment was used to construct the grades for the railroad tracks in the early years of Weston County. In 1889, a permanent railroad was laid through Weston County. The railroad brought people, commerce, and opportunity. The tracks that were established and placed in 1889 still serve Weston County and the surrounding area today.

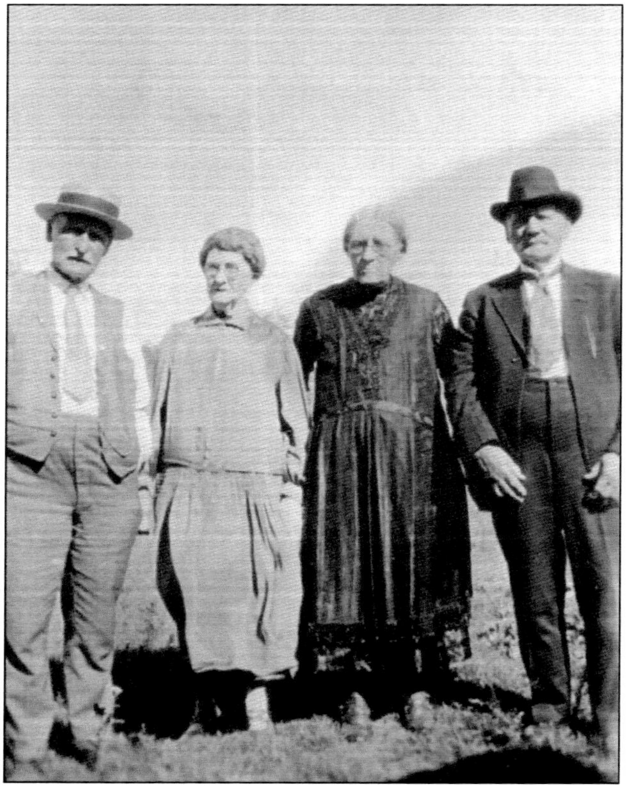

Deloss Tubbs. Wherever railroad tracks were laid, opportunists and entrepreneurs came ahead trying to grasp an opportunity. In 1889, Deloss heard a reliable rumor and came to Weston County to stake out lots and build his own town. His plan was to have a town built, ready, and waiting for the coming railroad. Pictured from left to right are Newton S. Tubbs, Rose Bard, and Deloss Tubbs.

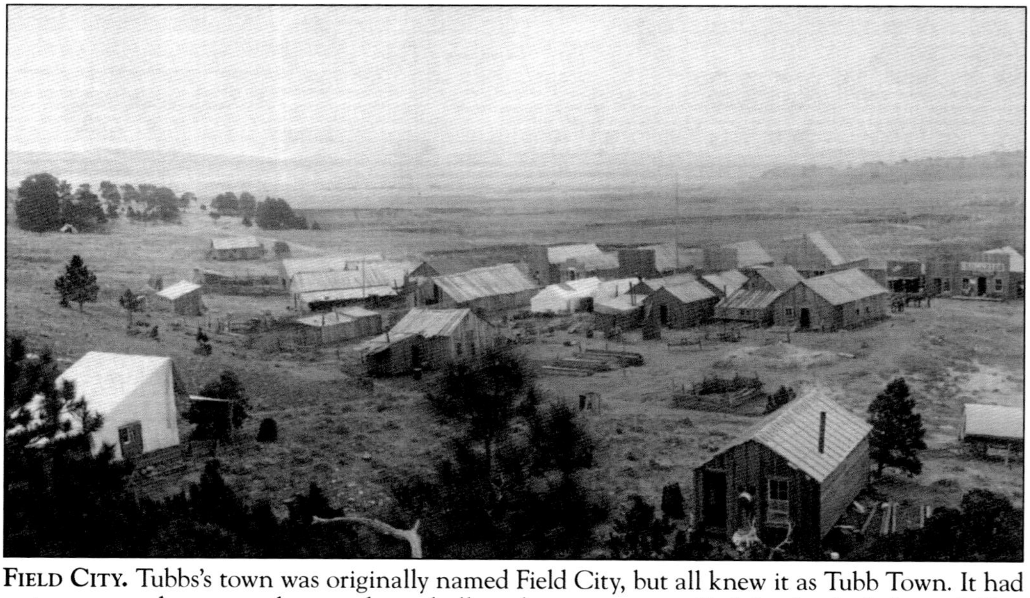

Field City. Tubbs's town was originally named Field City, but all knew it as Tubb Town. It had a store, an outhouse, a saloon, a dance hall, and a newspaper called the *Stockade Journal.* Two months later, fate played an evil hand. The railroad shifted course, and Tubb Town came to an end. The town picked up everything and moved a couple of miles west to where Newcastle was going to be built. (AMM.)

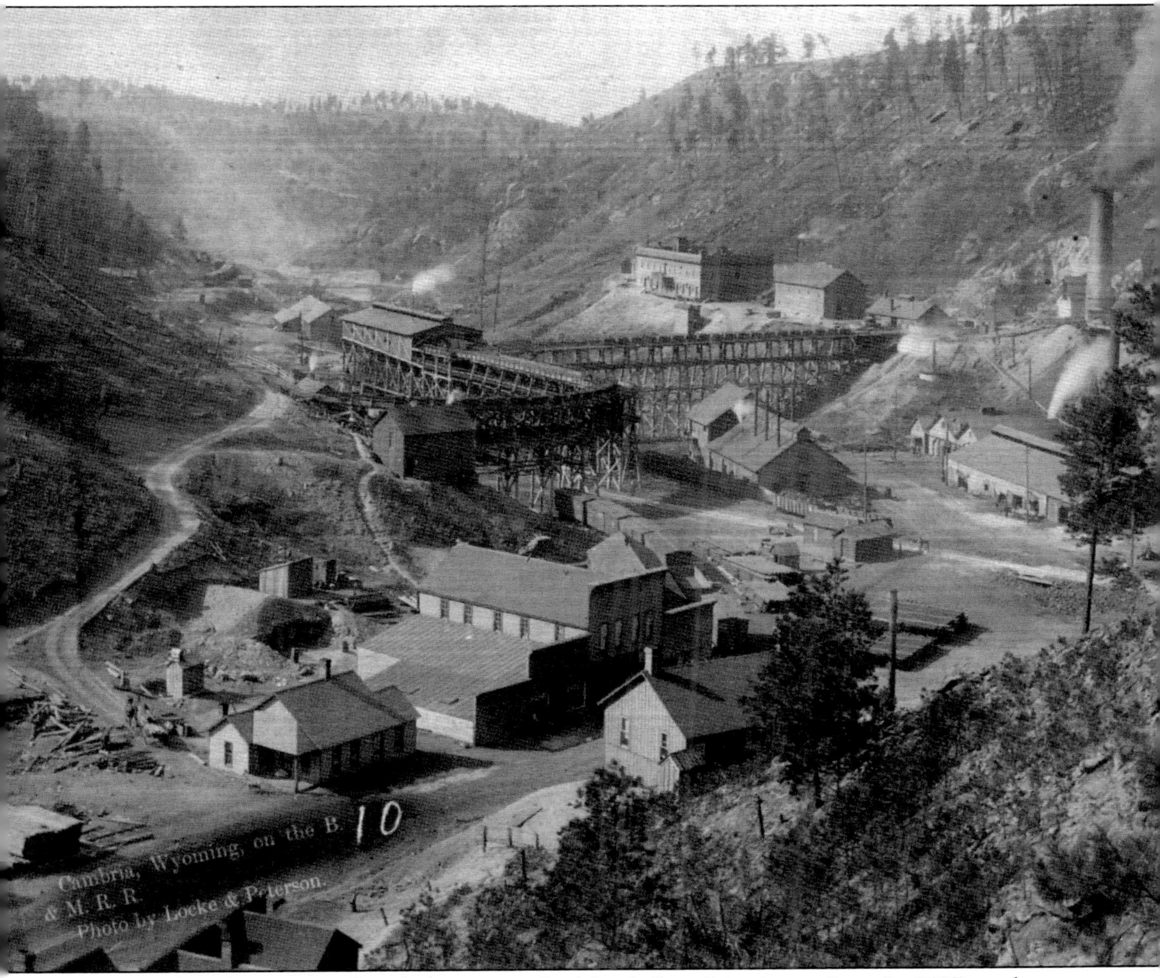

Cambria. The advancing railroad always searched for fuel to drive its engines. In 1887, coal was discovered in a canyon a few miles north of Tubb Town. Samples of the first coal discovery were tested and found to be lignite grade of bituminous coal. The order from the Kilpatrick brothers and Collins Company office read as follows: "Get the coal, get it quick, and get it all." They sent Frank Mondell to Cambria to set up mining operations. Soon after, a coal mine was established, and Cambria sprouted. Newcastle, which was closer to the planned railroad route than Tubb Town, was laid out in 1889. A spur rail line joined Newcastle and Cambria to bring the coal to the main railroad. The Cambria Fuel Company was formed to oversee the mining operation, and work started in October 1888. The next 40 years would see a flurry of activity and a generation of miners' families. (AMM.)

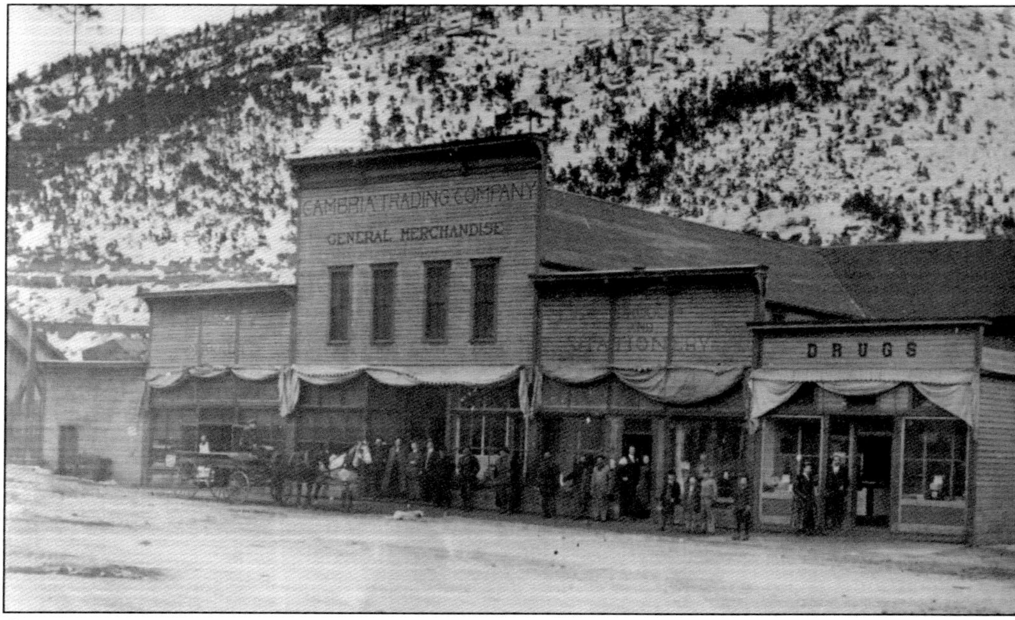

Cambria Fuel Company. Cambria Fuel Company began construction of a camp in October 1888. Frank Mondell was named manager, and Joseph Hemingway, a mining engineer, was made mine superintendent. The camp contained company-owned homes; stores, such as the Cambria Trading Company, which had an inventory that could rival any in the state of Wyoming; schools; churches; hotels; and lodge halls. (AMM.)

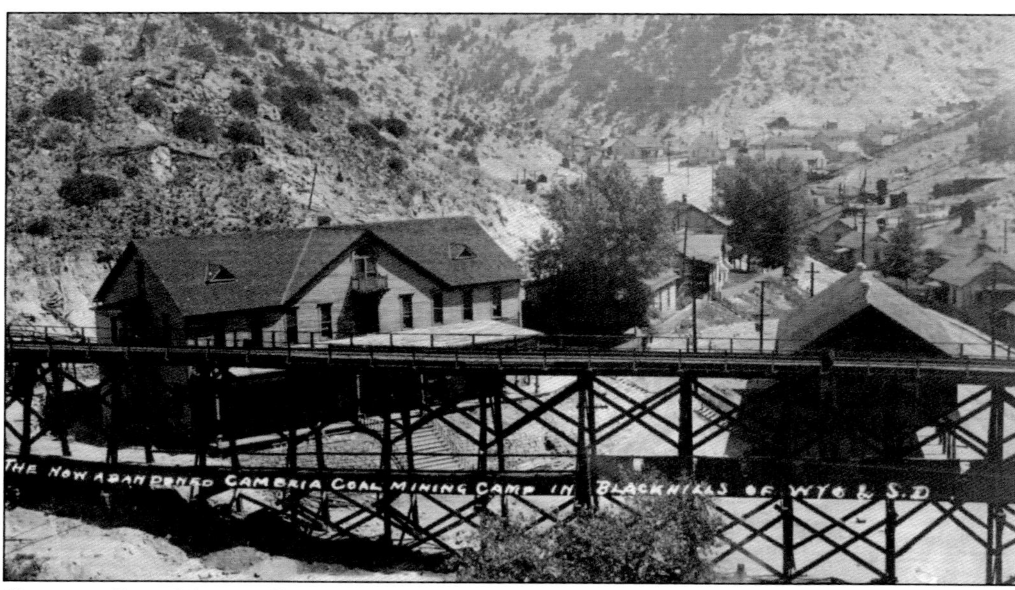

Cambria Coal-Mining Camp. Mining operations were set up in the middle of the canyon. Two mines were opened on either side of it. Jumbo Mine was opened on the east side of the canyon, and Antelope Mine was opened on the west side. On the right near the tipple is the opera house. Just behind it are the company stores, and up the canyon are the miners' homes. (AMM.)

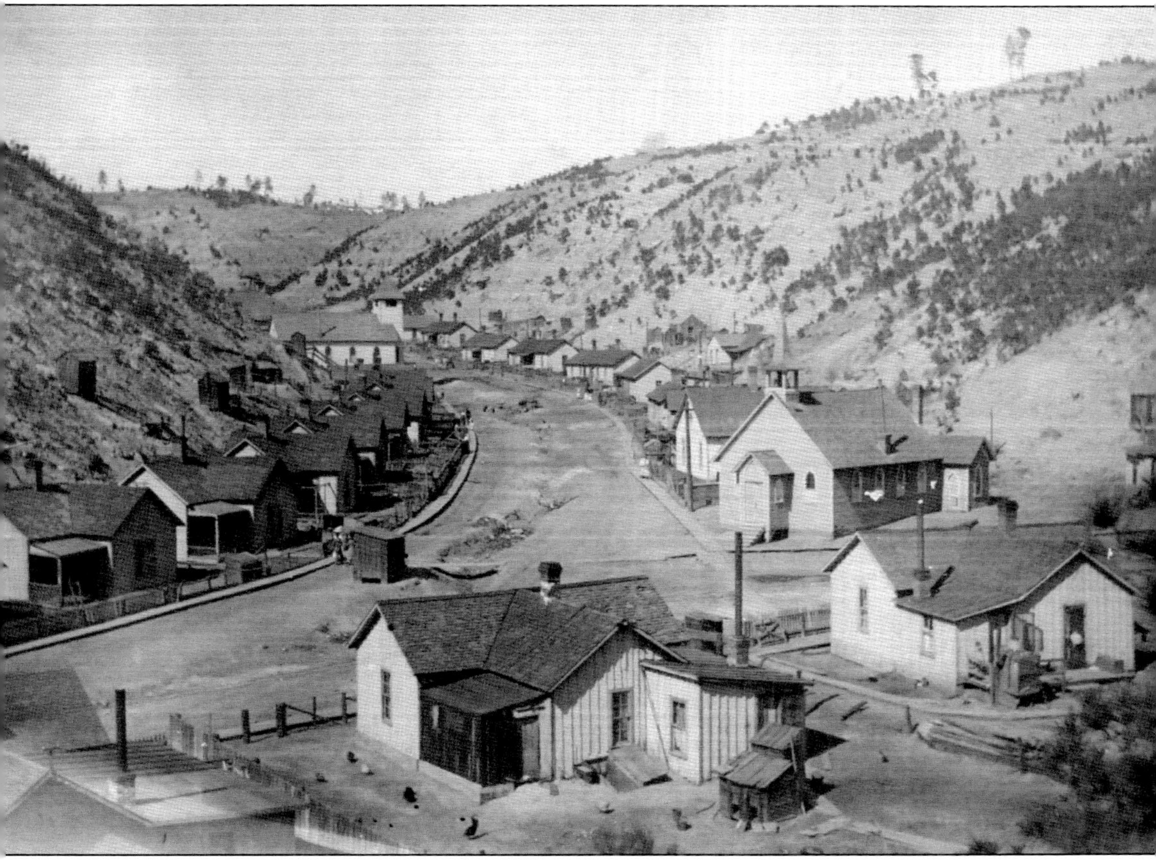

CAMBRIA HOMES. The company built homes for the miners and advertised worldwide for workers. Immigrants coming to this country heeded the called for workers, and at one time, people from 23 nationalities lived in Cambria. In the beginning stages of construction, Cambria was a series of scattered homestead shacks and campsites. Believing in vast coal reserves, Cambria Fuel Company built 150 homes. Besides the rows of homes, the town contained many amenities of comfortable living, such as public bathrooms, an opera house, and a hospital. Out of respect for their mother's wishes, the Kilpatrick brothers made Cambria a dry camp, and there were no saloons or gambling halls. At that time, the mine was considered to be very clean and safe because of its lack of poisonous gasses compared to other mines around the world. For immigrants, many who came from starvation situations, a job, a warm home, and generous, friendly credit at the company store must have seemed like paradise. (AMM.)

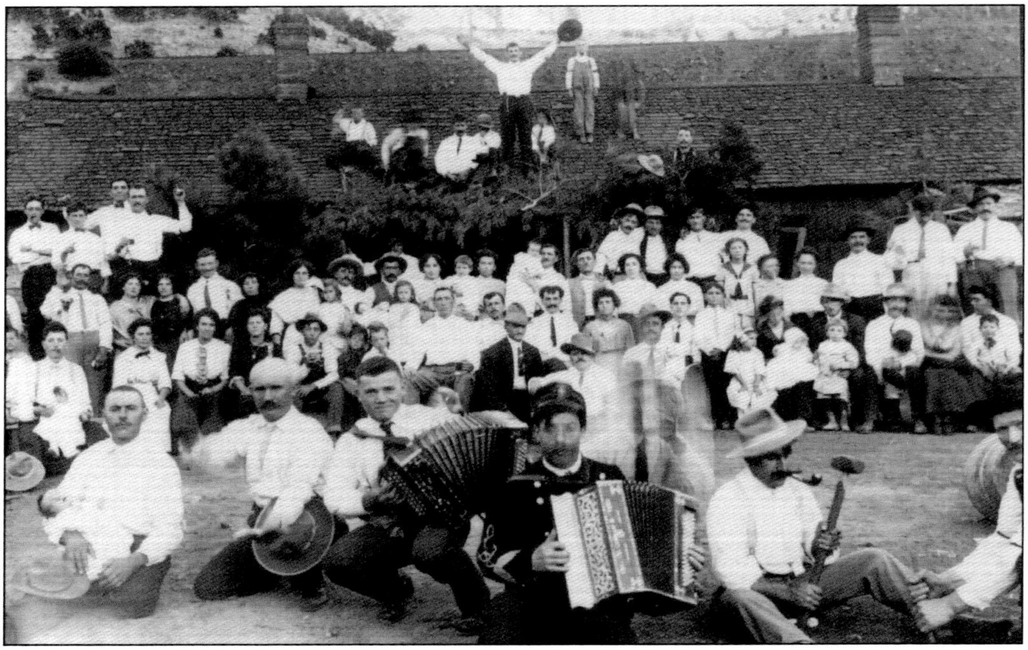

Ethnic Celebrations. By 1900, seven hundred fifty people were employed at Cambria, and the camp had a population of 1,500. At the same time, the United States was experiencing a wave of foreign immigration, and many of them came west to Cambria. At one time, people of 23 nationalities worked or lived in Cambria. Ethnic celebrations were part of the culture. (AMM.)

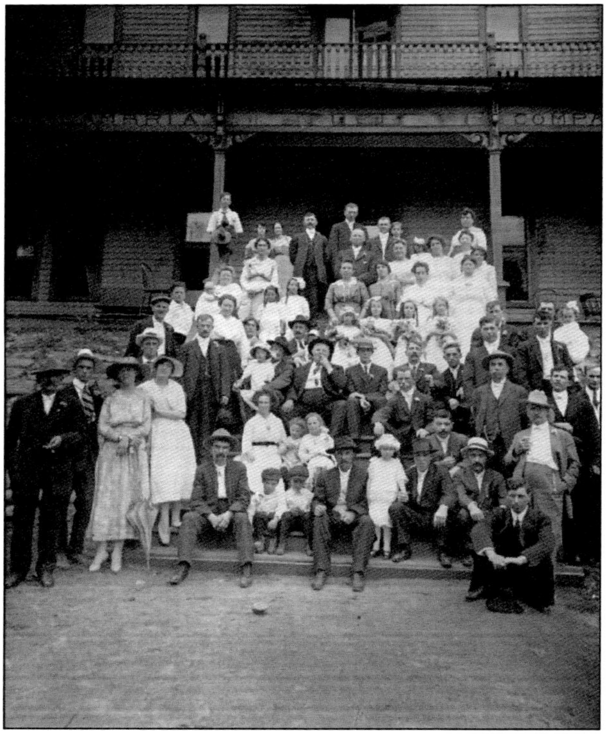

Festive Celebrations. With everyone dressed in their finest clothes, family celebrations included men and women and the young and old. Celebrations included weddings, confirmations, holidays, and ethnic traditions. Cambria Fuel Company made every effort to make life comfortable for its employees. The company did not work on Sundays. Although Cambria was "dry," a beer wagon was allowed to come out from Newcastle every day except Sunday. (AMM.)

Riley and Catherine Branscom. George Riley Branscom and Catherine Helen Beerbower were married in 1876 in Missouri. Around 1900, with their eight children and their covered wagon, they set out for the mining town of Cambria, Wyoming. They lived in a tent and their covered wagon during the first winter. In the spring, the Cambria Fuel Company built houses for the miners and their families, and Riley was assigned one of these homes.

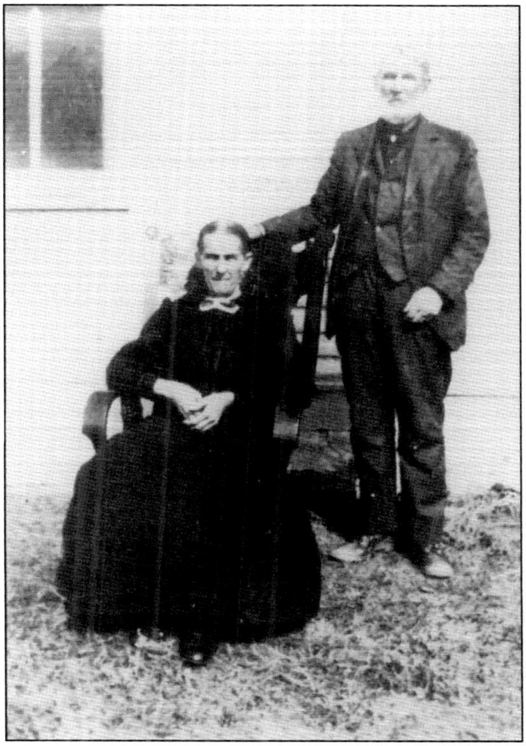

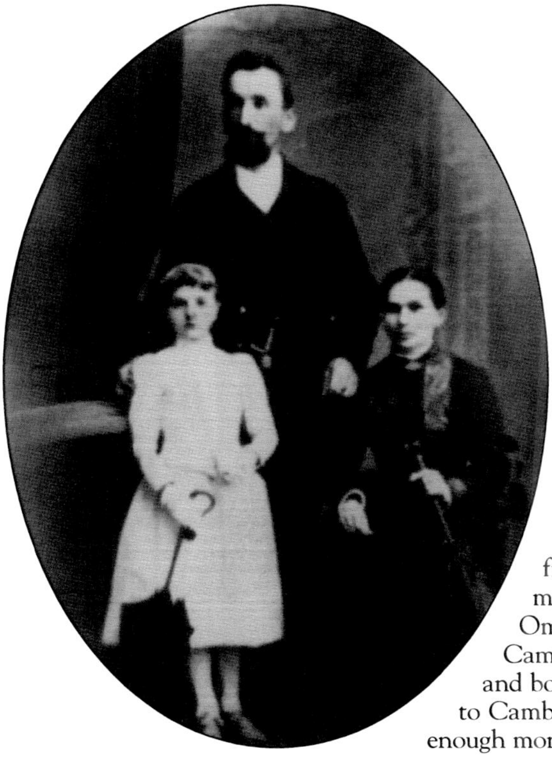

Ignatz and Ursula Kovac and Mary, Their Daughter. After coming to America from Austria, Ignatz worked in the iron ore mines in Pennsylvania and a slaughterhouse in Omaha, Nebraska. He was recruited to come to Cambria for work. Then he returned to Omaha and bought caps and watches. He took those back to Cambria and sold them to other miners, earning enough money to bring his family to join him.

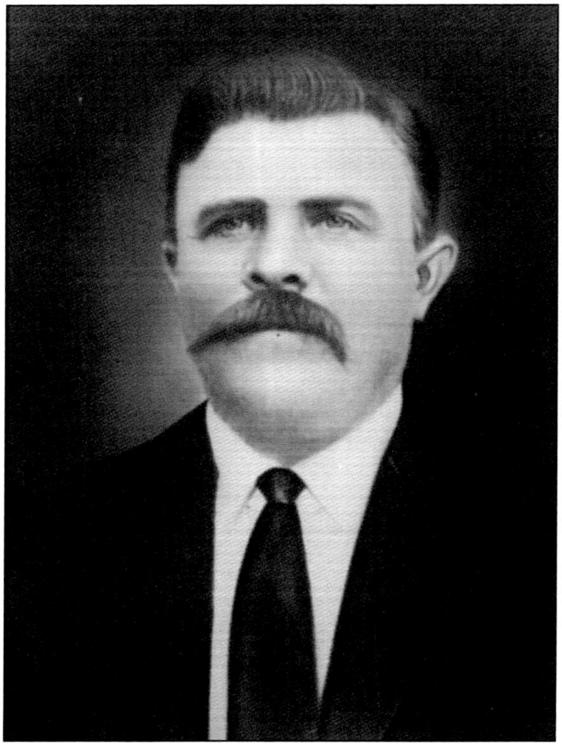

Stanley (Stanislaw Przybylski) Pzinski. Known as Stanislaw Przybylski in Poland, he fled to avoid the constant revolutions. In America, he became Stanley Pzinski and worked in mines in the East before making his way west to Cambria. Stanley spoke several languages, which was very helpful at Cambria, where people from many nationalities worked. He became a foreman of the coke ovens and homesteaded 17 miles north of the Cambria mines.

Andy Wocicki. Andy Wocicki was born in Warsaw, Poland, in 1879, arrived in the United States in 1907, and took a train to Cambria. He married Agnes Dominski two years later, and their wedding involved a three-day celebration. They homesteaded on Red Creek on the Canyon Springs. He worked in the mines during the week and walked to his homestead to work on weekends. Pictured is Andy Wocicki holding his namesake, Andy Podio.

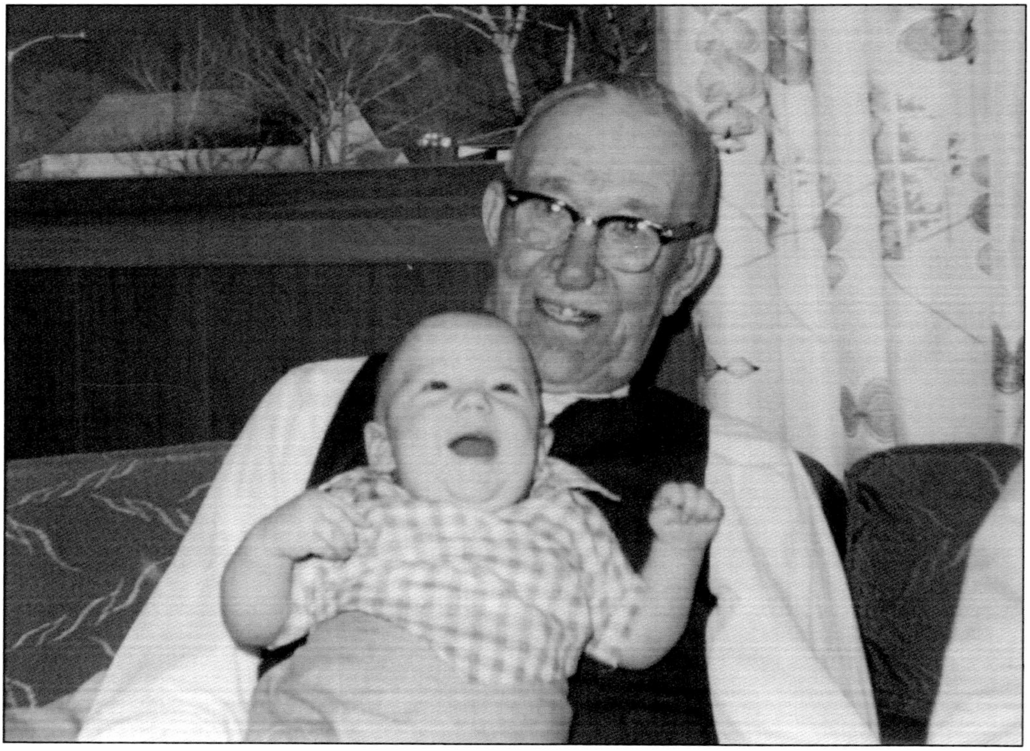

Matt and Rosi Perino. Matt and Rosi Perino were born in Northern Italy near the Swiss border in 1878 and 1886, respectively. Although living just three miles apart in Italy, they never met until they both traveled a world away to Cambria. Matt worked in the Cambria mines, and Rosi worked in her sister's boardinghouse for miners. They were married in Cambria in 1904.

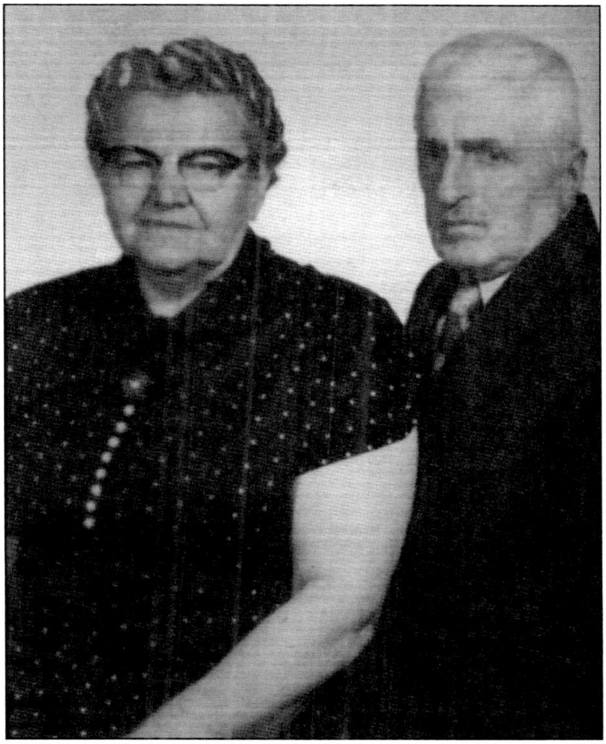

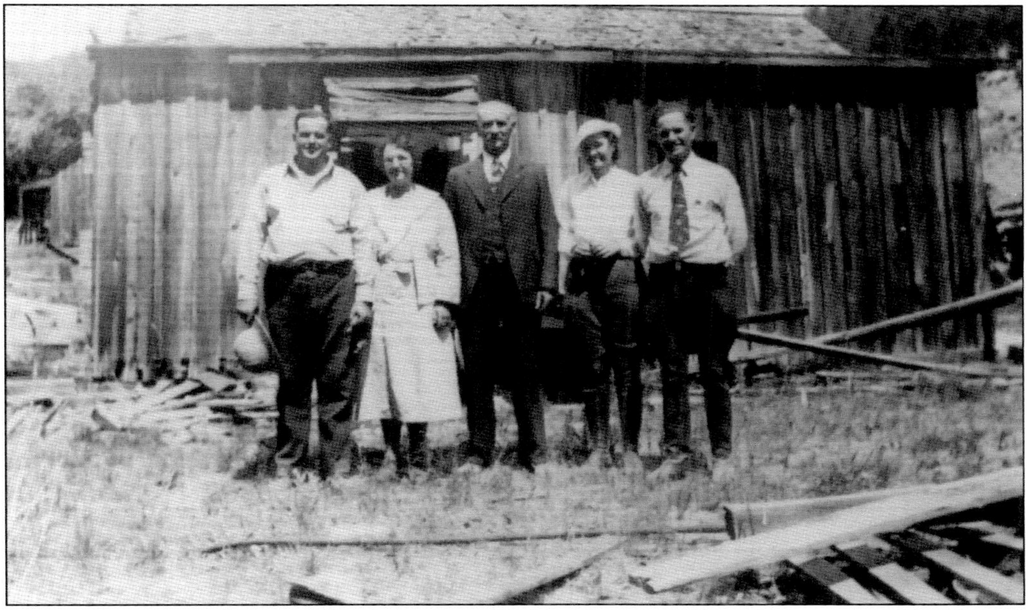

James William and Minnie May Cummings. Will was born in 1872 and Minnie in 1878. Married in 1897, they moved to Cambria in 1900. Will worked as a blacksmith for the Cambria Fuel Company. Minnie died suddenly in 1908. Will kept the family together and homesteaded in the Howard vicinity, located about 25 miles west of Newcastle. Pictured is the J. William Cummings family in 1936; from left to right are W. Ray, L. Gail, Will, Fay, and Leo.

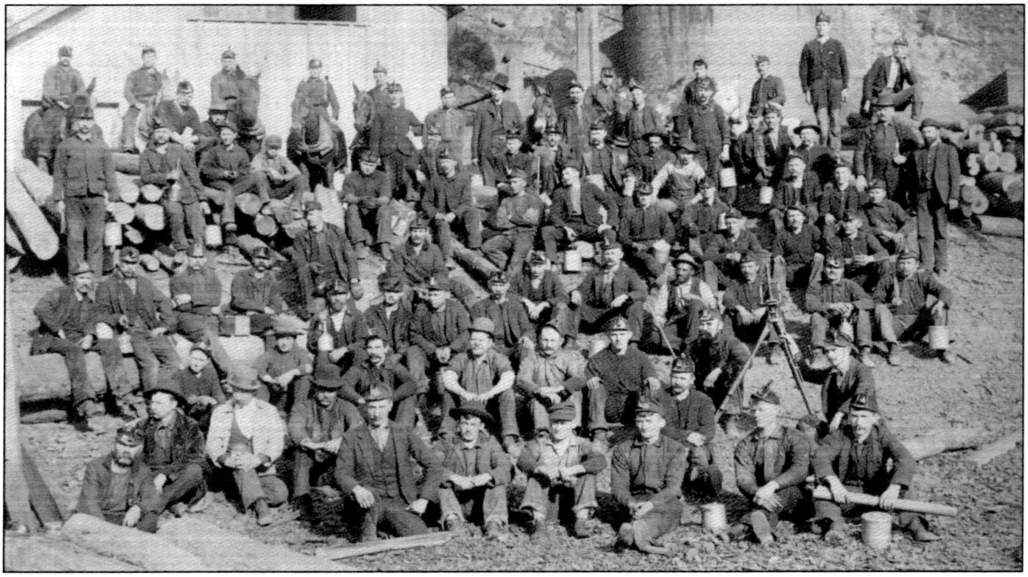

Cambria Miners. By 1900, a wave of foreign immigration hit the East Coast of the United States, and from that movement came people looking for a good place to work, an income, a warm home, and a chance for free land. Many came to Cambria and Weston County. Miners shipped their first trainload of coal from Cambria on December 30, 1889. (AMM.)

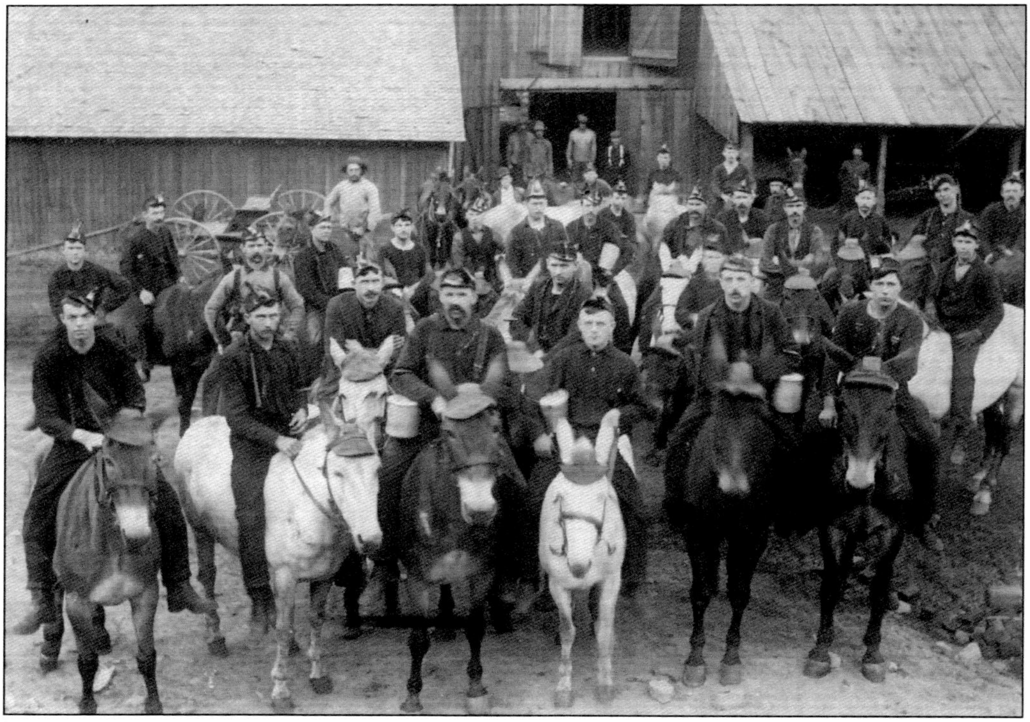

Mules in the Mines. Cambria coal miners were like other coal miners and used mechanical trains to get coal from the underground mines. However, mules were necessary to move the coal from small arms of the mine to central loading areas. (AMM.)

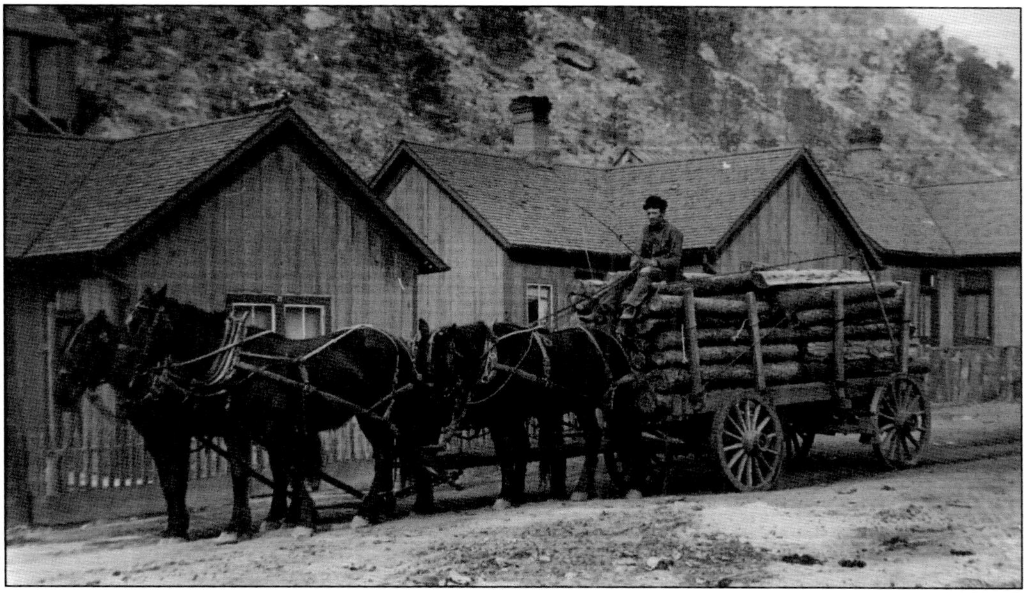

Keeping the Mines Open. Besides the miners, who worked inside mines, many men worked outside the mines to provide supplies. William J. McMoran hauled mine props to Cambria. Mine props or mine timbers were lengths of lumber used to prop up the roofs of tunnels in coal mines. (AMM.)

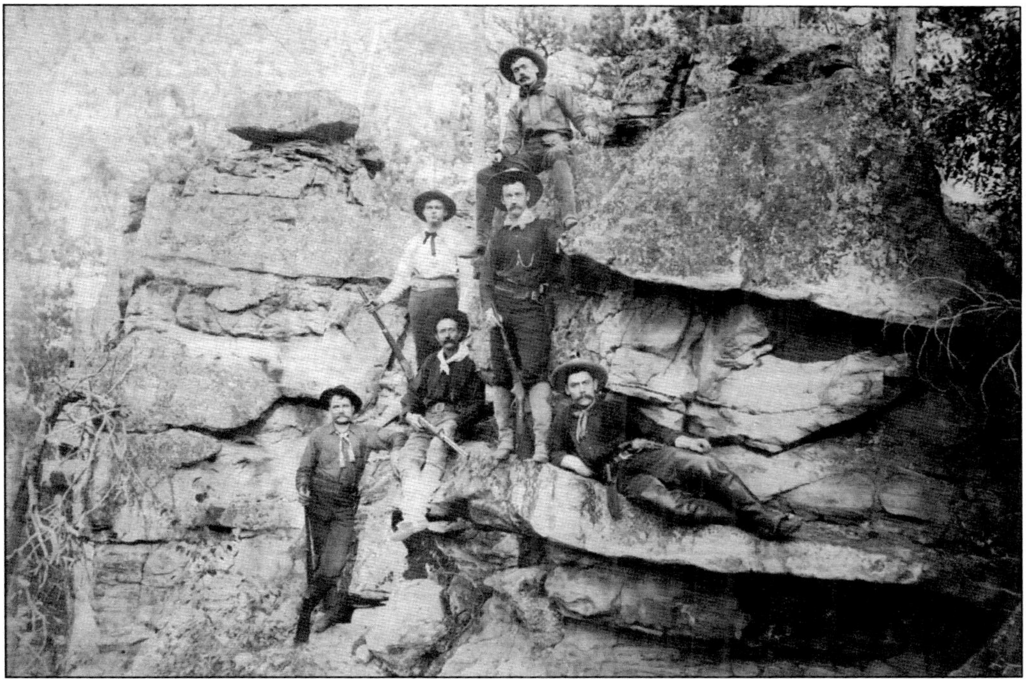

Cave Springs Canyon. A favorite place to visit west of Cambria for miners and their families was Cave Springs Canyon. One of the miners enjoying himself was Seth Alan Robinson, the reclining gentleman at lower right, who was the brother of Nellie Geraldine Robinson, the wife of Louis Charles Thoeming. (AMM.)

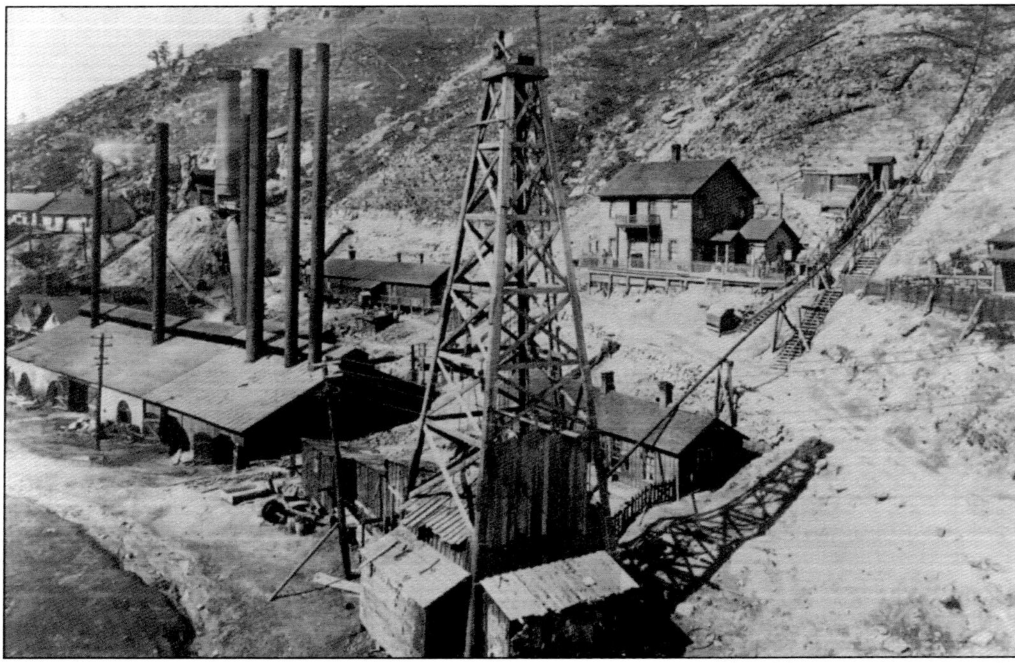

CAMBRIA SCHOOL. When men came to work, many with families, a school became a priority. The Antelope Table School was built on top of the valley, and children had to climb 365 steps to get to school. Those miners who lived outside of the canyon climbed down into the mines to get to work, and children who lived in the canyon climbed up the steps to their school. (AMM.)

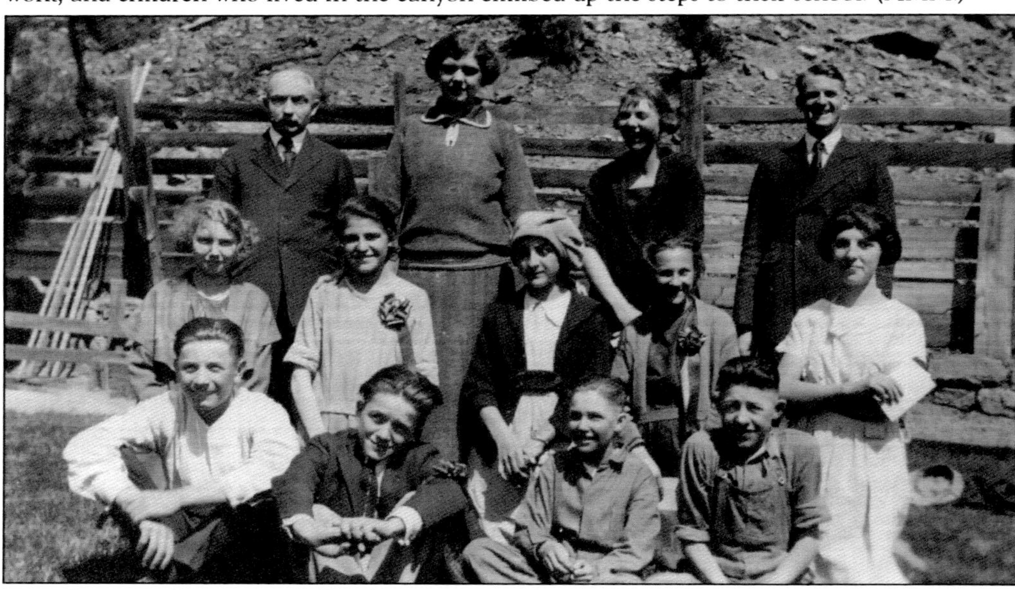

1923 CAMBRIA GRADUATES. Ella Christensen was the only graduating high school student in 1923. The other students were graduating from eighth grade. The photograph shows, from left to right, (first row) Joe Weigher, Arthur Giles, Dennis Routes, and James Musset; (second row) Dora Westova, Mary Bartalemeo, Lena Cardacia, Lily Corozza, and Norina Rizzi; (third row) Mr. Hale, principal and teacher; Miss Sparks, English and languages; Ella Christensen; and Mr. Elder. (AMM.)

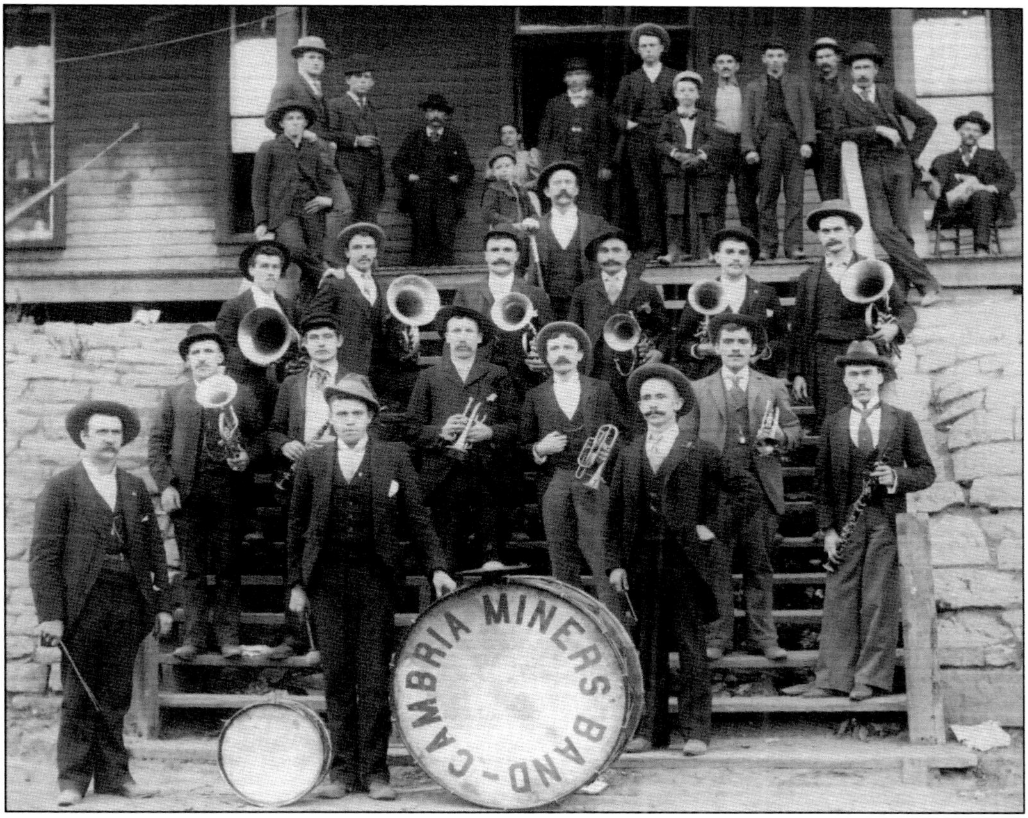

CAMBRIA MINERS BAND. With hard work aside, Cambria was a social place. Weddings and celebrations sometimes lasted for three days. Music was loved and valued. It was said that if one could play a musical instrument or play baseball, he or she was guaranteed employment at Cambria. The Cambria Opera House was the cultural center of the coal-mining town. The floor, which was made of oak and finely waxed, was a focal point of the hall. (AMM.)

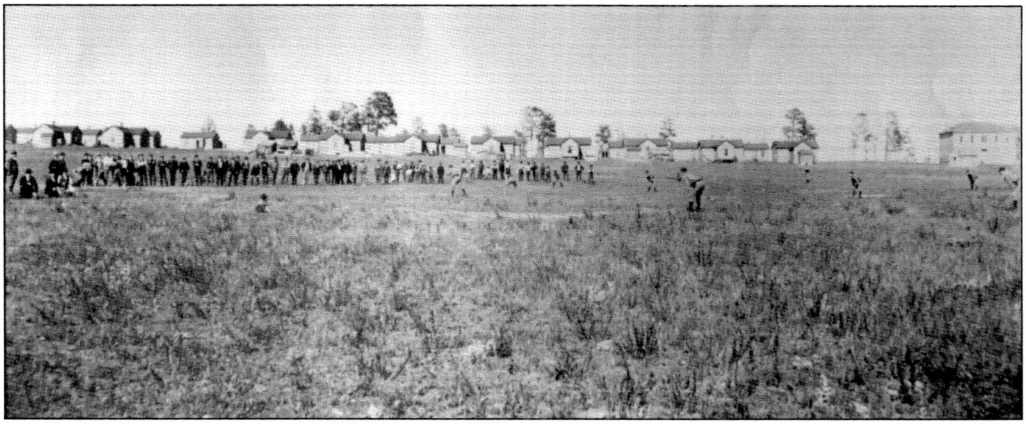

BASEBALL AT ANTELOPE CITY. Entertainment was necessary for miners and their families due to the hard work and isolated living arrangements. Besides music, people participated in athletic events, baseball being a primary American pastime. On June 16, 1894, the Never Sweats competed with the McGees in a baseball game at Cambria, Wyoming, on the hill (Antelope Table). (AMM.)

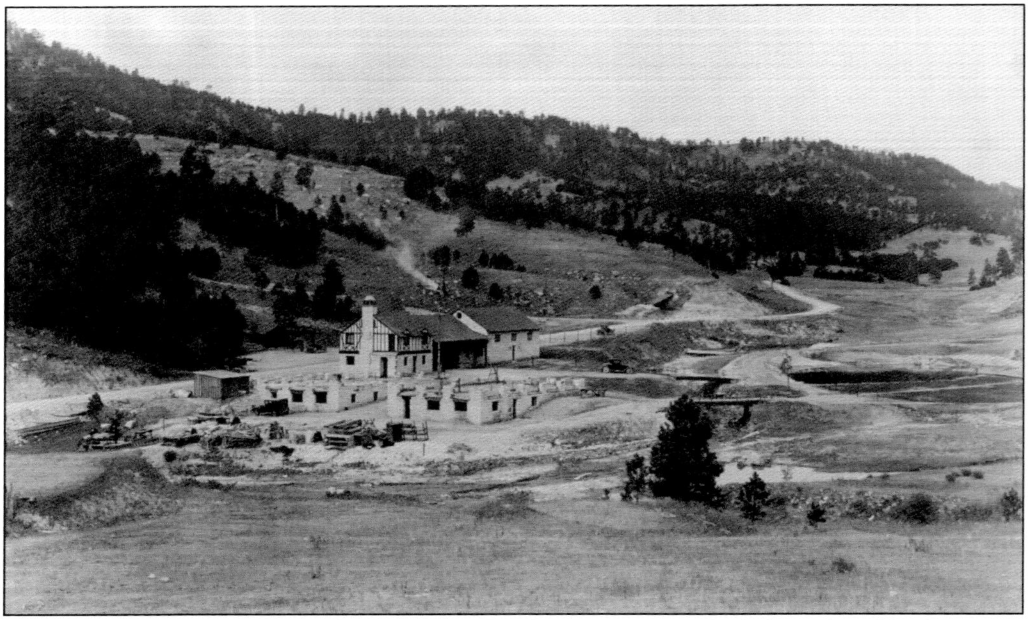

CAMBRIA INN. In 1924, under the direction of architect J.T. Rosenthal, the railroad built a resort for the miners and their families. When the building was completed in 1927, it was called the Cambria Inn. Unfortunately, the beautiful resort was finished just as the coal veins played out in the Cambria mines. (AMM.)

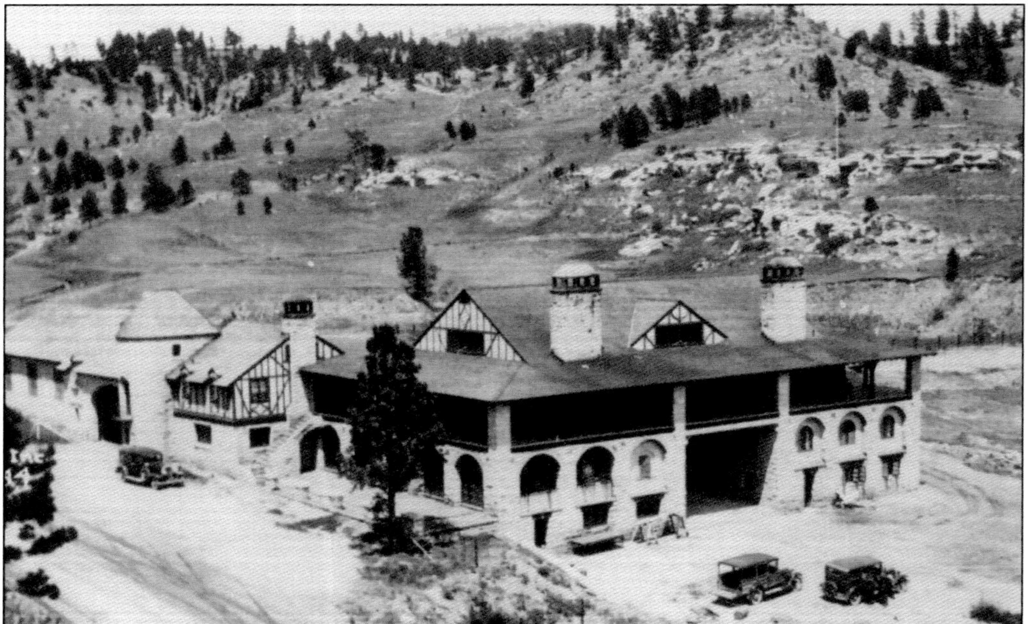

FLYING V. After the Cambria mines closed, the vast track of land surrounding the mines and the Cambria Inn were leased by the Driskell Cattle Company. They branded their cattle with the Flying V brand. Cambria Inn has had several owners over the years. In one of the changes, the hotel's name was changed to the Flying V after the cattle brand. (AMM.)

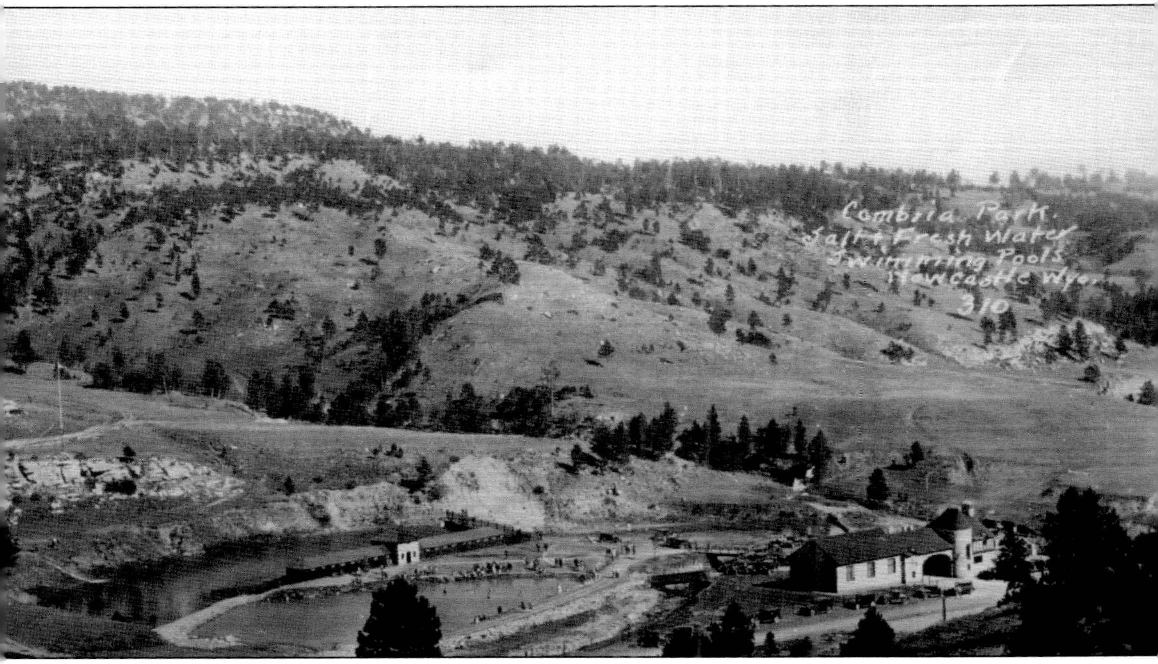

Cambria Casino Park. The Flying V was also called the Cambria Casino Park and served as a resort and retreat for the workers and families of Cambria. The railroad established a museum as a memorial to the Cambria miners in the chapel that was built alongside. It was dedicated to Thomas Wolfe, the first president of the Cambria Fuel Company. The Flying V never realized its dream or purpose. The historic lodge has served as a guest ranch, country club complete with a nine-hole golf course, gambling casino, ministerial college in the 1940s, hunting lodge, and restaurant. (AMM.)

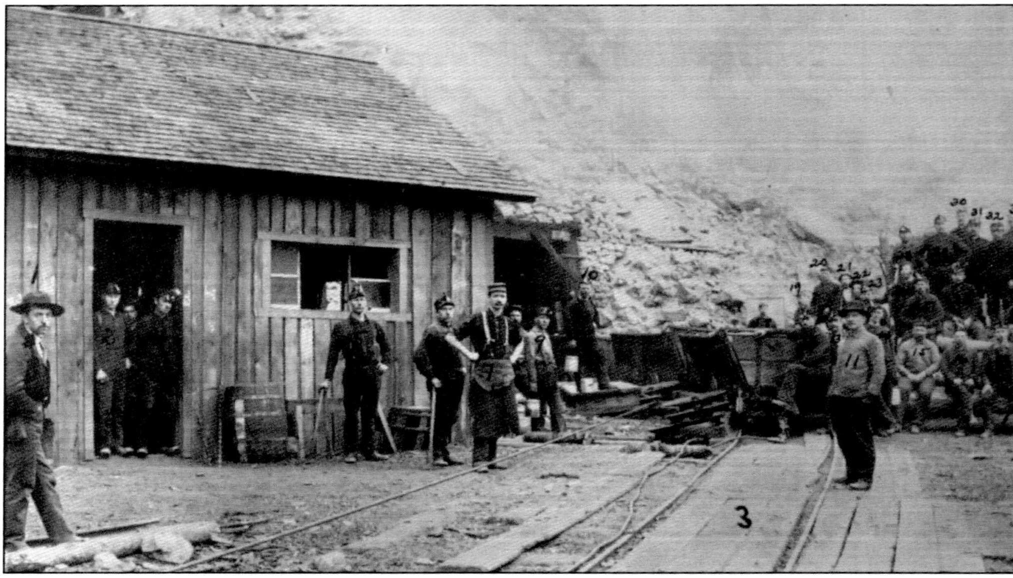

CAMBRIA MINERS. For almost 40 years, Cambria prospered. It was said that there were enough coal resources there to "fuel the fires of hell for an eternity," but the reserves had been grossly exaggerated. In 1928, the coal veins ran out. After a frantic search for more veins, none could be found. In its time, Cambria produced approximately 13 million tons of coal at an estimated value of $20 million. On March 15, 1928, at 4:30 p.m., the mine whistle blew for the last time. The town was dismantled. (AMM.)

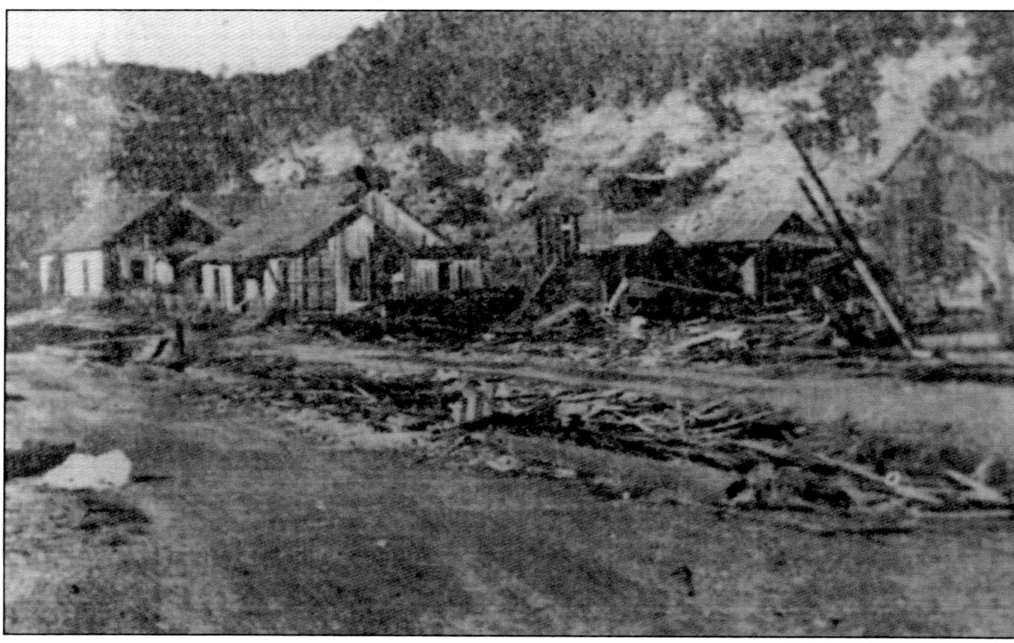

THE END OF AN ERA. Cambria disappeared, with buildings being torn down and their lumber being used elsewhere. All that is left today are memories of a town, a way of life, and a place that still holds a spot in the heart of Weston County as one of the greatest moments in its history and development. (AMM.)

Five

Weston County Towns

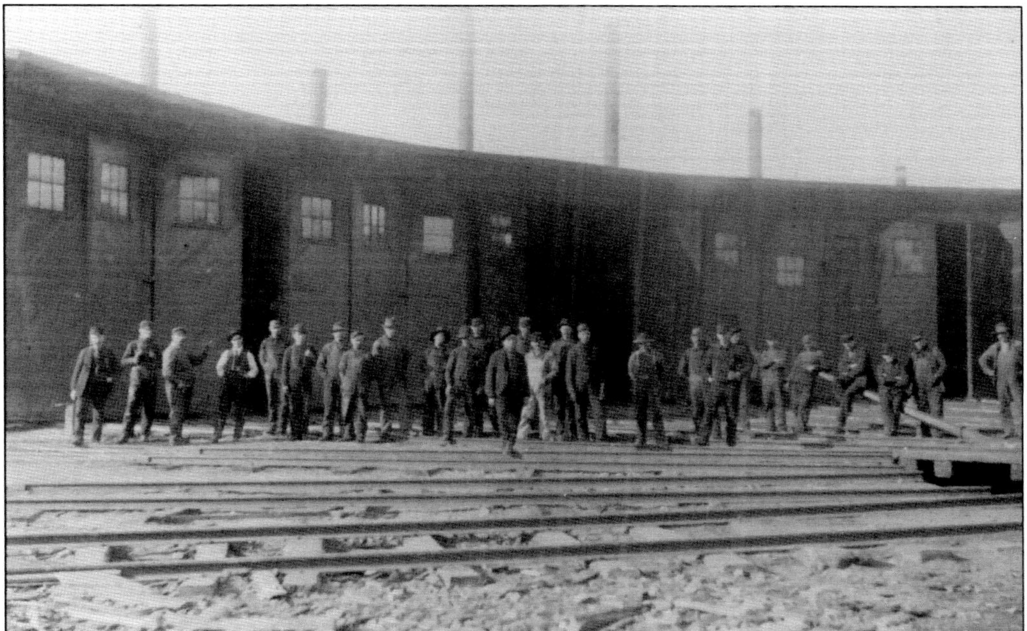

Cambria Connected to Newcastle. The railroad first established Newcastle as an important place on its ever-westerly route. Newcastle would be a crucial juncture between the railroad and the spur line that ran to Cambria. Coal coming down the spur line to Newcastle would keep the train engines fuelled and running. The picture shows workers at the roundhouse by the tracks in early Newcastle.

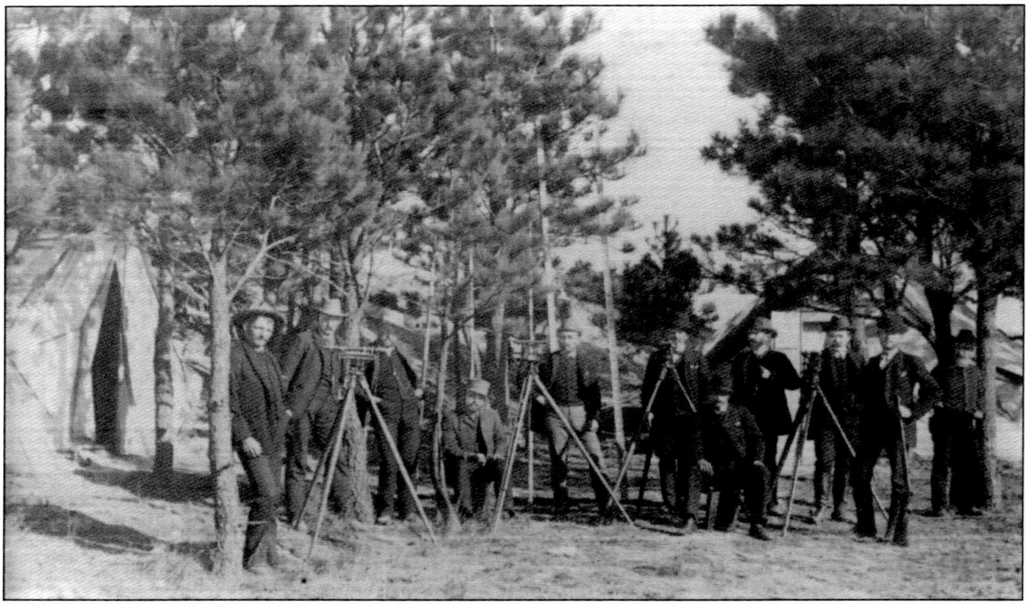

The Naming of Newcastle. In July 1889, a large camp of the Kilpatrick and Collins Construction Company arrived onsite. W.H. Kilpatrick, second from left, surveyed for the railroad coming into Newcastle. J.H. Hemingway, a superintendent at the Cambria Coal Company, was given the honor of naming the new city. He called it Newcastle after his hometown, Newcastle upon Tyne, a coal-mining center in England. (AMM.)

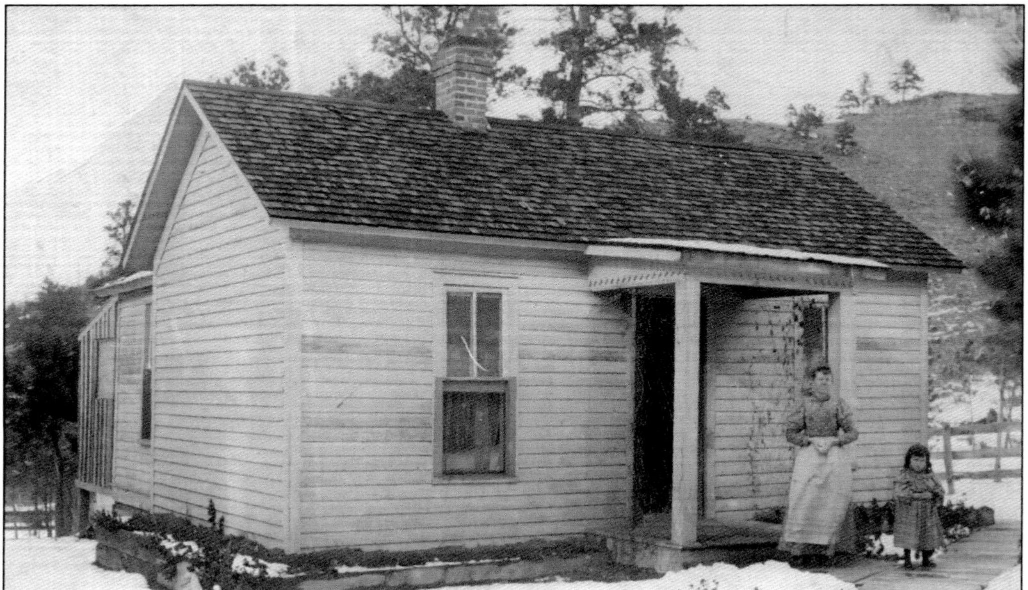

Early Newcastle. On September 10, 1889, grading and filling had progressed far enough that lots went on sale. A 25-foot lot sold for $1,500. By that evening, $30,000 worth of lots had been sold. Among the first to buy lots was Peter J. Kinney, a man of Irish parentage who called Newcastle home for nearly 40 years. Pictured are his wife, Ethel, and their daughter Ruth Rachael at their home.

FRANK MONDELL. In October 1889, Newcastle was incorporated. The first election was held on November 12 that year, and Frank Mondell was elected mayor. Born in 1860, Mondell came to the area in 1888 under orders from the Kilpatrick brothers to find coal for the building of the Burlington Railroad. He was elected to the first state legislature in 1890 and to Congress in 1894. He served Weston County in many capacities during his life. (AMM.)

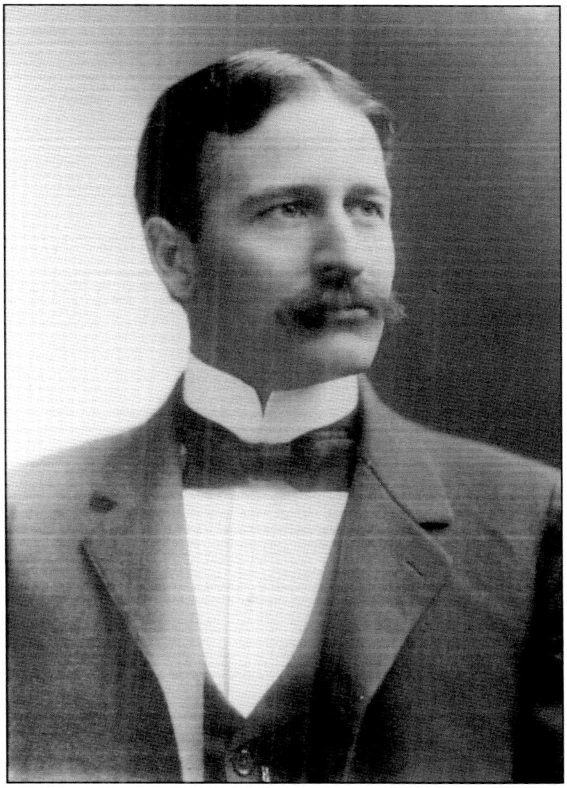

MONDELL HOUSE. Demolished in 1946 to accommodate the construction of the Weston County Memorial Hospital, the Mondell house was home to Frank Wheeler and Ida Harris Mondell. Frank supervised the operations to start mining in Cambria, and his name is tied to several institutions in Weston County, such as Mondell Airport and Mondell Heights Home. Congressman Mondell authored the 1909 Homestead Act, originally known as the Mondell Act. (AMM.)

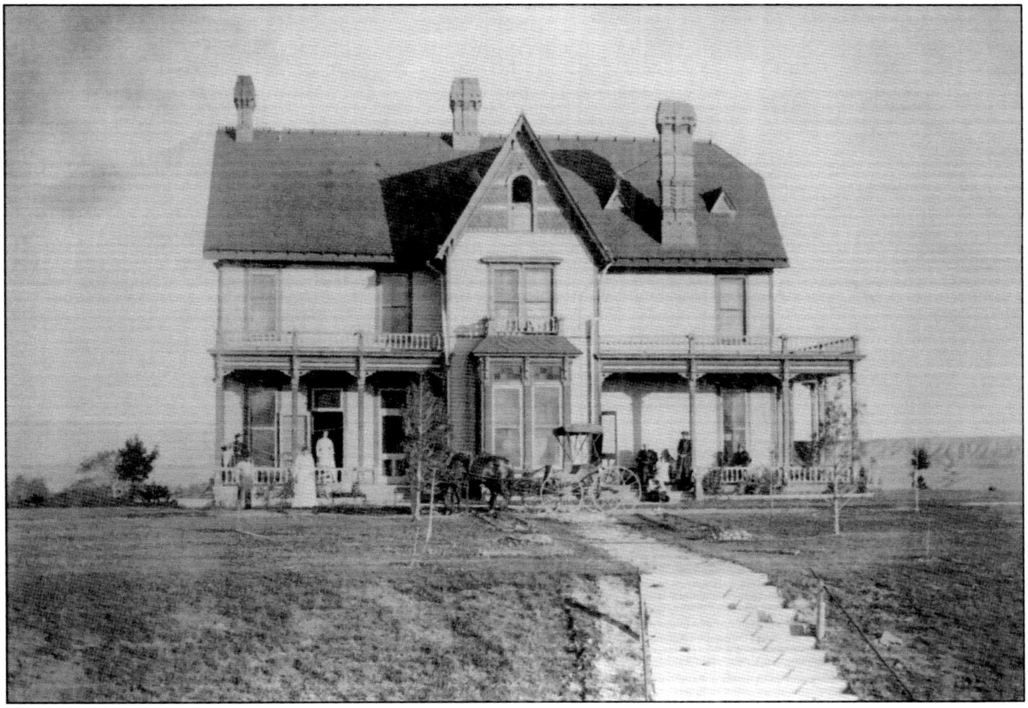

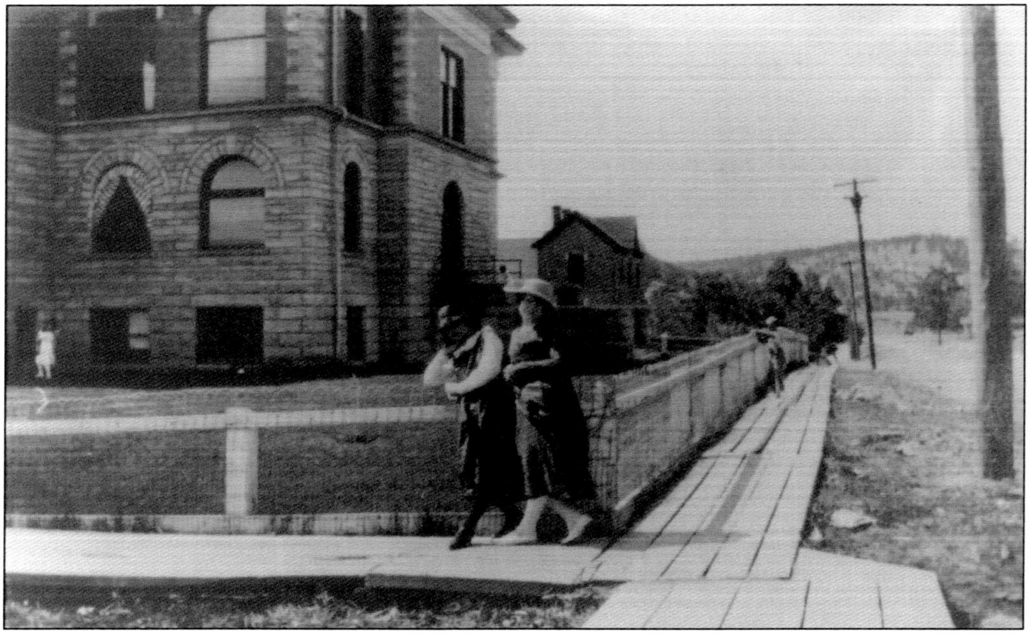

Early Law and Order. Early Newcastle was a rowdy town, full of cowboys, dancing girls, saloons, miners, railroad workers, and construction crews, who after a day's work liked to cut loose and have a little fun. The Weston County Courthouse on the left and old jailhouse in the background of this photograph served their purposes in keeping law and order. For the most part, Newcastle was a law-abiding place.

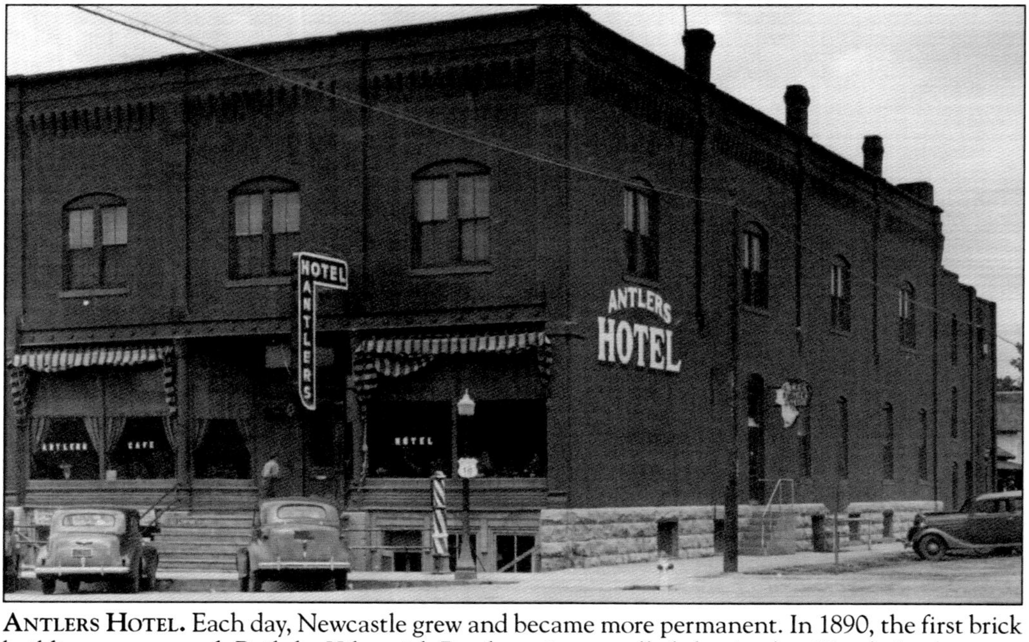

Antlers Hotel. Each day, Newcastle grew and became more permanent. In 1890, the first brick building was erected. Built by Kilpatrick Brothers, it was called the Antlers Hotel. At the time, it was a grand hotel. Over the years, it has served many other purposes, and it is still used today, although not as a hotel. (AMM.)

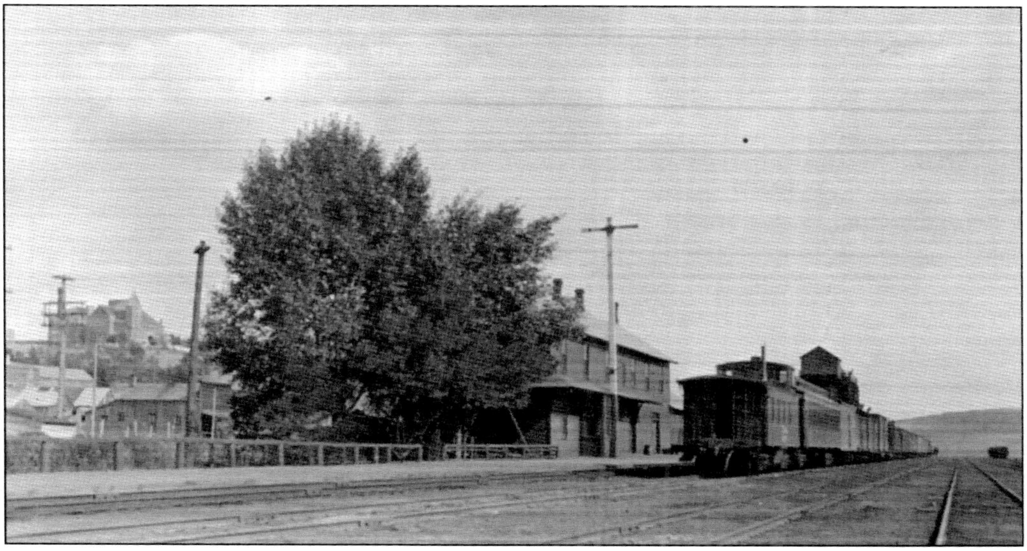

Newcastle Train Depot. In November 1889, the first passenger railroad arrived in Newcastle. The first depot was a house unloaded off a flatcar. That day, telegraph lines were installed, and a message was sent that said, "Newcastle is connected to the railroad." In 1936, a modern depot replaced the one that had been hauled in on a flatcar. (AMM.)

Ida Jarvis. In 1916, Ida Jarvis was one of many newcomers who arrived at the Newcastle depot. When Ida started her schooling, she only spoke French. She learned English and finished school with "normal training," which qualified her to teach. She taught in Wyoming at the Red Butte School north of Newcastle and in South Dakota and Nebraska. She worked as a governess and a night telephone operator. Then she returned to Wyoming to teach. Secretly, she married Robert Elliott at Christmastime in 1921. They kept it secret because teachers were not allowed to be married. (Courtesy of Bobbi Jo Stith.)

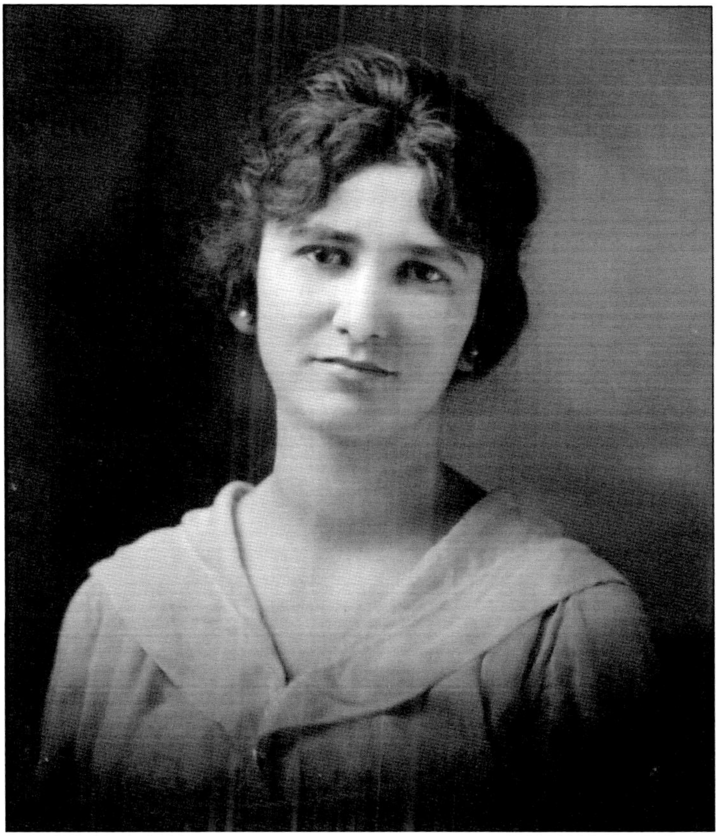

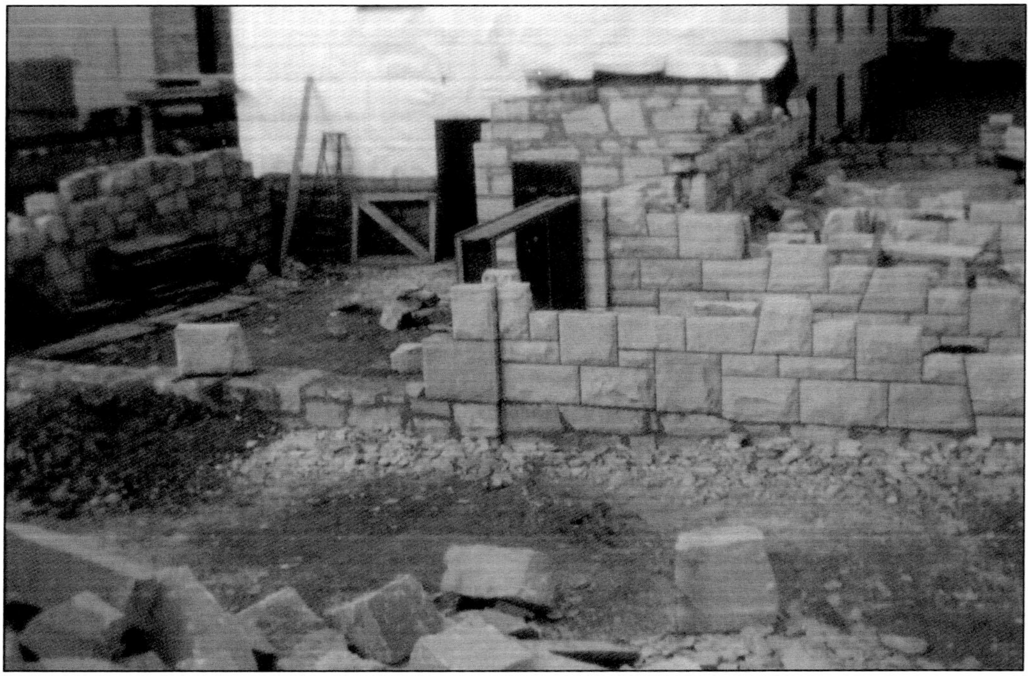

Early Downtown Newcastle. Towns built along the railroad either survived and thrived or died out. Brick or stone buildings gave Newcastle a feeling of permanence. It was a railroad town that thrived. To this day, it serves as the county seat and the center of Weston County. The upper photograph shows early stone construction of Toomey's Mill, a flour mill originally built in 1905. On the right in the lower photograph are the steps to the courthouse and county offices. On the left is the Nichols Block. Both buildings were designed and construction was overseen by Charles A. Randall.

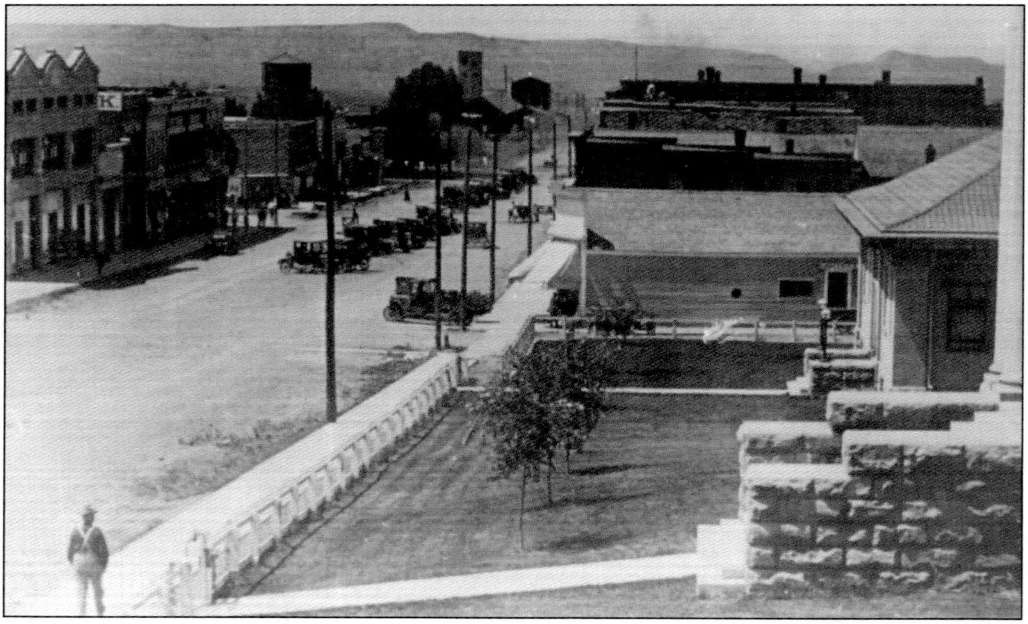

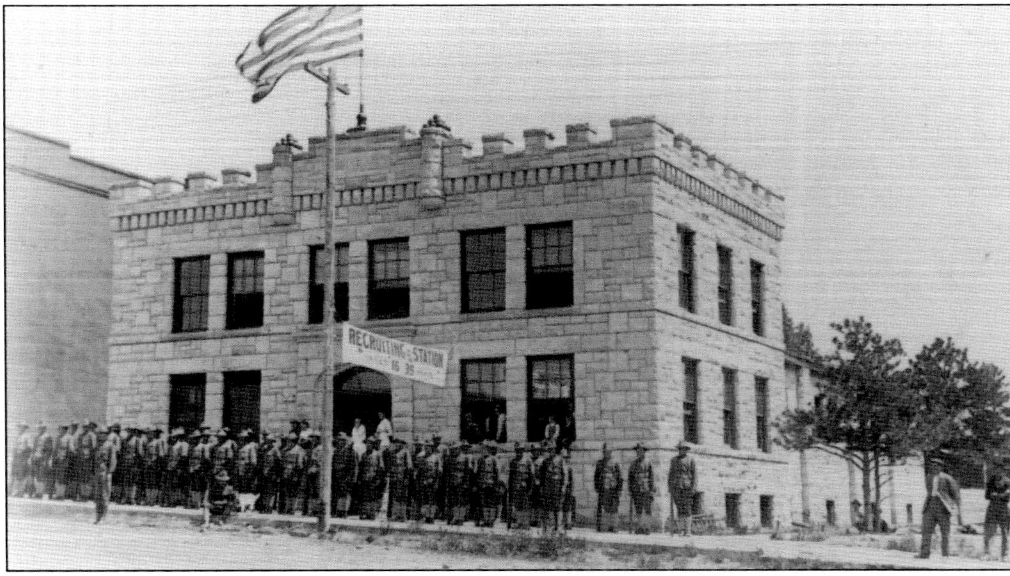

WYOMING NATIONAL GUARD ARMORY. One of Newcastle's early, beautiful stone buildings was the National Guard Armory on Main Street. The first troop, Company A, was organized in Newcastle in 1899 under the command of Captain Gates. The building was two stories high and had a basement. It was completed in 1914 at a cost of $15,000, sold to Continental Oil in 1960, and dismantled, making room for the present-day post office.

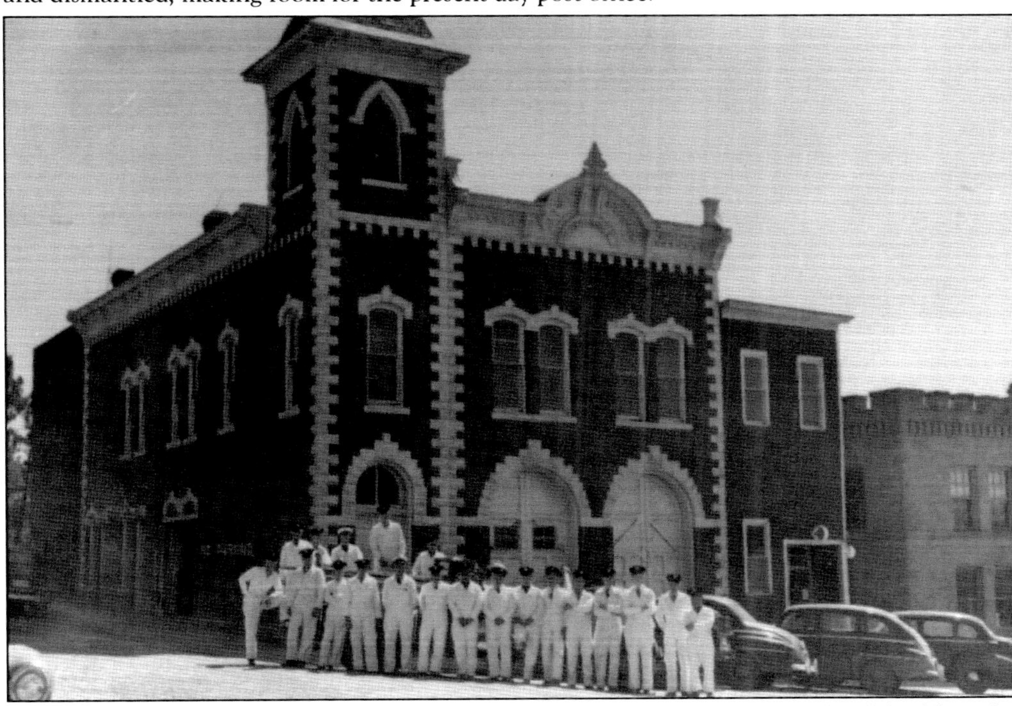

NEWCASTLE CITY HALL. The early Newcastle City Hall was housed in a fine brick building that also provided a home to Newcastle's early fire department. Shown here is Newcastle's volunteer fire department in 1940 with city hall in the background.

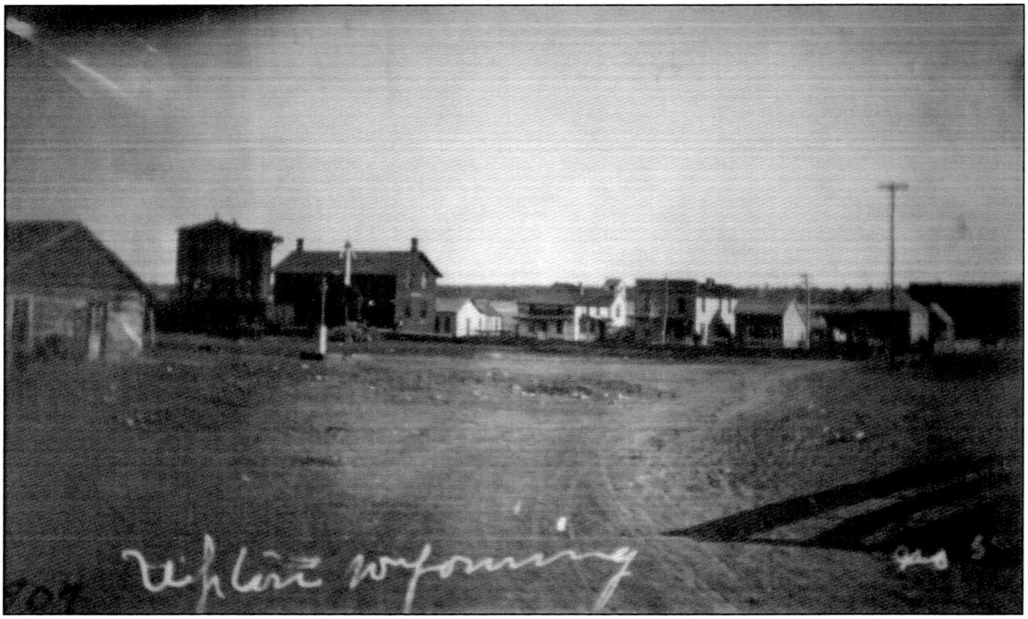

Early Upton. Down the tracks about 29 miles west of Newcastle, a band of settlers established Iron Town, a camp on the banks of Iron Creek, named for its metallic brackish water. The photograph shows Upton after its beginnings at Iron Town, when it was no longer a camp along the creek. The main street ran parallel to the railroad track, where a coal chute and waterline serviced railroad engines.

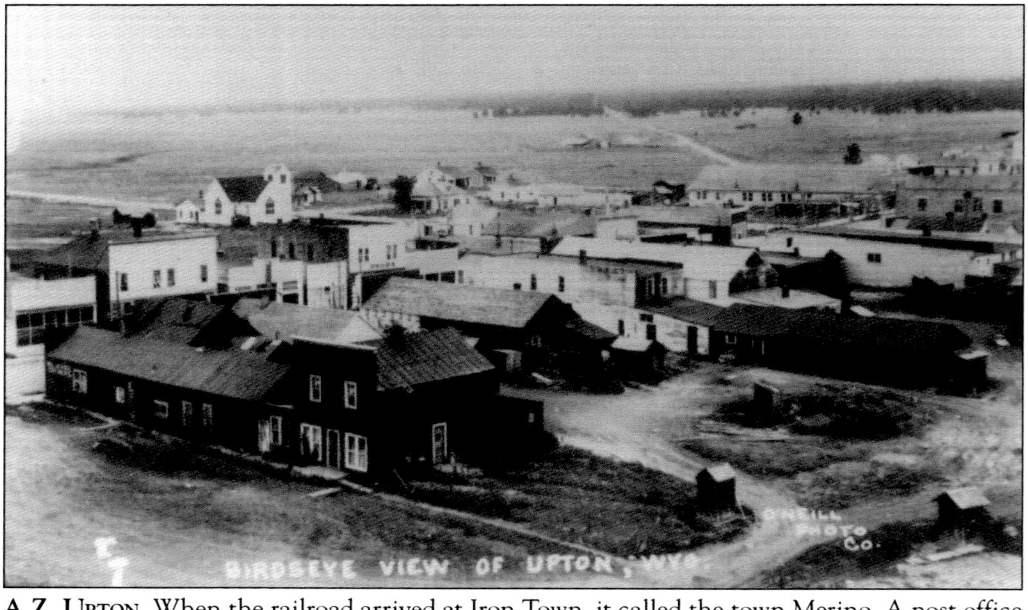

A.Z. Upton. When the railroad arrived at Iron Town, it called the town Merino. A post office was established in 1890, and the little town thrived for a year. When the railroad moved on, the post office closed. However, in 1892, the railroad established a depot and supply station at Merino. In 1901, the town's name was changed to Upton in honor of railroad employee A.Z. (also known as George) Upton.

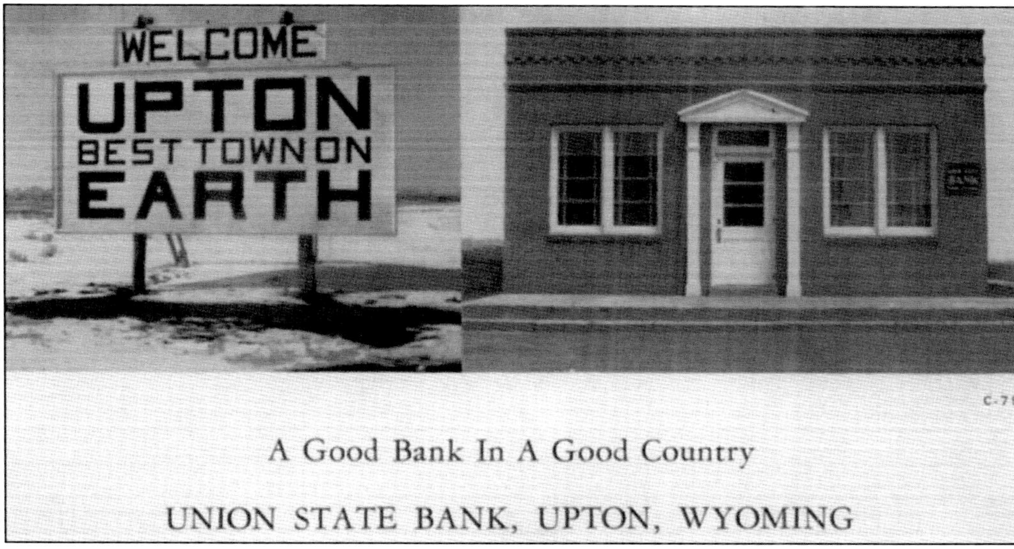

BEST TOWN ON EARTH. A.Z. Upton is given credit for the town's slogan "Upton: the Best Town on Earth." Used to promote the town, the slogan originated when Upton claimed the population doubled with his marriage. It was more legend than truth, as there were other residents living in Upton at the time. Pictured is a postcard from the Upton State Bank using the advertising slogan. Today, the slogan is painted on Upton's new water tower.

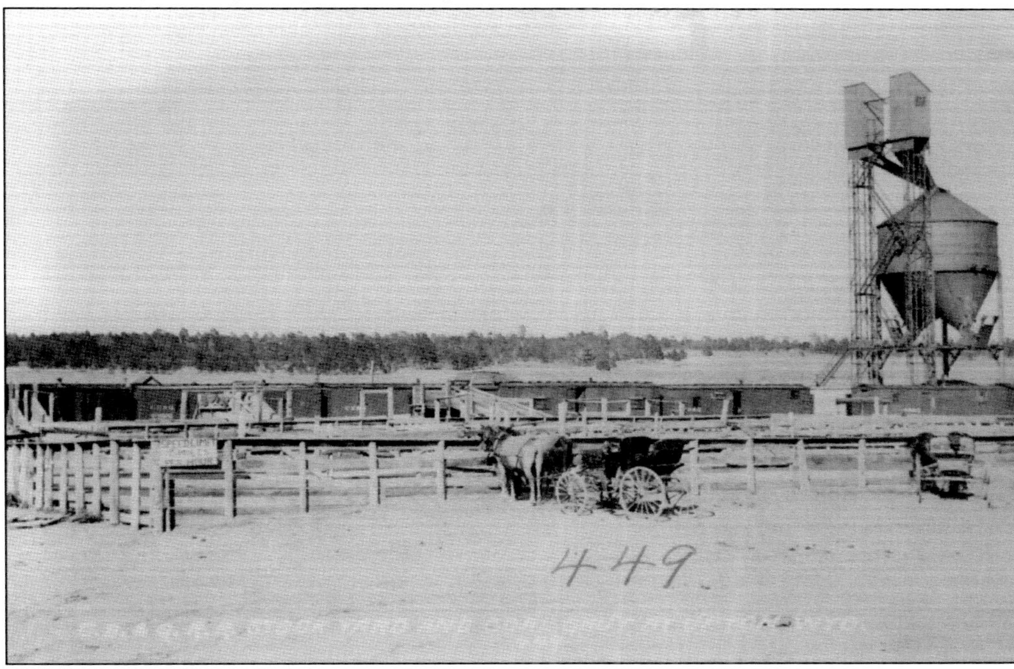

CB&Q RAILROAD. The Chicago, Burlington & Quincy Railroad took an active interest in seeing Upton develop. Water systems were built, and a coal chute was erected. To accommodate buildings and businesses that were springing up along the tracks, Pine Street was constructed from the tracks to the timber north of town. It remains a busy street in Upton today. Shown in the picture are the stockyard and coal chute in early Upton.

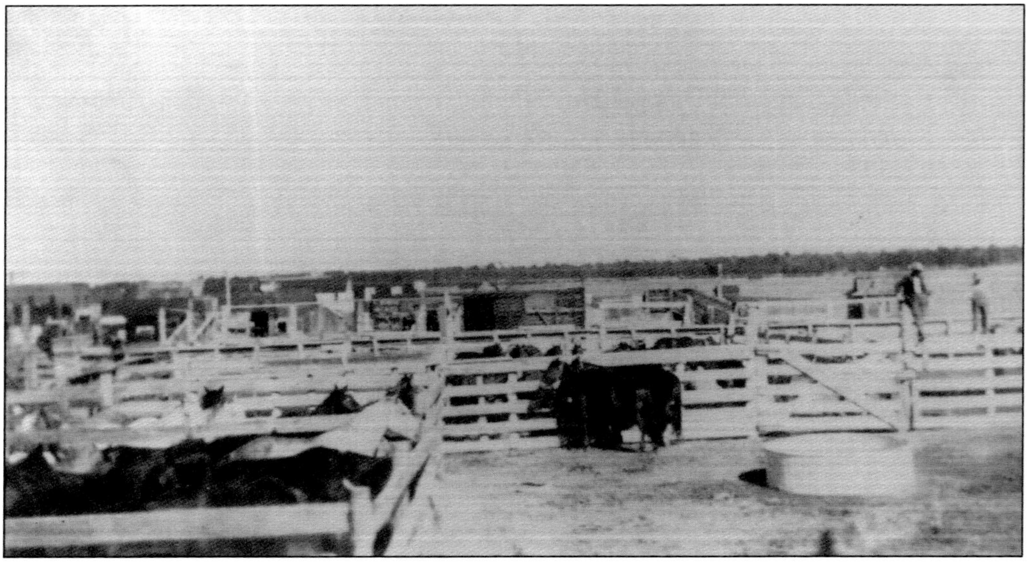

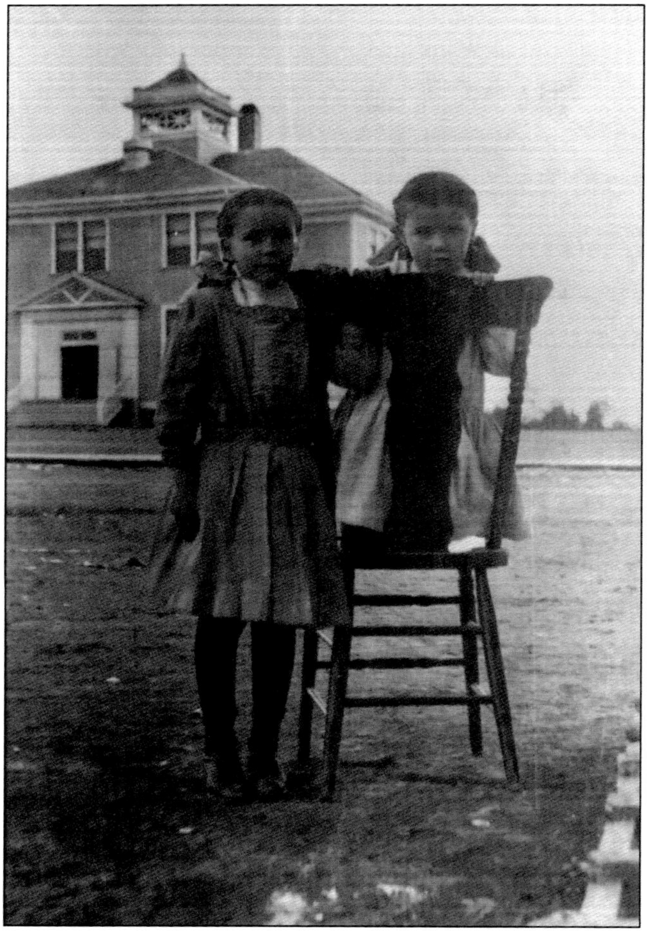

Livestock Corrals. A set of corrals was established at Upton earlier for sheep shearing and horse roundups. The railroad rebuilt those corrals for shipping local livestock on the rails. The corrals became a popular place for shearing sheep, wild horse roundups, horse sales, and rodeos that might last a whole weekend. At this time, Upton began to thrive, and it is a viable community today.

Foltz Daughters. Taken in 1912 or 1913, this picture shows Ruth Foltz Giffin on the left and Maxine Foltz Pridgeon on the right in front of the Upton School. They came to their family homestead southeast of Upton in April 1910. Both attended Upton schools, married local men (Ruth married Lloyd Giffin, and Maxine married Henry Pridgeon), and raised families in Weston County.

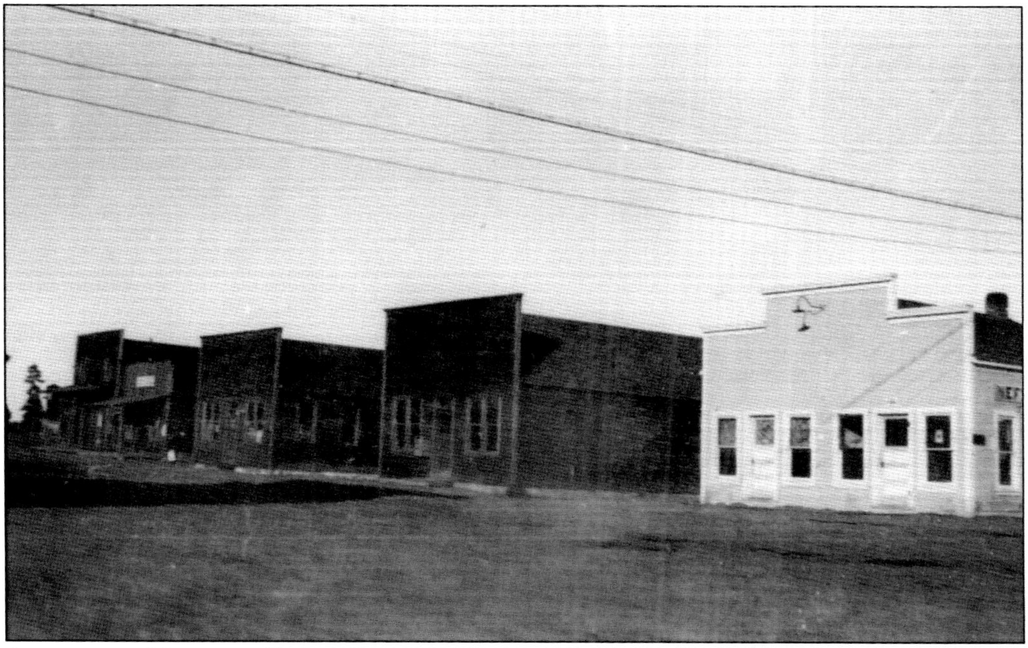

APOSTLE TO NEFSY TO OSAGE. Between Upton and Newcastle on the rail tracks is the little town of Osage. When John Nefsy first discovered oil in 1910, the new town was officially called Apostle after railroad employee George A. Apostle. In 1920, Nefsy made a successful plea to the postmaster general in Washington, DC, to rename the town Nefsy; it was to no avail, though. On November 29, 1920, the legal name was changed to Osage.

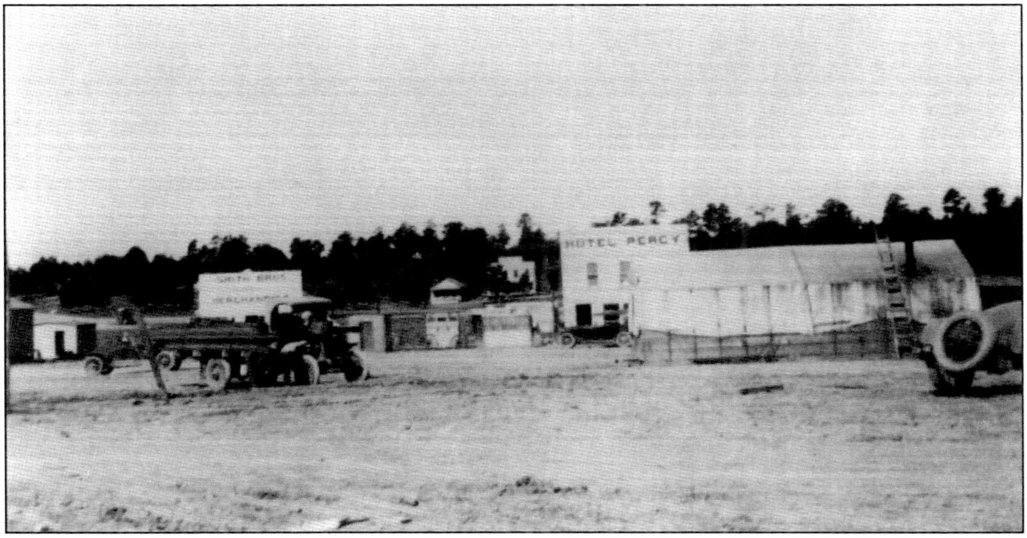

OSAGE OIL BOOM AND BUST. In 1920, a gusher oil well was struck in the Osage oil field. It caused a sensation throughout the United States, and people poured into the little town. The townspeople have tried several times to incorporate, but the propositions fail. The fortunes of the little community have ridden the wave of the oil industry's boom-and-bust cycles. Tent businesses were not uncommon (lower right) during the early boom days.

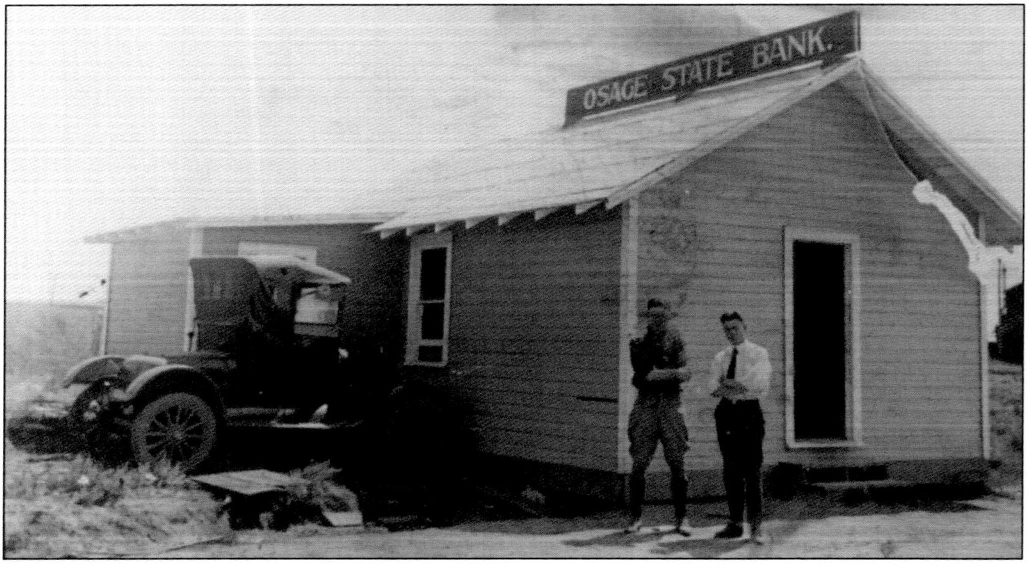

Osage State Bank. By 1920, the population of Osage was 500 persons. Although Osage had a thriving business district, many people lived in tents and barns. The business district consisted of three hotels, a lumber company, a feed store, a furniture store, an electric light plant, grocery stores, cafés, a drugstore, a bathhouse, a bank, and a newspaper. Osage built schools for its children, and one such school was named after an early Osage teacher, Kathrine "Kitty" O'Connell Moats.

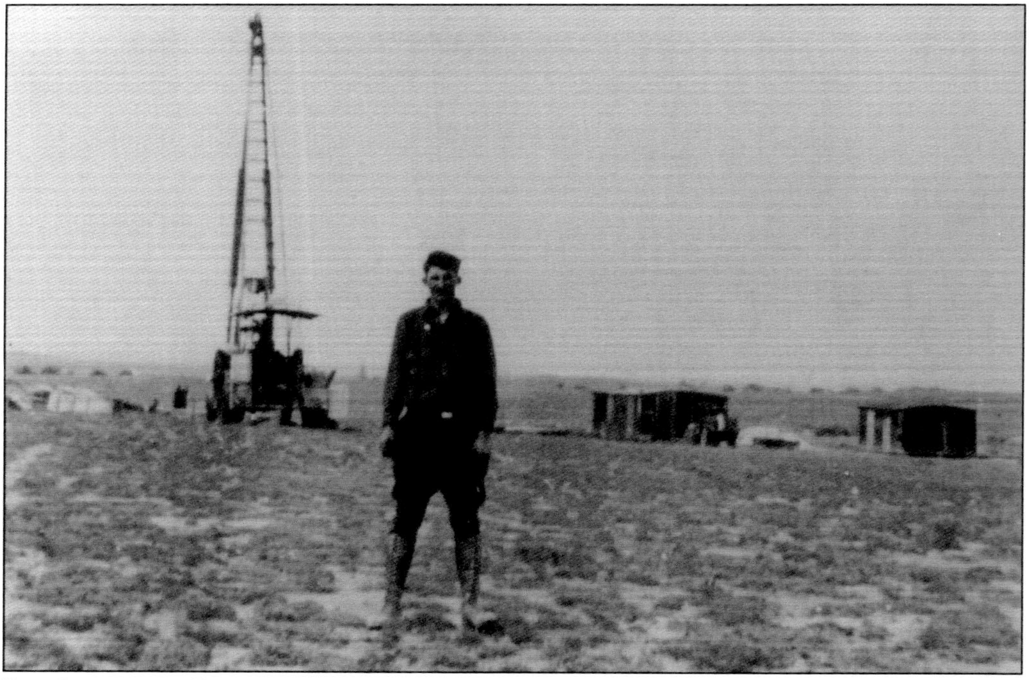

Ben Strickling. Born in 1901 in West Virginia, Ben chose oil field work over farming and left home after high school. In 1920, he invested in an oil field company with Joe Dornacher, and the two of them settled on a lease in the Osage oil field. Ben is pictured at the first camp and oil rig in Wyoming owned by High Test Oil Company.

Six

Making a Living

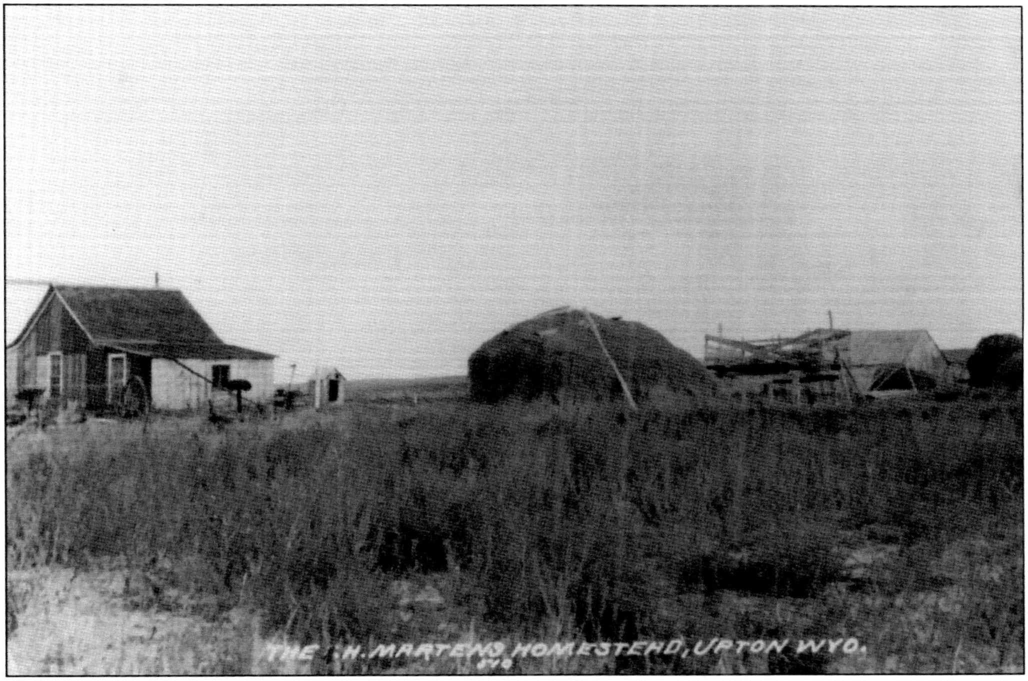

Henry P. and Clara C. Martens Homestead. While the railroad was the driving force for the development of Weston County's towns, it was also the means for bringing settlers and homesteaders. Born in 1883 to German immigrant parents, Henry homesteaded on Buffalo Creek southeast of Upton in 1914. Clara Willadson was born in 1890 to Danish immigrant parents and also homesteaded in the same area. Henry and Clara were married in 1915.

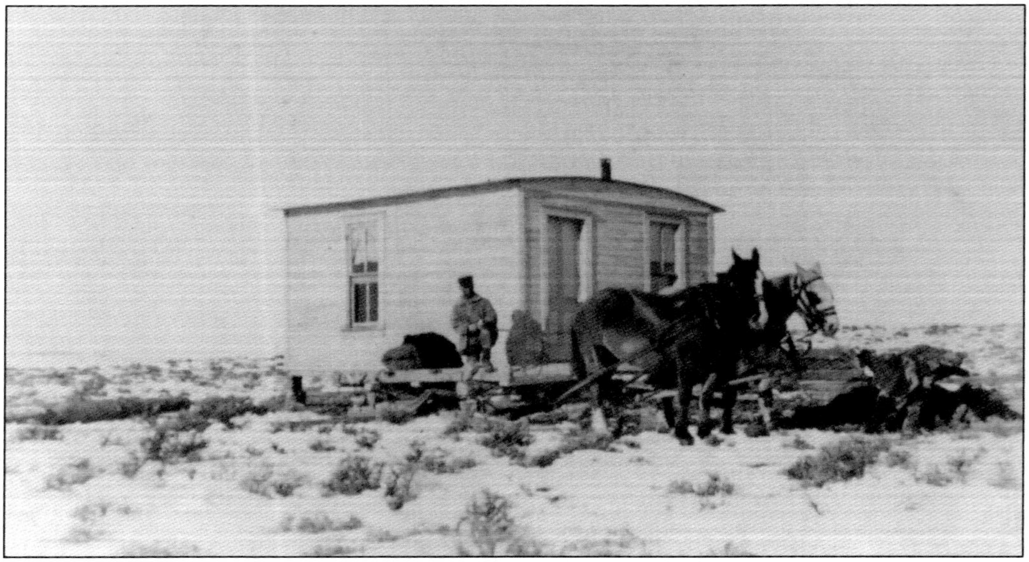

John H. Lane Sr. Some homesteaders came by train. One could get an immigrant car that provided a boxcar full of wagons, implements, animals, and all that was needed to homestead. The family rode in the passenger cars while someone, usually a male, rode in the boxcar with the stock and equipment. John H. Lane Sr. is pictured at his homestead north of Upton. His team was named Nig and Bird.

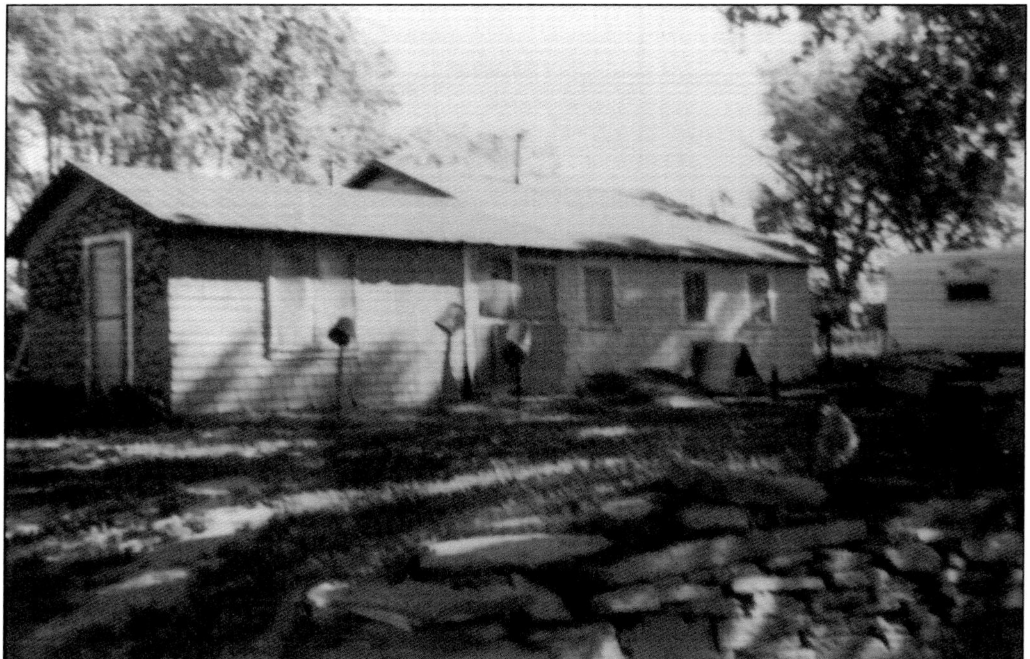

Orville and Ilene (Finn) Whitney Sod Home. Life on a homestead was not easy. Building materials were hard to come by. The eastern side of the county sits near large timber areas with accessible wood, while the western and southern parts of the county are rough sage-covered prairies without timber. A few sod homes were built like this one in 1928.

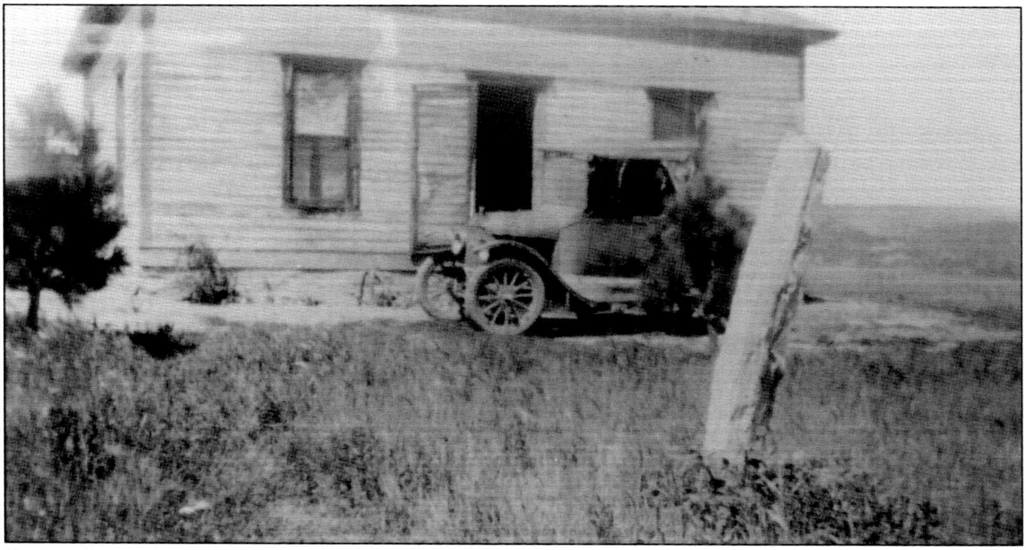

Raven Mail Carriers. Carrying mail from Upton to Raven with a team and buggy, Orie Johnson was the first mail carrier to the Raven Post Office. The second mailman was Fred Messersmith, who drove the Ford shown in this 1920s picture at the Walter Williams ranch home. Besides the mail, the carriers would take cream and eggs to stores for the farmers and would bring groceries ordered by homesteaders.

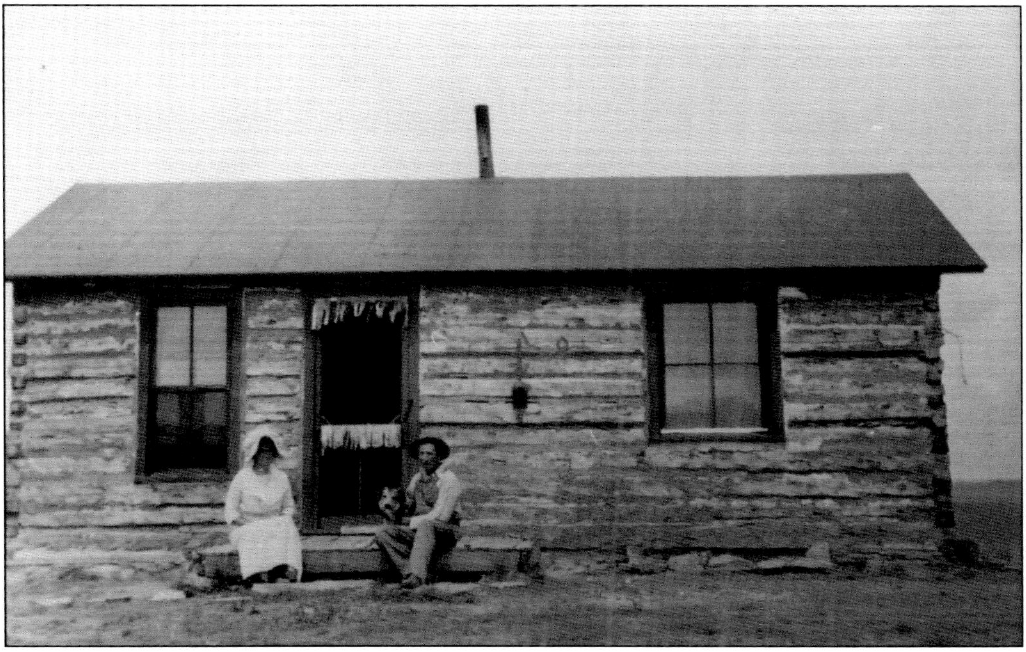

Louise Rankin Homestead. Some ingenious, or perhaps desperate, homesteaders even made homes in little dugouts buried in the side of a hill. Other more fortunate homesteaders had homes like this homestead of Louise Rankin. The picture shows Rankin and her brother Robert Rankin visiting in front of the house in 1913.

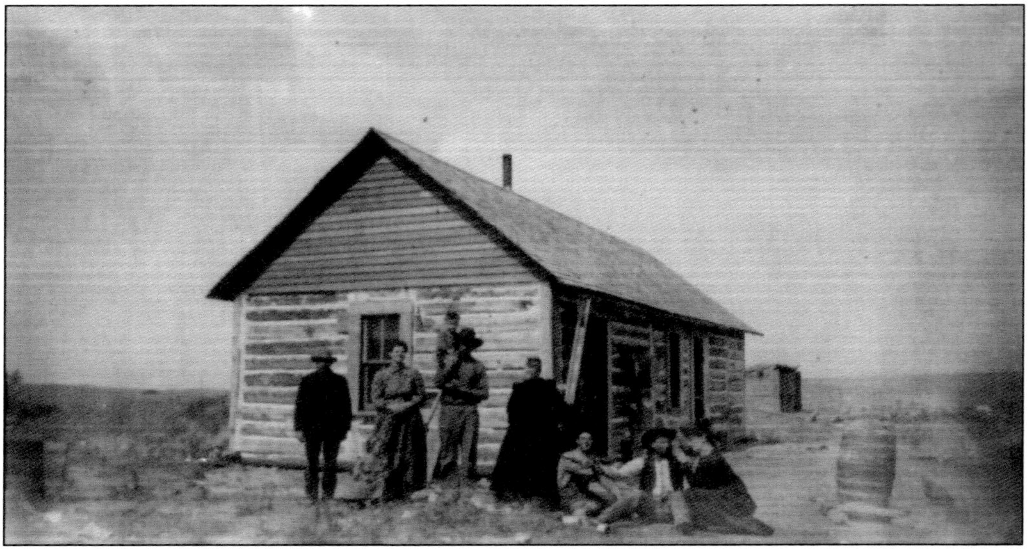

John Dunham Homestead. To say that life on a homestead in Weston County was hard would be a gross understatement. Rainfall was minimal, 11 to 17 inches a year. Pictured is the John J. Dunham home in 1905. From left to right are John Irland, Bertha Dunham, Amelia Dunham, George Dunham on the shoulders of John Dunham, Mrs. George Hopf, Joe Klodt, S.C. Holst, and Mary Holst.

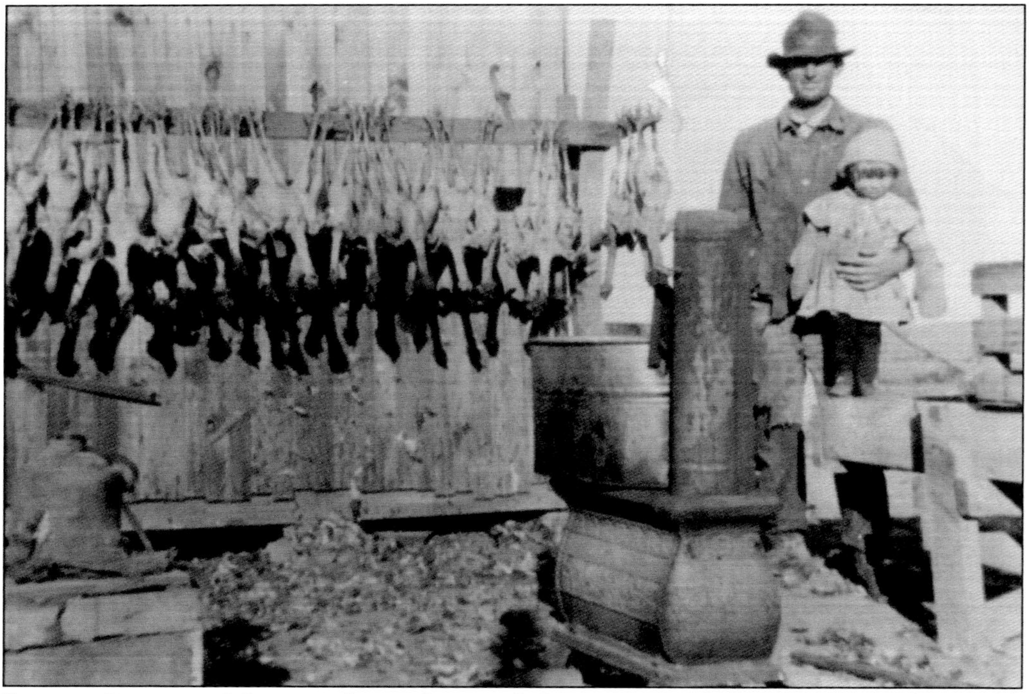

Raising Chickens. Many people supplemented their meager incomes in any way they could. Some worked at jobs off their homestead, while a good wife took care of the land, chores, and family. Some milked cows and sold cream in towns. Some raised poultry and sold the meat and eggs. This is Charlie Benne and daughter Jane with butchered chickens for sale and eating.

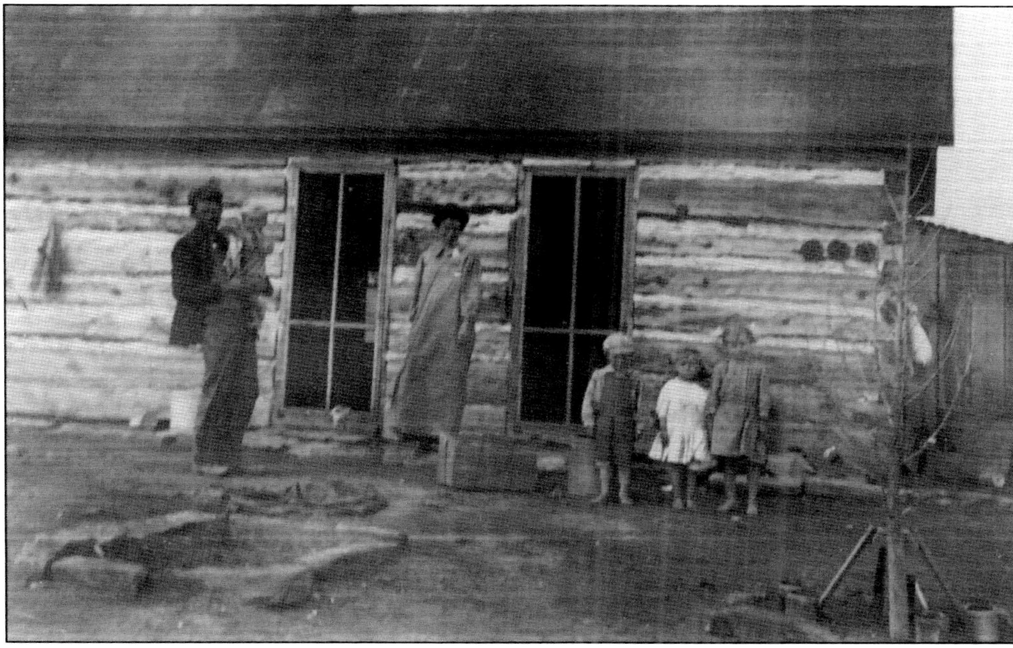

Foltz Homestead. Too many homesteaders went broke and left the country. Many of them said they left their homesteads for health reasons. If one asked an old-timer what that meant, he would sadly say that they were "sick and tired of starving to death." The homestead dream—free land, something for nothing—seemed too good to be true. For many, it was. The William H. Foltz family homesteaded four miles southeast of Upton in 1910. William H. Foltz, holding Paul, is pictured with, from left to right, Mildred E. (Doll) Foltz, Ralph, Maxine, and Ruth Foltz.

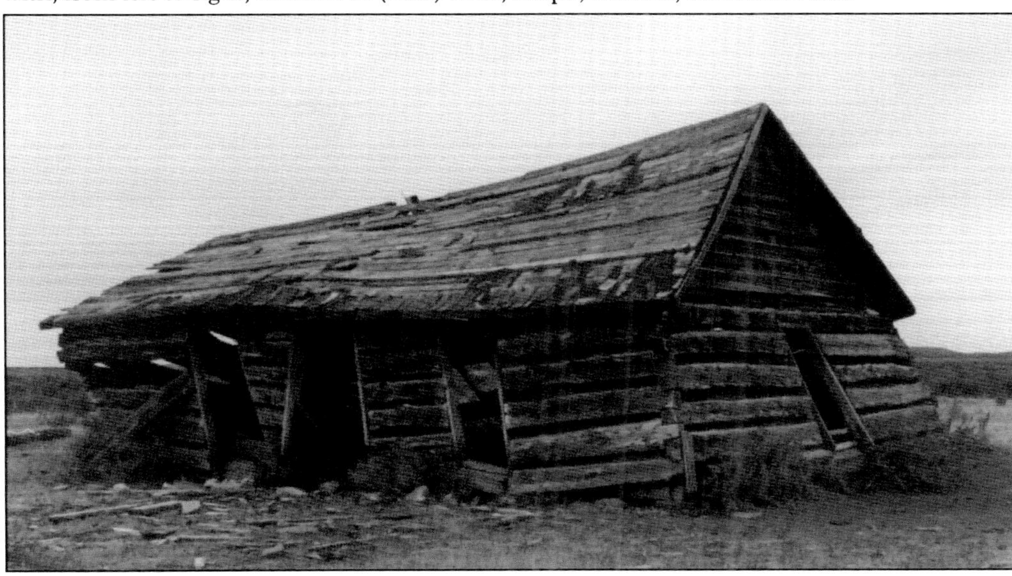

Abandoned Foltz Homestead. It was a disillusioned and defeated people who left the country. The federal government ended open grazing and homesteading in the 1930s. Some people stayed on in the county and found opportunities in their established homesteads or in other businesses and pursuits. Other homesteads, like the Foltz homestead, were abandoned.

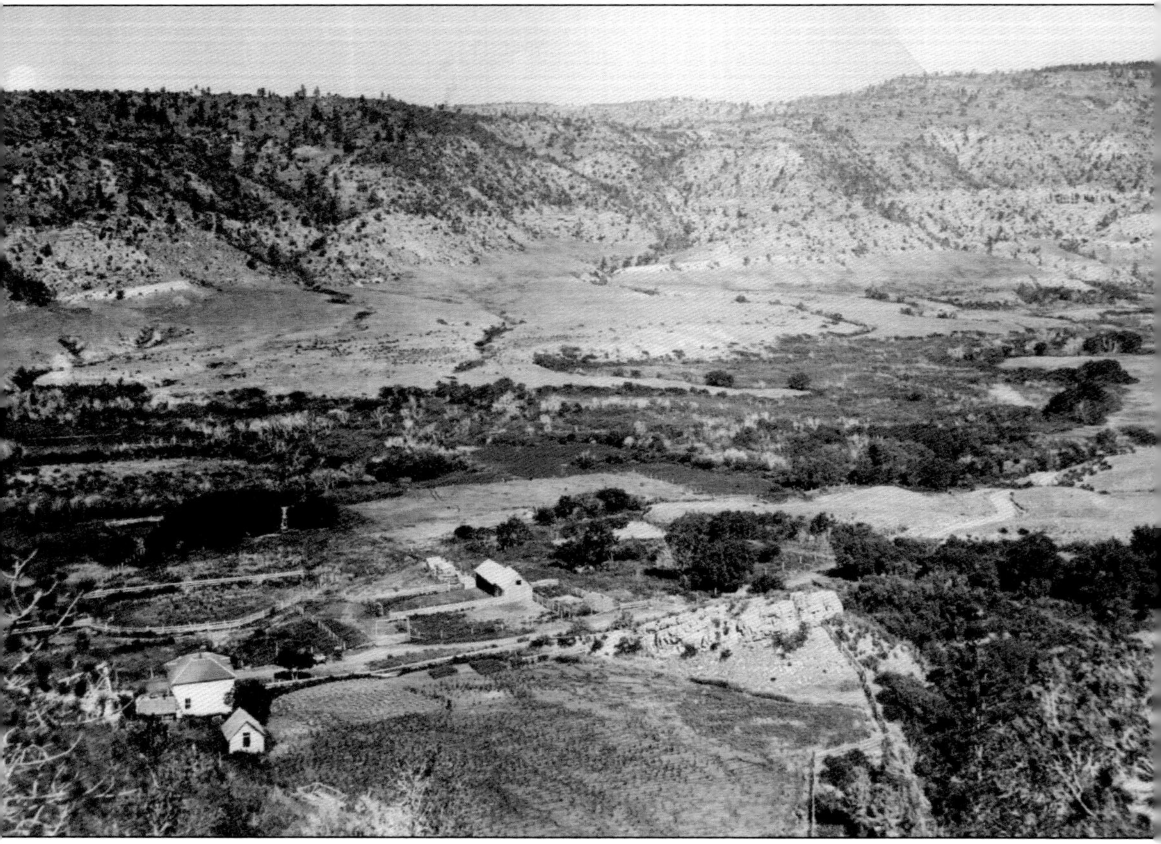

FROM HOMESTEAD TO RANCH. Some homesteaders, for whatever reasons and good fortunes, were able to make it work. But more than good fortune, it took plain old persistence and hard work, hard work, and hard work. They often purchased the homesteads of the neighbors who could not make a go of it. Those people were able to put together enough land to make a living with their expanded holdings. They became the backbone of the agricultural industry in Weston County. Pictured is Robert Harper's ranch on Beaver Creek near Newcastle. Robert A. Harper purchased the ranch in 1897 from Fod Hansen. His son Robert J. Harper was born in 1919 and continued ranching until his death at 90 years old. (AMM.)

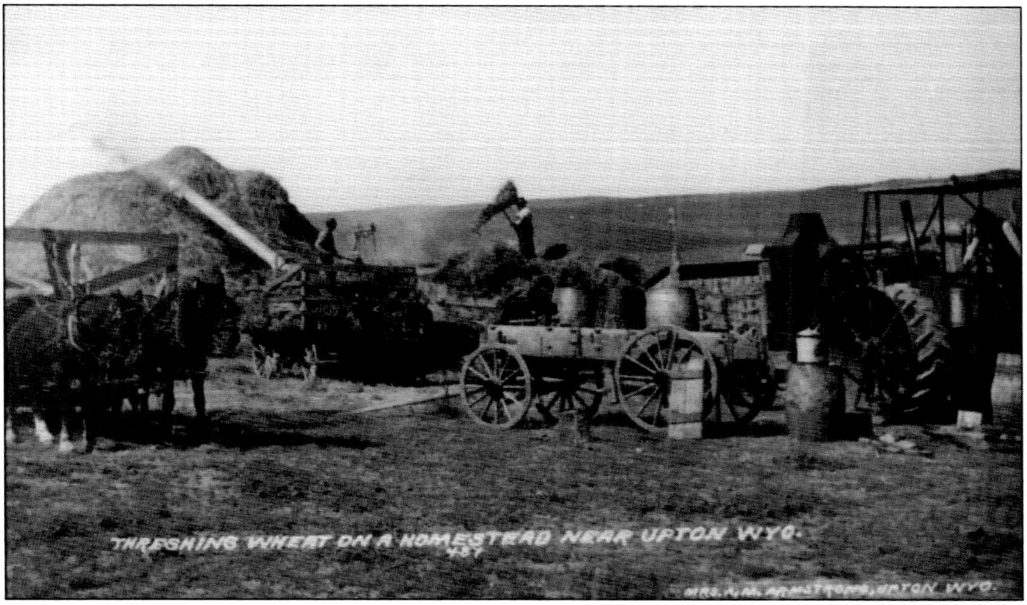

THRESHING GRAIN. Some parts of Weston County were ideal for small grain production. In the early 1900s, the Agricultural Extension Services introduced dry farming methods. These methods helped make small grain production a viable enterprise in early county history. This threshing crew was working near Upton with a steam engine thresher. Most of Weston County was a dryland agricultural enterprise.

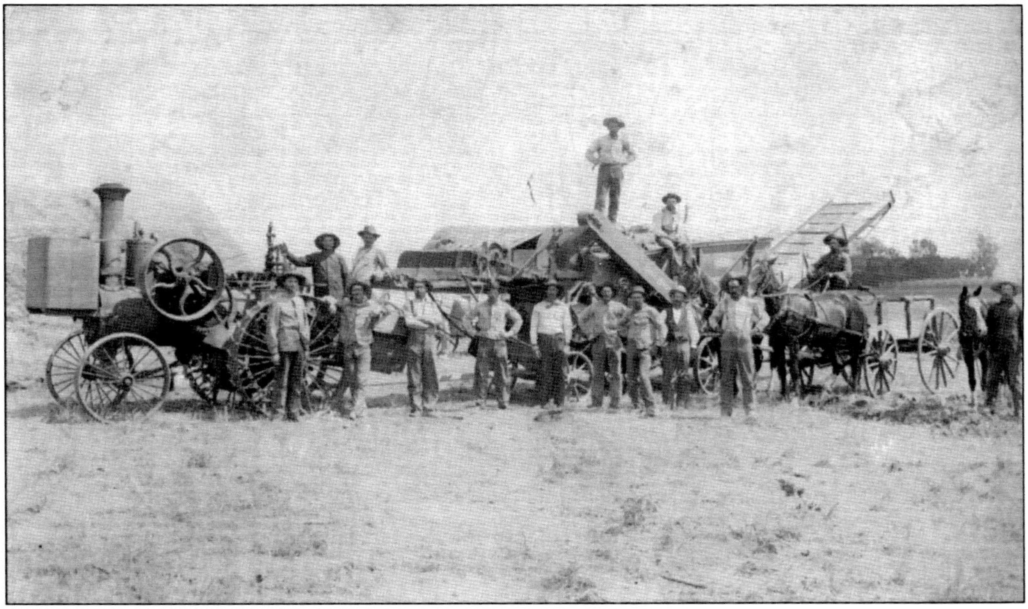

HIRED THRESHERS. In 1910, the Dry Farming Homestead Act was passed, providing new incentive for more homesteaders to come to Wyoming. Even with the added acreage, it was still difficult to make a living on a homestead. Not everyone could afford a threshing machine and a tractor. So some people, who were fortunate to own their own equipment, hired out to thresh for others in the community.

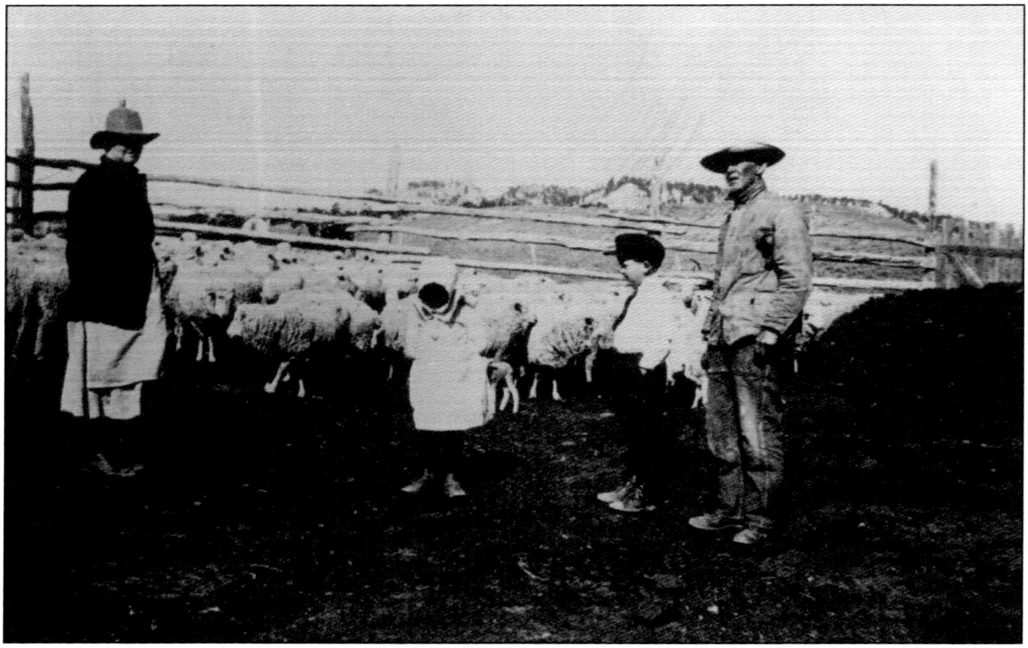

Sheep Farming. Homesteaders were credited with bringing the first sheep to the county. It took less capital to buy into the sheep business than it did the cattle business. As an added benefit, sheep provided two incomes with wool and meat production sales. Edward and Charlotte Noe and their children, Mary and Tommy, are with their sheep.

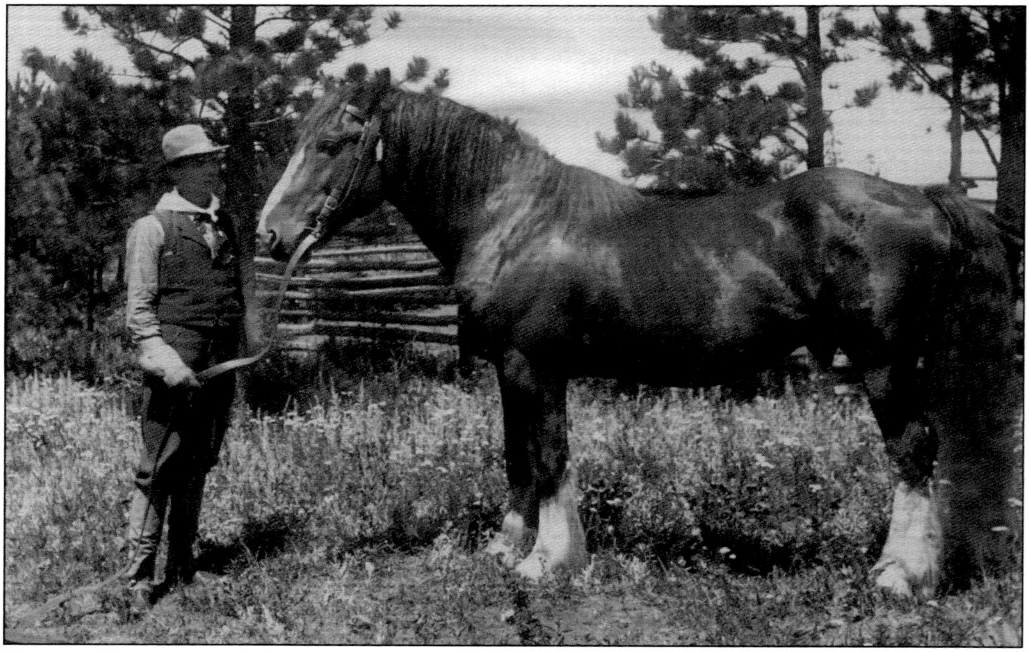

Horses. Horses provided transportation and power for getting work done. In early-day Weston County, gathering wild horses and breaking and marketing them was a profitable business. Horses provided transportation and a workforce. Pictured is George R. Shane in Cambria.

BLACKSMITH SHOP. Like the auto repair shop today, the blacksmith shop kept horses shod and wagon wheels in good repair. Blacksmiths would be involved in functional work, such as making tools, equipment, and implements and maintenance and repairs for both domestic and agricultural clients. Their work as farriers included not only horses but also oxen and donkeys. Before coming to Wyoming, Henry P. Martens was an apprentice blacksmith and received his diploma.

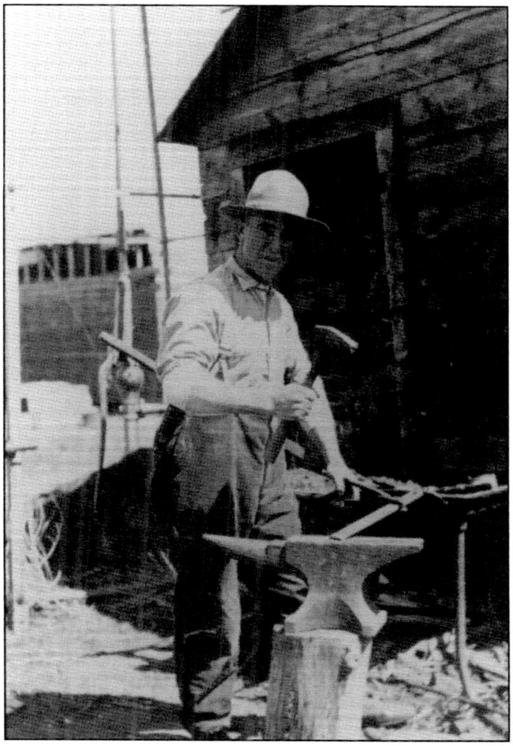

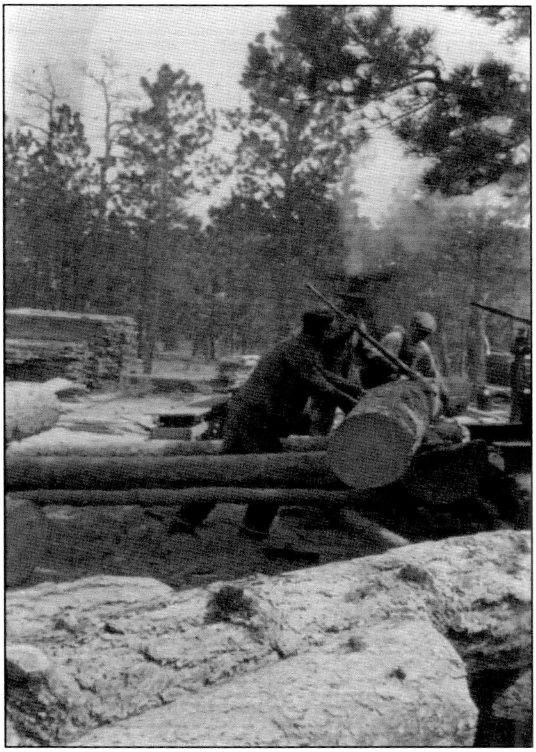

TIMBER AND LOGGERS. The northeastern part of the county is dense with heavy forestland. This timber provided homesteaders with building materials, heat, and jobs both to supplement homestead incomes and as businesses and employment opportunities. Pictured are Mike Materi and other workers at a sawmill in 1927.

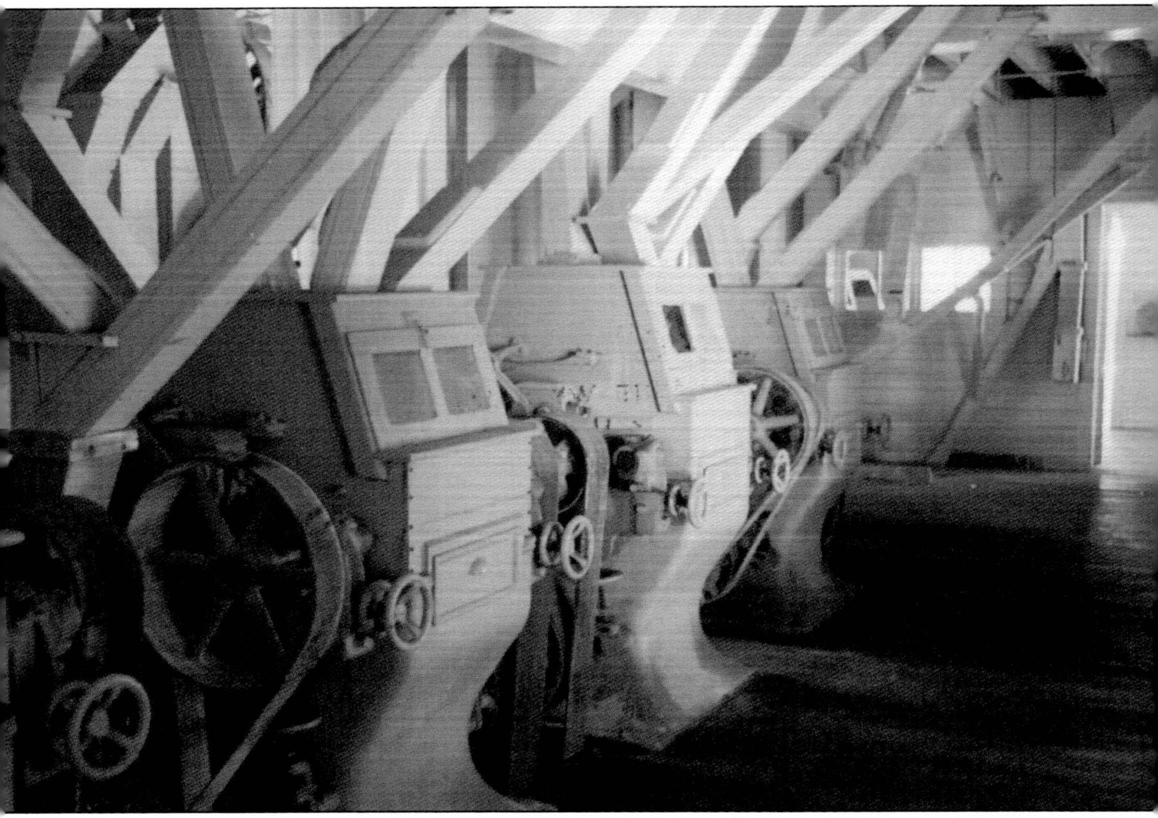

TOOMEYS MILL. In 1905, George C. Getchell built a large flour mill in Newcastle. Later, it was purchased by Howard Toomey. One of Toomey's most famous products was flapjack flour packaged in bright yellow packages. The mill, built of locally quarried sandstone, was a Weston county landmark that served local grain producers, cooks, and bakers. In 1965, the mill discontinued operations, and the building and business became a restaurant. After being sold in 2011, it was demolished to make room for a convenience store. (Courtesy of Beck Decker.)

David Norris, World War I Soldier. On April 16, 1917, the United States entered World War I. Prior to that, Weston County led an agrarian way of life. Once the United States entered the war, the county participated in the war effort with food drives, rationing, and soldiers. World War I soldier David Norris and other young Weston County men left for the war that dramatically changed life in Weston County.

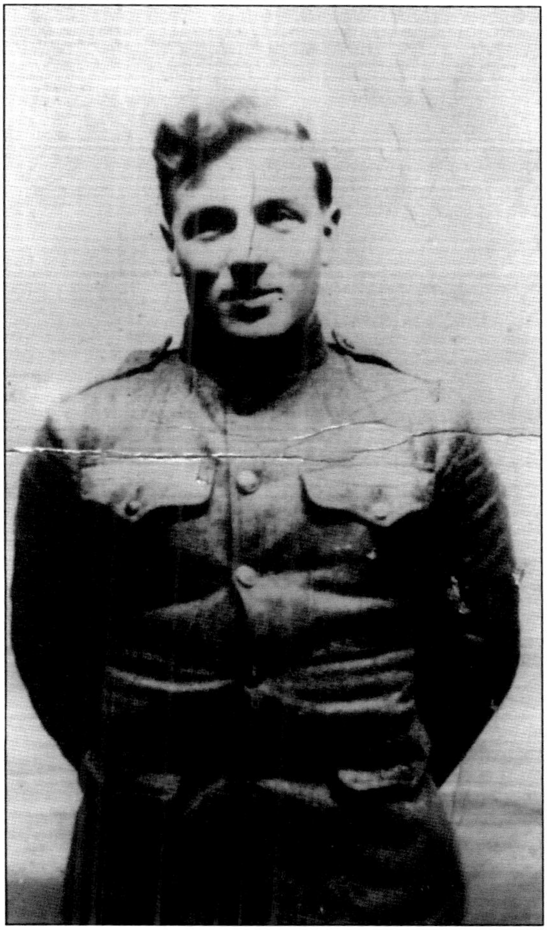

"We Haul Anything." O.M. Willis was happy to have a job in 1926, and his motto was printed on his truck: "We haul anything, anywhere, anytime." He was helping Myra Allen move from Star Butte School on the Jonasson Ranch on Skull Creek.

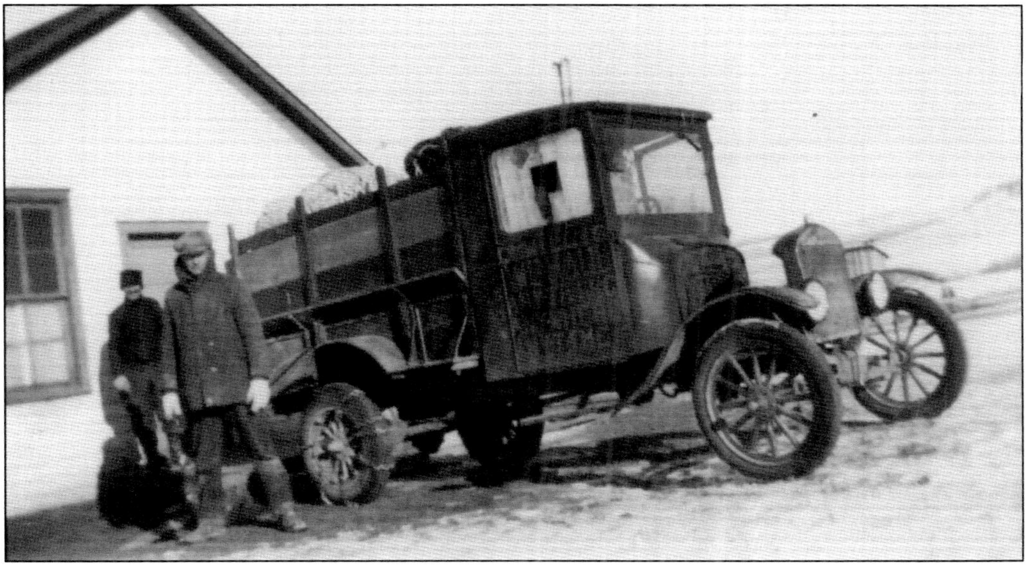

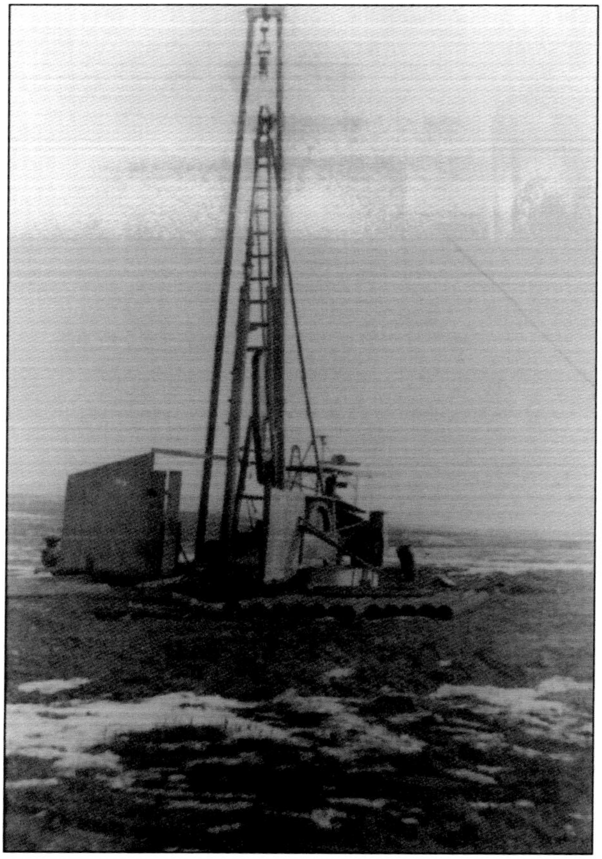

Weston County Oil. World War I increased the demand for oil and petroleum products. That there was oil in the county was no secret. Oil seeped from the ground and flowed into pools of water. The oil was skimmed from the pools, strained, mixed with flour, and sold as wagon axle grease. In 1920, the High Test Company moved an oil-drilling rig in from Ohio to tap into Weston County's rich reserves.

Osage Lunch. During the war, the demand for gas and petroleum products rose, and the price of crude oil went up. In March 1920, a gusher well was struck in the Osage oil field on Poison Creek, and Osage turned into a bustling community. Developers, speculators, investors, and get-rich-quick scammers poured into Osage along with workers. While businesses thrived, they operated out of tents and shacks of all kinds.

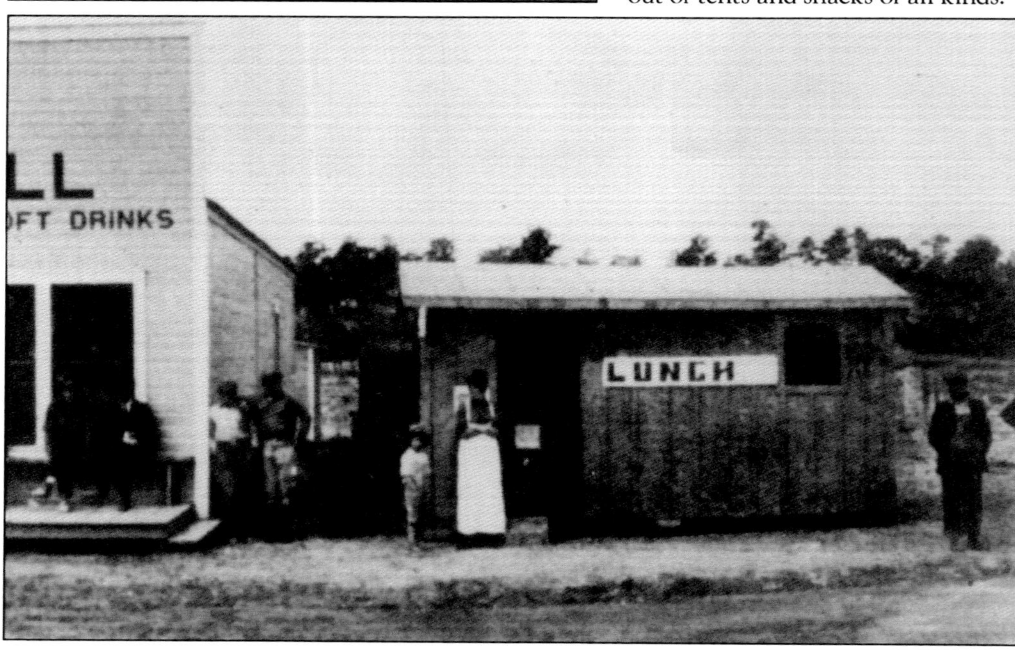

First Wooden Oil-Drilling Rig in Weston County. Rigs and equipment moved into the county from everywhere. This was the first wooden oil-drilling rig in Weston County. Standing at the extreme left is oilman Vernie Gose; William "Bill" Hockett is fourth from the left; and the man on the extreme right is John Brorby. The first location it drilled was a dry hole, which is the nature of the game. Some are gushers, some are not, and some are bone dry.

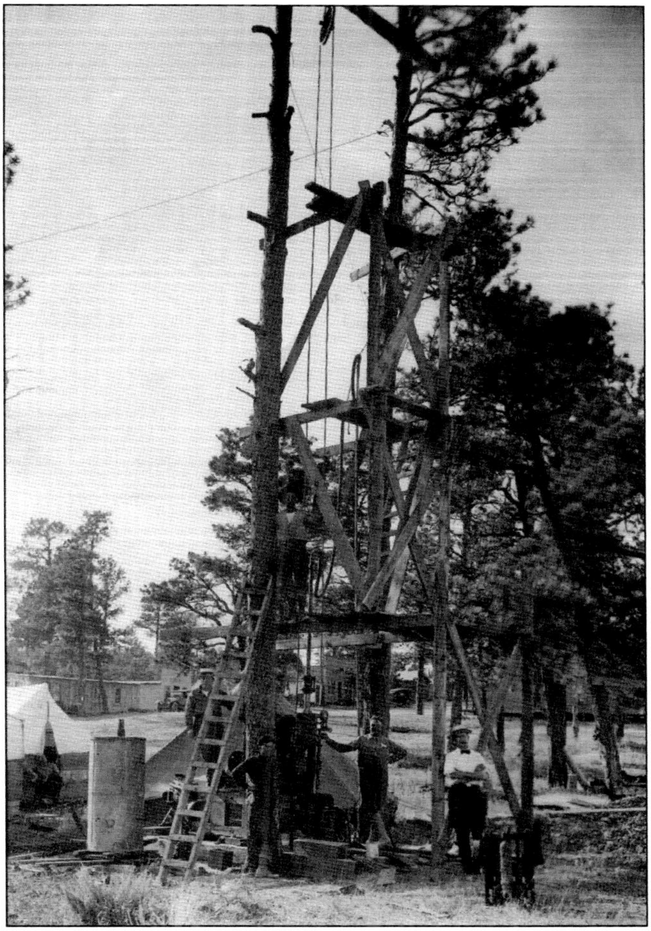

Osage Oil Field Camp. Life in an oil field camp was not luxurious. Portable sheds served as home to several people. Moving equipment and rigs was a major undertaking. Neither rain, sleet, nor snow stopped the mail or the activity in the oil field, or oil patch as locals call it. Here, workers dig their vehicle out of the snow in an Osage oil field camp in 1926.

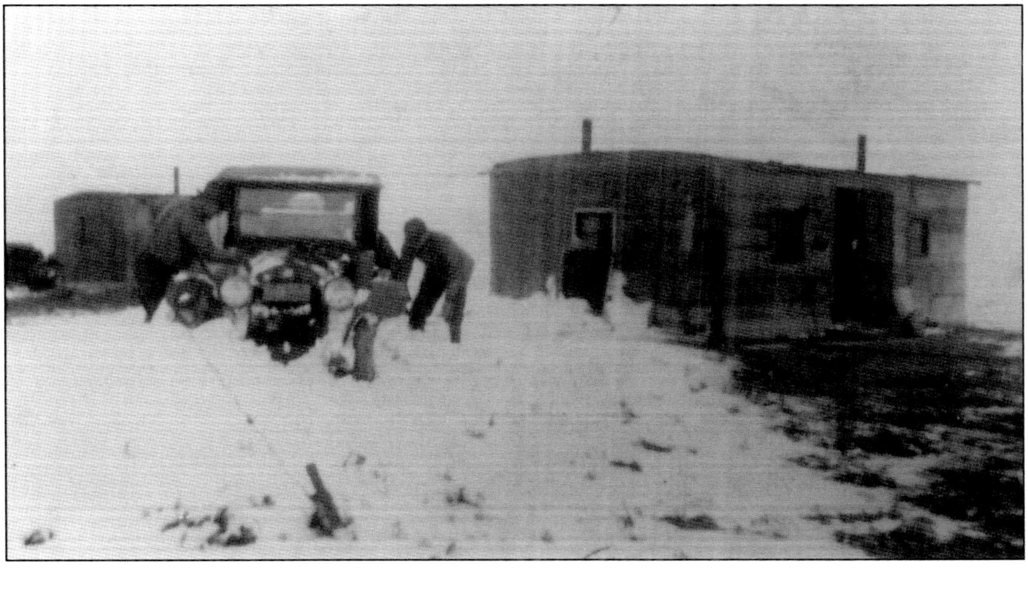

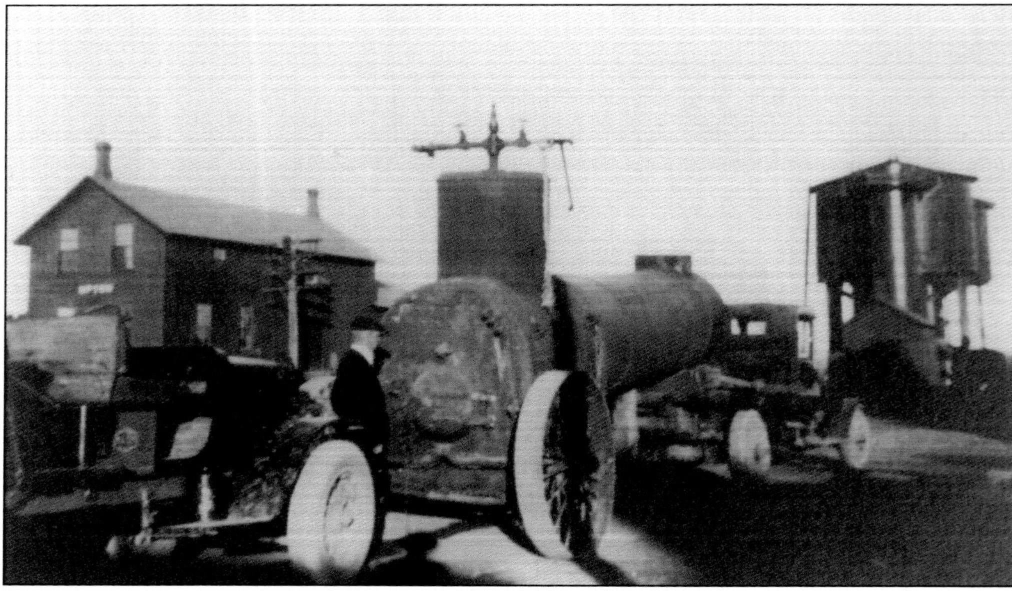

Gose Drilling Equipment. Drilling equipment purchased by the Gose Oil Company arrived at the Upton train depot. It is ready to move out to the field. Even with the difficulty of moving oil field equipment with horses or tractors, it did not take long for drilling rigs to become a standard part of the Weston County landscape.

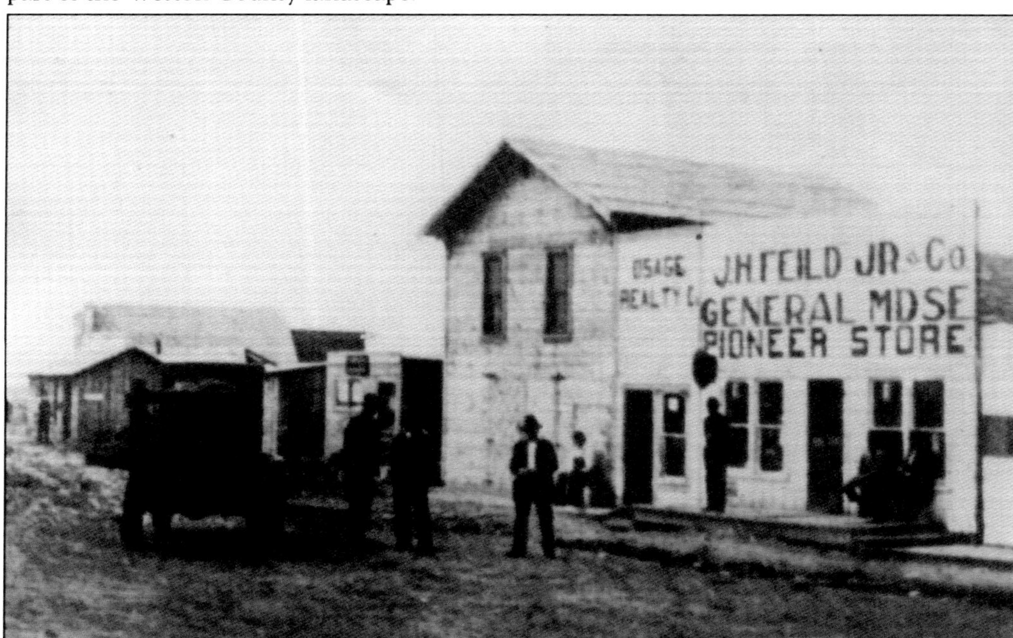

Osage Reality. When the oil boom was on, everyone wanted to get in on the play. General merchandise stores, such as the J.H. Field Jr. Co. General Merchandise Pioneer Store, were part of Osage's boom in the 1920s. Osage Realty served its purposes even though tents were pitched anywhere and little rough shacks thrown together. When oil did well, everyone did well. This is the nature of an oil boom.

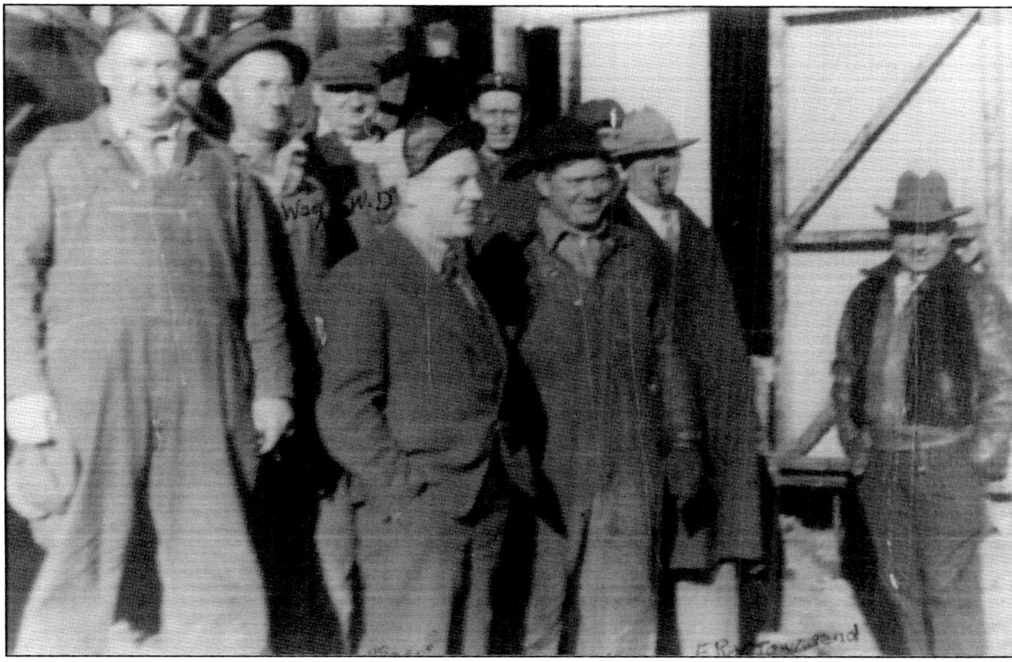

OSAGE UPTON OIL COMPANY. William D. Townsend Sr. homesteaded in Weston County in 1912. In 1918, he went to Osage, where he helped form the Osage Upton Oil Company, developed a refinery that had the ability refine 300 barrels of crude oil a day, and made it possible to take oil from the wellhead to the gas tank. Shown here are, from left to right, Don Townsend, "Wog" Townsend, W.D. Townsend, "Spec" Elwin Townsend, unidentified, Clint Townsend, unidentified, E. Roy Townsend, and Thede Lull.

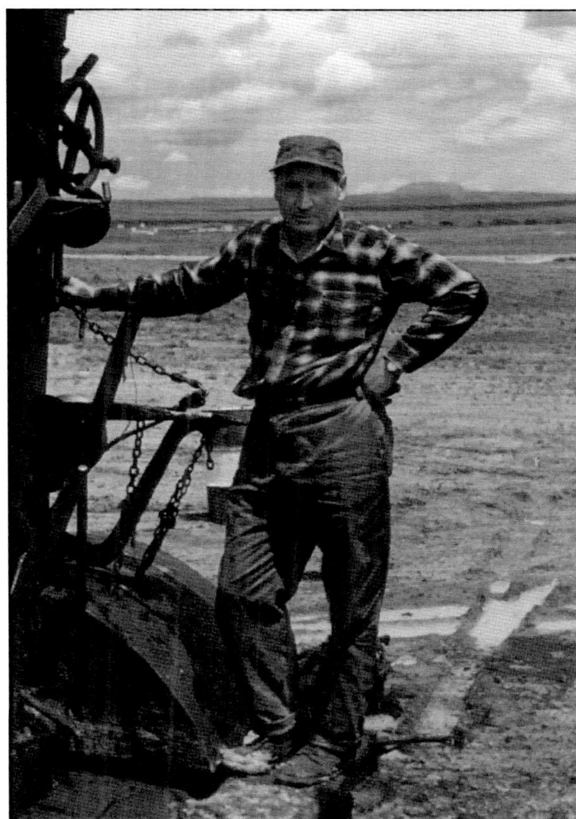

WILLIAM "BILL" D. TOWNSEND. Having come to the Osage oil field when he was 19 years old, William Townsend II eventually took over the leadership of the Townsend Company. Later, a third generation, including his three sons, assumed control of the company. William Townsend III ran the ranching part, Charles ran the oil field, and Mark ran the shop and employees. For three generations, the Townsend family provided employment to countless residents in Weston County.

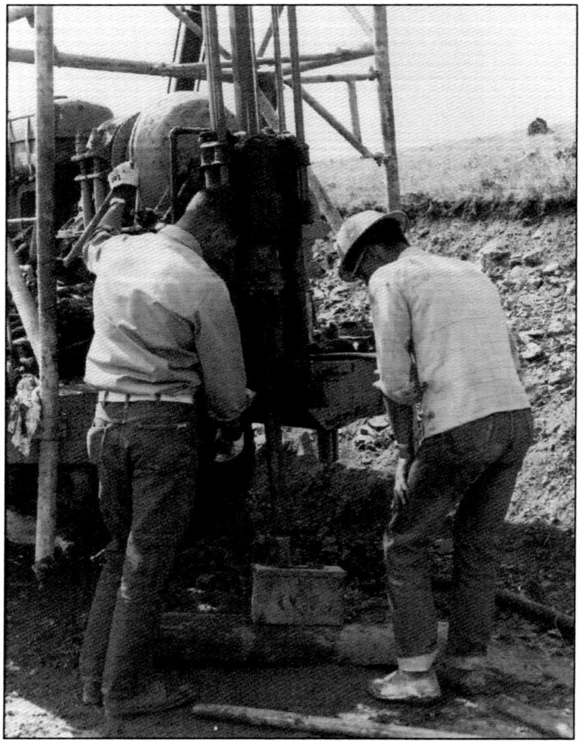

Lawrence Materi. In 1924, Lawrence Materi (right) was born on his family's Weston County homestead. In 1954, he established Materi Exploration with his partner and brother-in-law John Nelson. He is shown here with Steve Pummel and his first rotary drilling rig. Although his operations spanned the entire Rocky Mountain region, he chose to make Weston County his home. He served the county by employing many people over the years. (Courtesy of Liz Materi Barritt.)

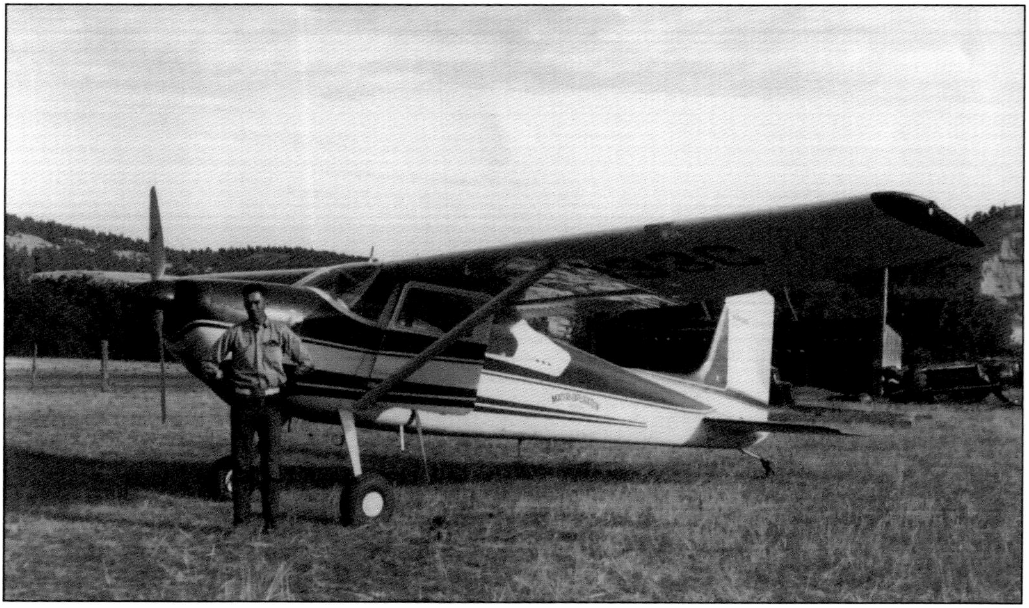

Materi Exploration. This 1954 military trainer was acquired by Lawrence Materi in the early days of Materi Exploration, a contract drilling business. He carried a magnetometer onboard and flew many treacherous hours exploring for minerals. For 35 years, the plane carried equipment and personnel for the business and was used as a helping hand for people in need of medical assistance and search and rescue. (Courtesy of Yvonne Materi Barritt.)

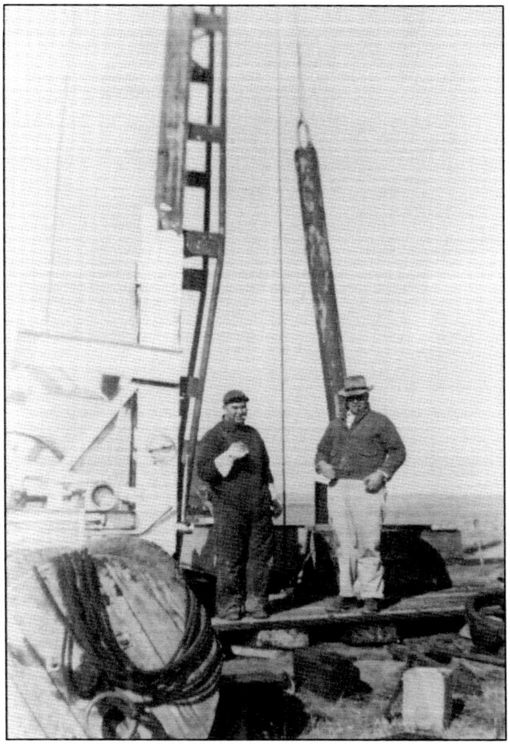

Osage Ironworks. During the Osage oil rush of 1920, Weston County rode the wave of prosperity, but it was short lived. When World War I ended, the high demand for petroleum products ended also. In spite of that decline, Gordon Paulley, owner of Osage Ironworks, built his first drilling rig in 1936. On the left is Gordon Paulley, and on the right is prominent oilman Harry Thorson with a drilling rig that Gordon built in 1947.

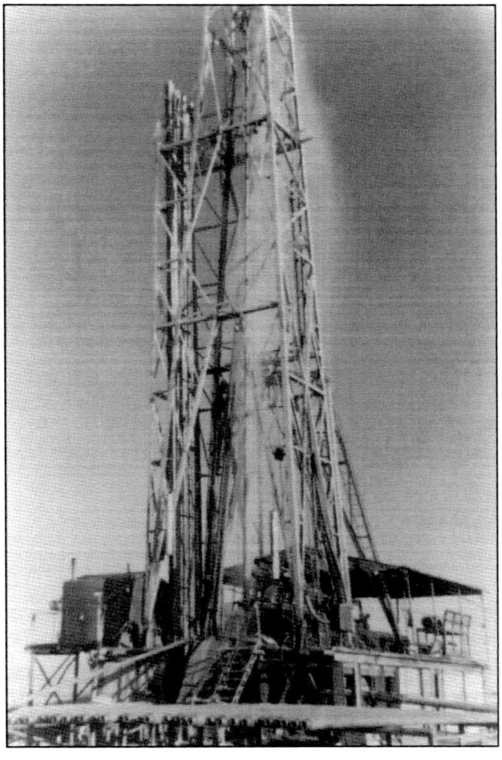

A Gusher. In the 1950s, Weston County was blessed with another oil boom. Shown is oil shooting out the top of the No. 3 well on the Joe Shostack lease in 1952. During this rush, lights on the many drilling rigs outside of Osage made it look like a large city at night. The boom then bust of the 1920s and 1950s set a pattern for the Weston County economy. (Courtesy of Ed Mundell.)

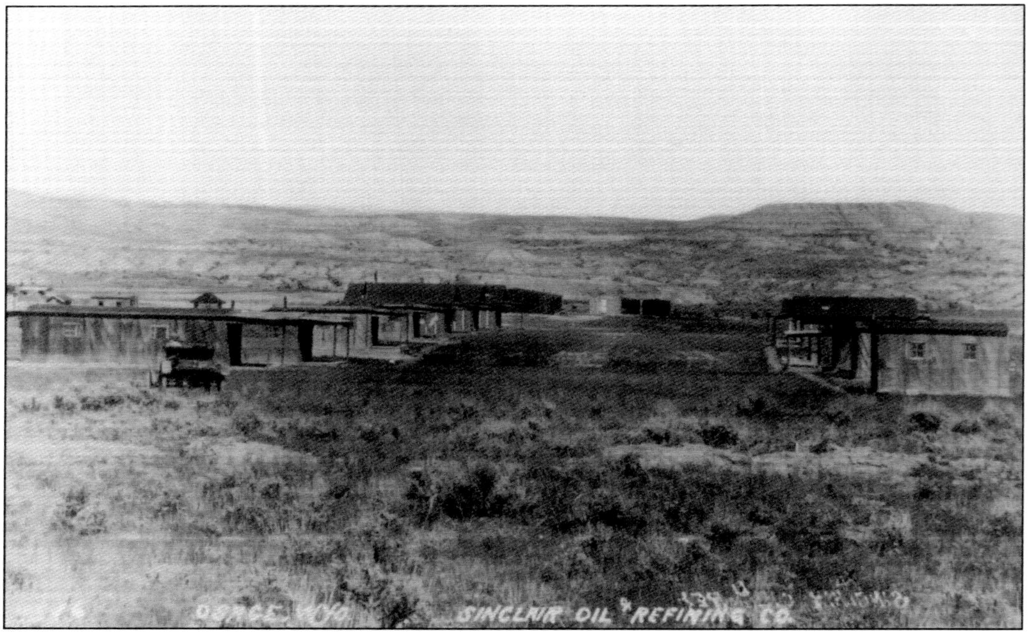

Sinclair Refinery. Although many people did it, distilling one's own crude to make gasoline was not without risks. Fires and explosions were always possible. Refining became a serious business, and refineries sprouted up around the county. Pictured here is the Sinclair Refining camp located south of Osage. Small refineries and family-owned refineries operated in early Weston County.

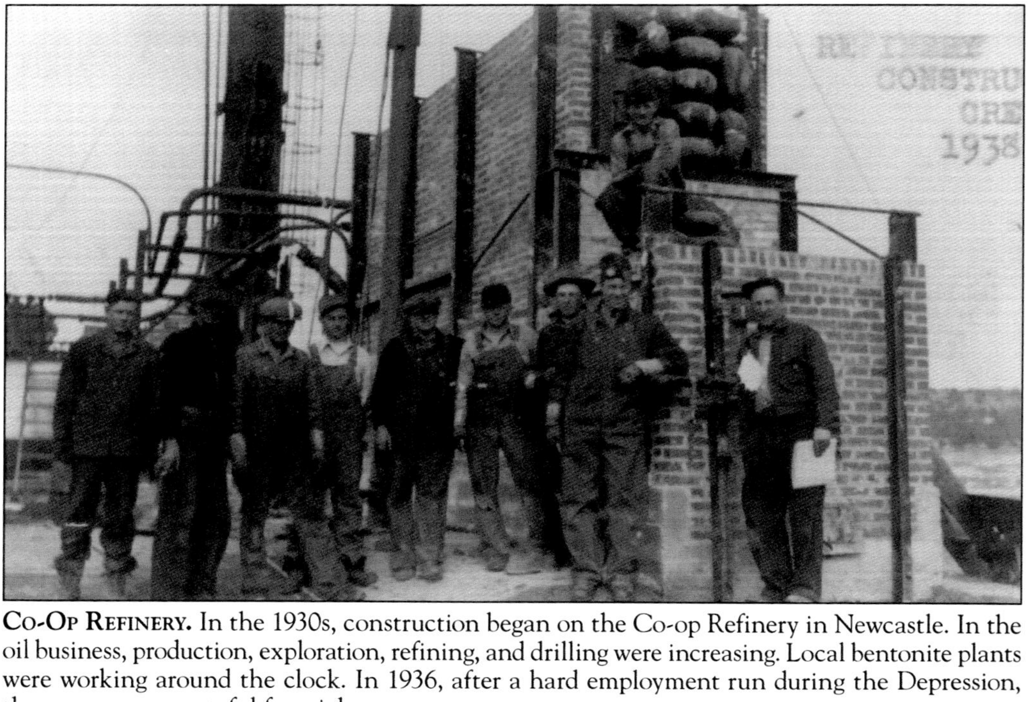

Co-Op Refinery. In the 1930s, construction began on the Co-op Refinery in Newcastle. In the oil business, production, exploration, refining, and drilling were increasing. Local bentonite plants were working around the clock. In 1936, after a hard employment run during the Depression, these men were grateful for a job.

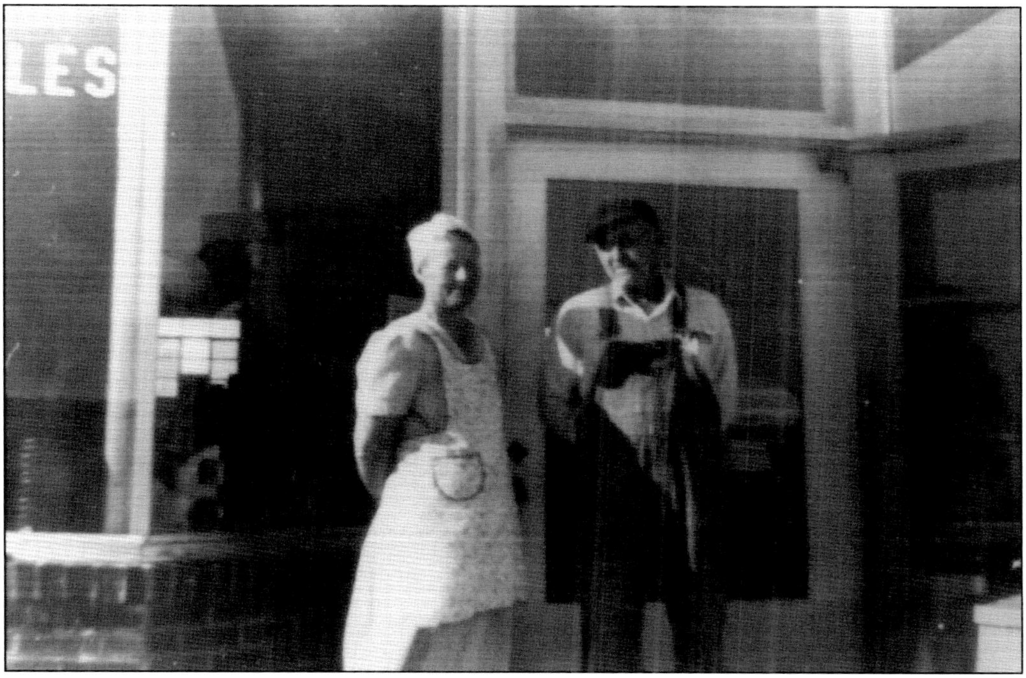

UPTON GROCERY AND REFINERY. Mike Materi decided to get into the refining business himself. He bought a little gas station/grocery store/refinery outside of Upton and called it Upton Grocery and Refinery. His business did so well that he built a new, larger building in 1944 and stocked it with groceries and hardware. Mike and Edna Materi are pictured in front of their store.

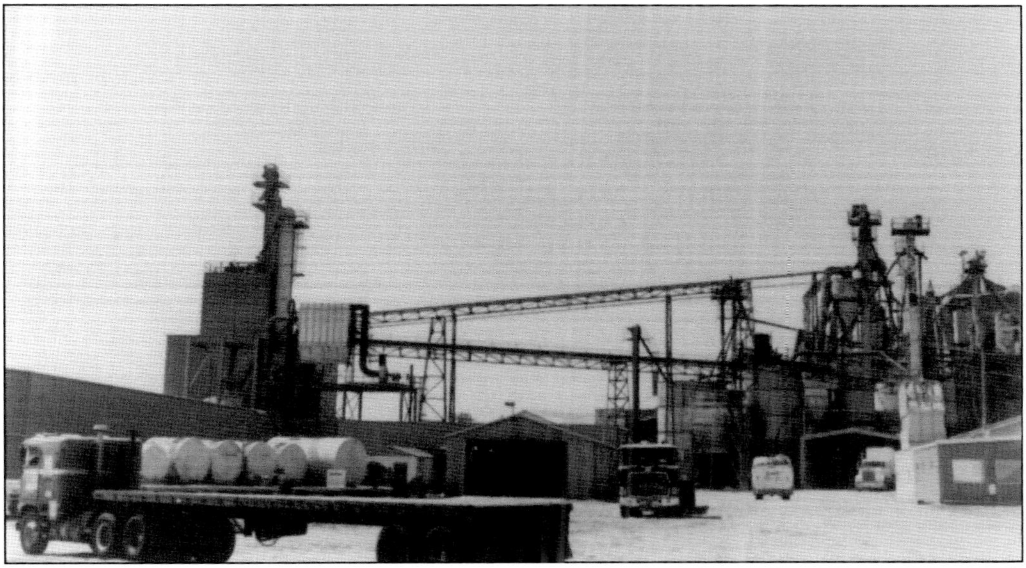

AMERICAN COLLOID, 1944. The oil boom gave rise to a sister industry, bentonite mining. Beds of volcanic clay or bentonite were found in Weston County. The clay was mined, dried, and used in rotary oil well drilling to flush drill cuttings from the well. Although the Clay Spur bentonite refining plant built near Osage was the first bentonite refining plant in the world, American Colloid built a plant at Upton in 1928.

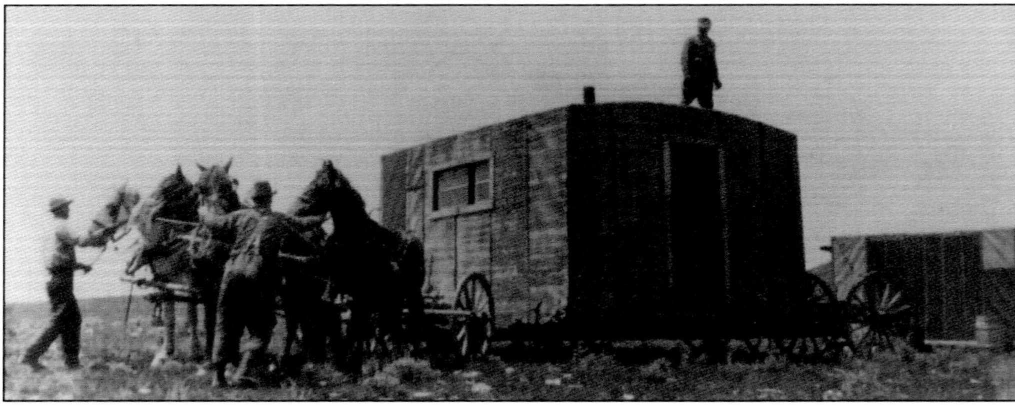

Early Days in the Osage Oil Field. Work was the first and most important requirement that allowed people to come and stay in Weston County. Most jobs revolved around the county's rich natural resources and agricultural assets or businesses that served them. Here, oil field workers are seen moving a building used in the oil field. Moving buildings and heavy equipment with horses was the way to get things done in the early days.

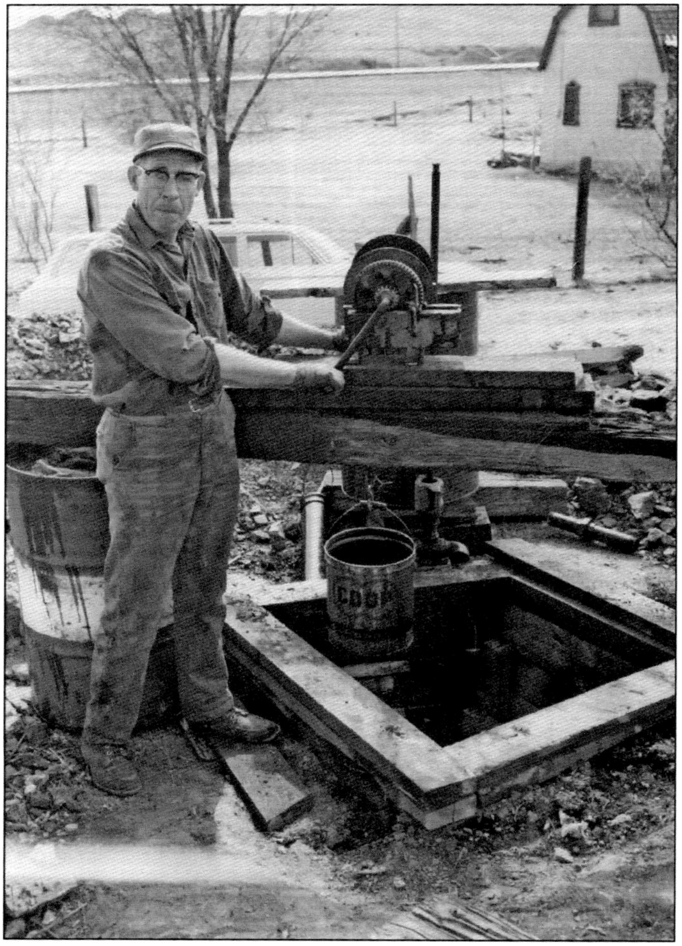

Al Smith and Accidental Oil Company. Al Smith came to Weston County in about 1958 and worked as a contract driller in the oil fields. While drilling a water well on property east of Newcastle, he found oil at about 30 feet. Some five to seven years later, he purchased an oil lease on the property and set his mind to fulfill his dream of producing oil at the location. On the property, he built the only hand-dug oil well in the world and from that oil production launched Accidental Oil Company in 1967. Shown here is Al Smith bringing rocks up from the hand-dug well. (AMM.)

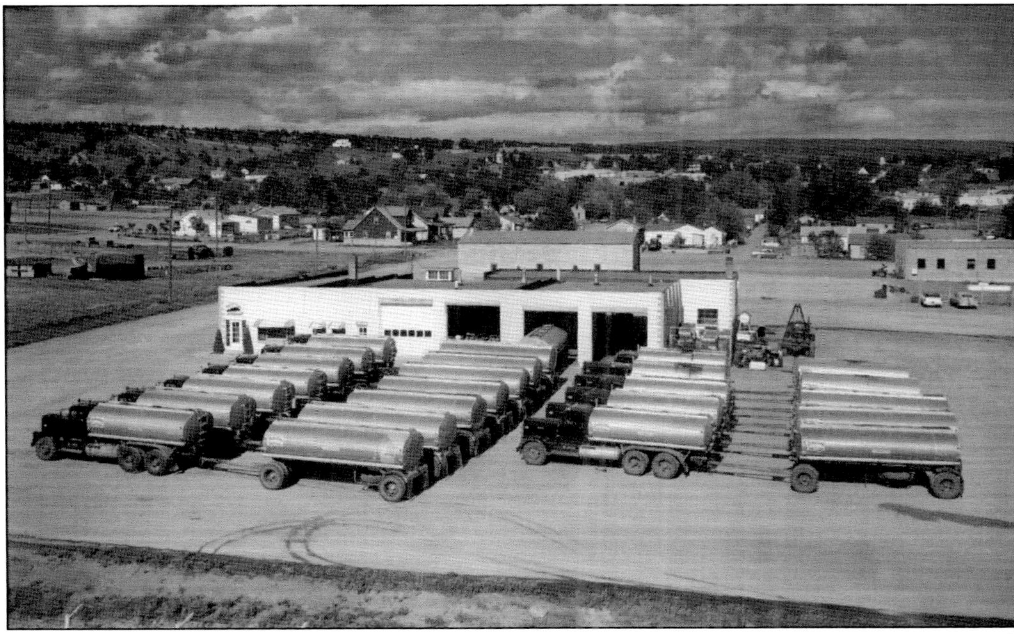

JOHNSTON'S FUEL LINERS. Johnston's Fuel Liners came to Weston County during the post–World War II period to service the 1950s oil boom. The company established its headquarters in Newcastle. Pictured is its first terminal and equipment in the 1940s. The company's purpose was to transport crude oil to refineries. With Eldon Johnston's leadership, the company soon became very busy. In order to maintain the workforce it needed, it had to deal with a housing shortage. The company built the first substantial housing development in Newcastle after the war. Pictured below are, from left to right, Wilson Burnette, Rose Goodson, Wanda Liamos, Dean Fulk, Bob Archer, Walt Litman,and Gordon Pecha. (Both, AMM.)

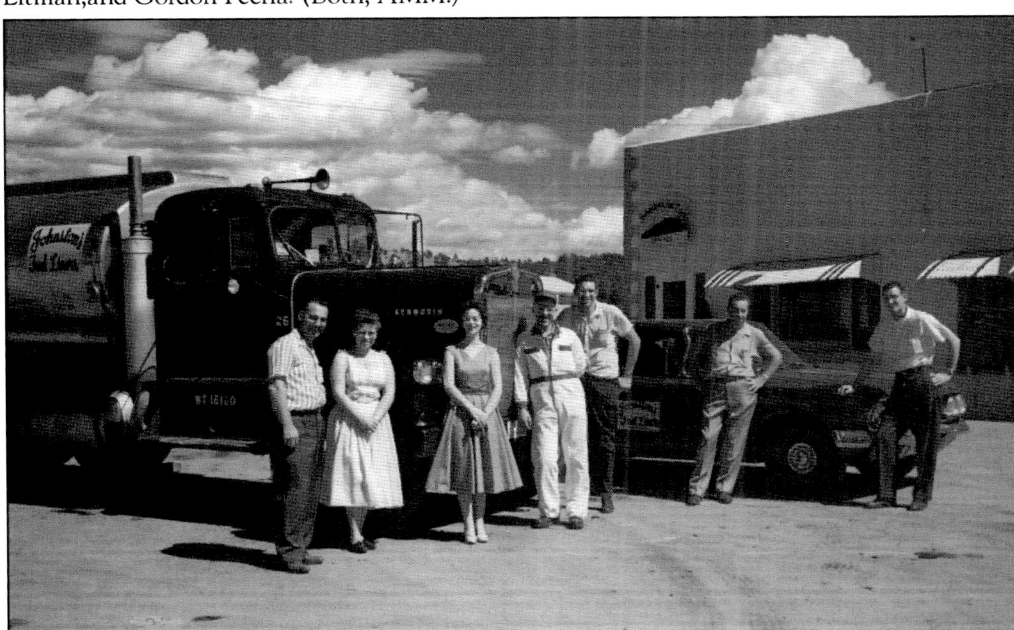

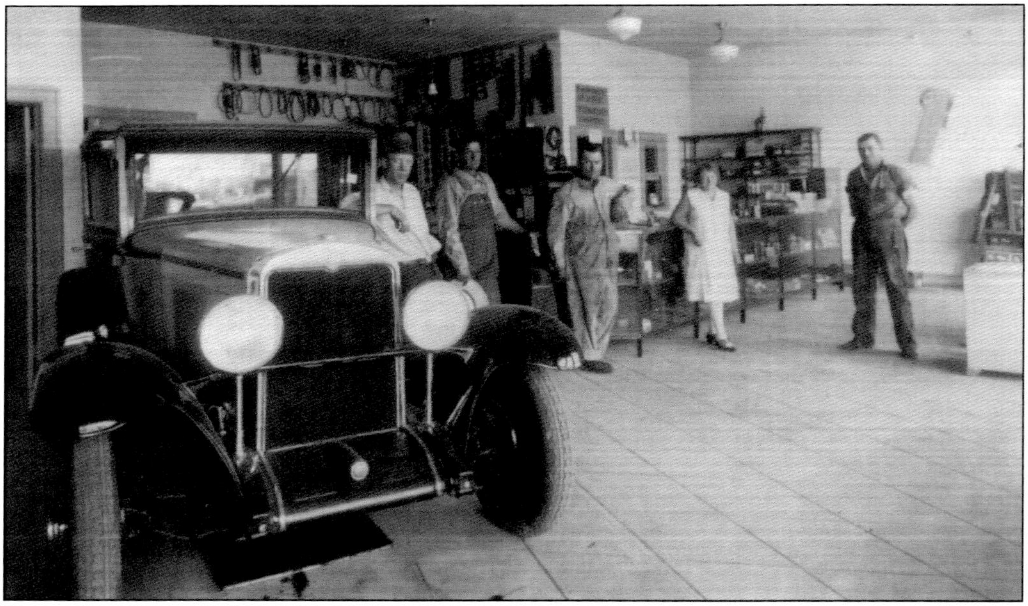

PRINGLE MOTORS. In the mid-1920s, Pringle Motors started business in Upton. Homer and Margaret Pringle, along with Bill Meek, sold, serviced, and repaired Chevrolets and Buicks. Pictured in the Pringle Motors Co. showroom in 1929 are, from left to right, Homer Pringle, Willard Canfield, John Lane, Margaret Pringle, and Ben Bershide. In 1978, the business burned down, and the decision was made not to rebuild it.

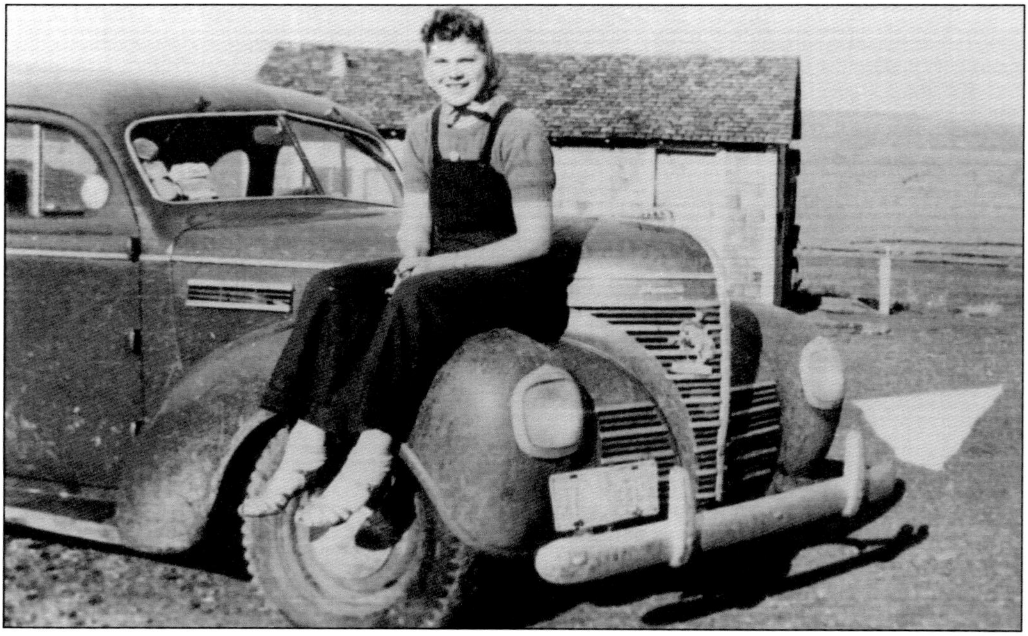

PLYMOUTH, AN AMERICAN SYMBOL. The motorized car ultimately became a symbol of American independence and prosperity. Weston County, with its mineral production, played a large part in keeping that symbol running. In this 1940 photograph, Dorothy Middleton Cowger is shown sitting on a Plymouth.

Seven

A Community

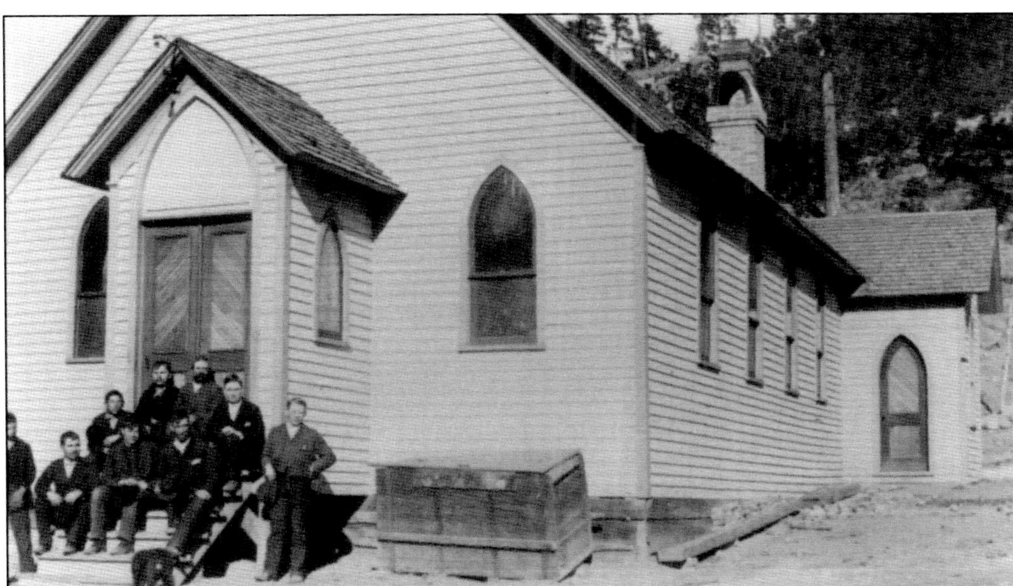

St. David's Episcopal Church in Cambria. When people worked and built places to live, the need to develop a community was a priority. Important to building a community was attention to people's spiritual needs. Early residents gathered together whenever and wherever they could, especially when a circuit preacher happened to be passing through.

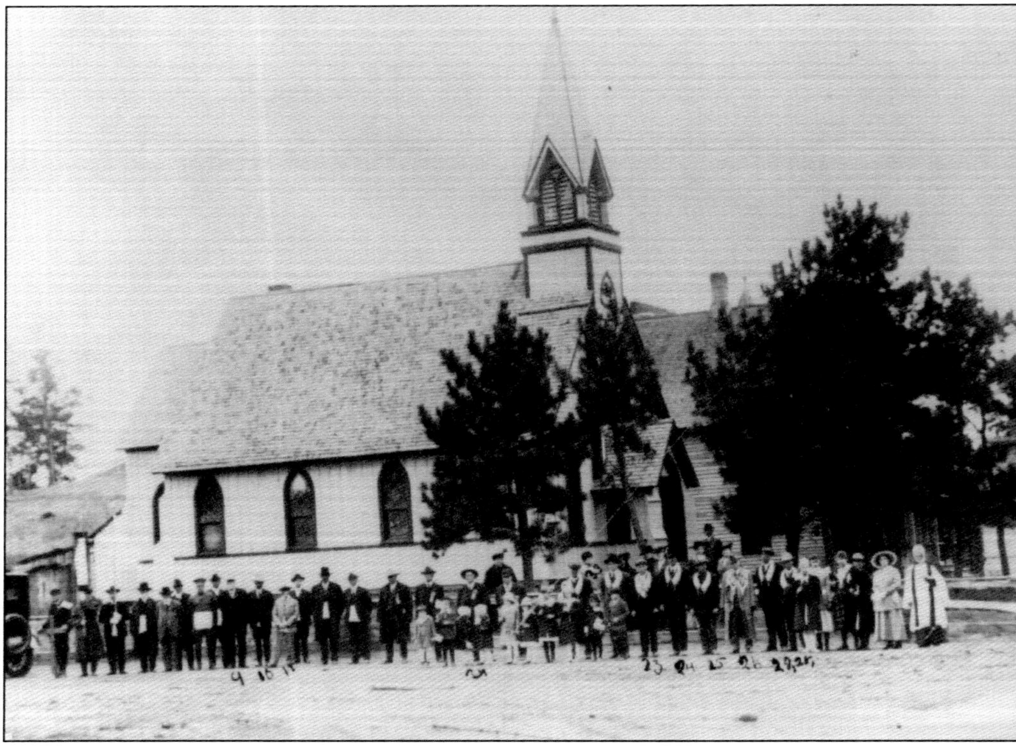

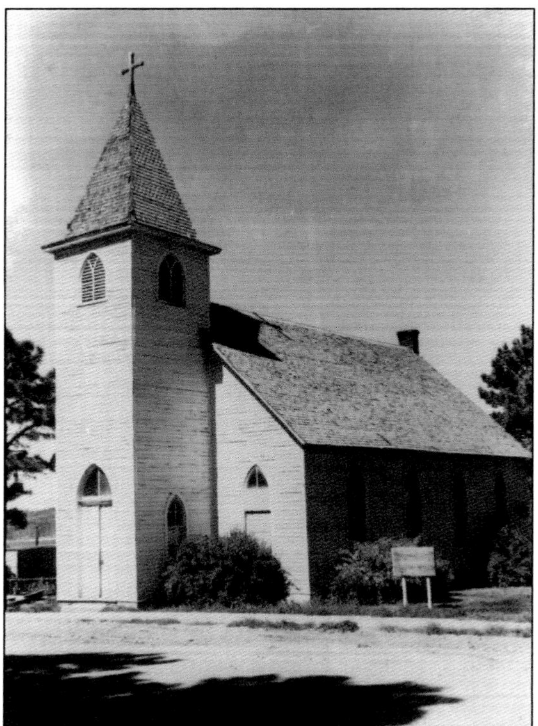

Oldest Church in Weston County. The Episcopal congregation was active in Newcastle in 1889, meeting in Meyer Frank's Hall. The construction of Christ Church Episcopal was completed in 1890 at a cost of $2,500. Pictured is the congregation at Christ Church Episcopal.

Corpus Christi Church. Under the guidance of Father Cassidy of Hot Springs, South Dakota, the Newcastle Catholics began construction of a church in 1892. The Lincoln Land Company donated one lot, and the new church was officially opened in January 1893. Benches were made of rough wood, and the people knelt on the floor.

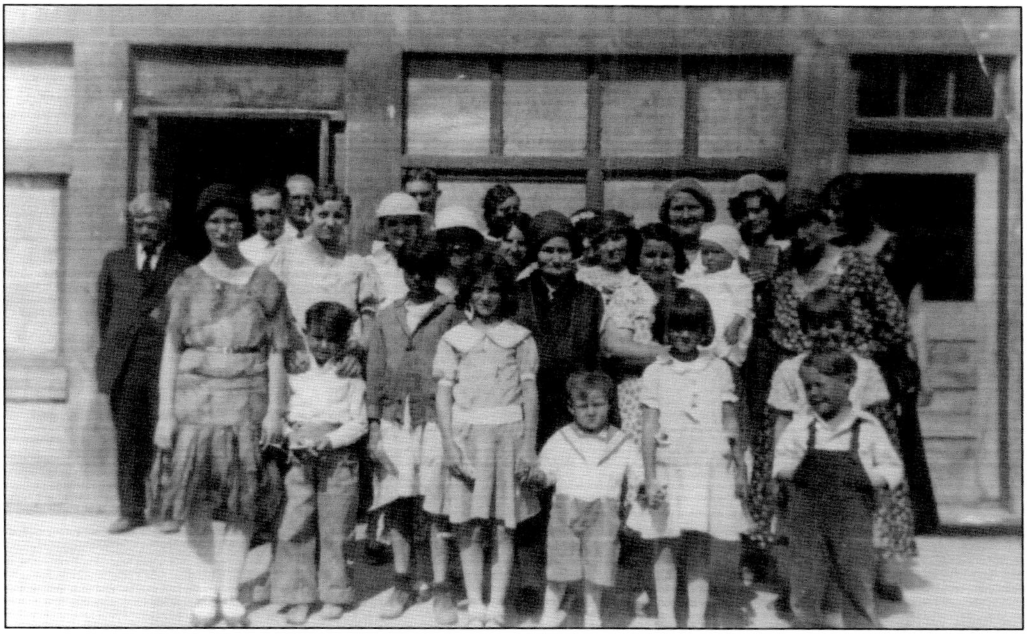

Assembly of God Church. The Assembly of God Church first met in November 1931. Shown are faithful followers in 1933–1934. Some of the people shown are "Grandpa John" Cullum, Willie Anderson, Lloyd McIntosh, Ray Forbes, Hazel Cullum, Ariel McIntosh, Mina Arnold, Dora June Combs, Maureen Combs, Marie Fenner, Goldie Stevens, "Grandma Cullum," Mrs. Fenner, Mrs. Copley holding Jane, Florence Combs, Goldie Portwood Poppleton, Jeanie Glaringhouse, Howard Copley, Patty Glaringhouse, Bessie Combs, and Glen McIntosh.

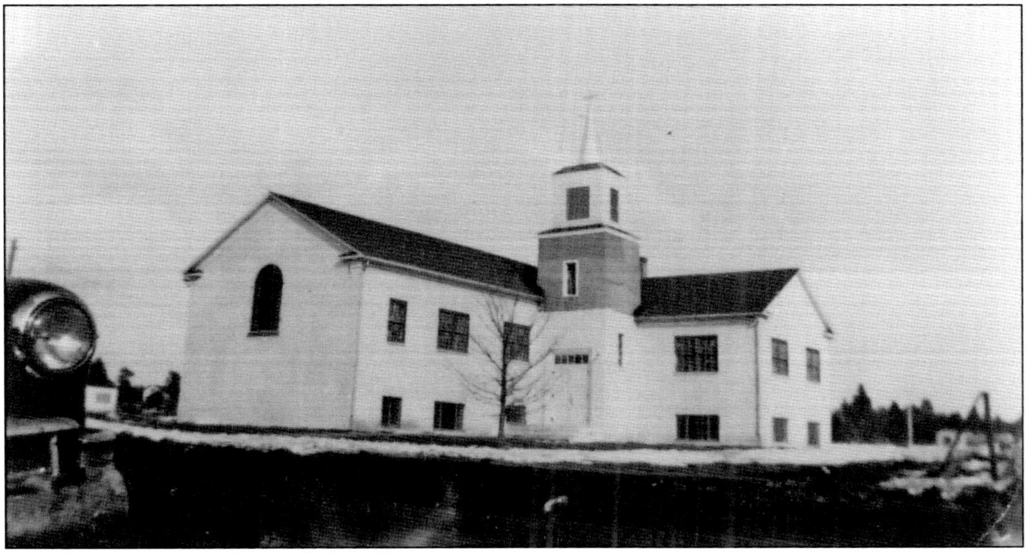

Upton Community Methodist Church. The Upton Methodist community began in 1899, and its first church was built in 1908 on land donated by CB&Q Railroad Company. From 1949 to 1953, new planning and construction culminated in the incorporation of a new church under the name of the Community Methodist Church at a cost of $34,000. Shown is the church in 1953 at the dedication.

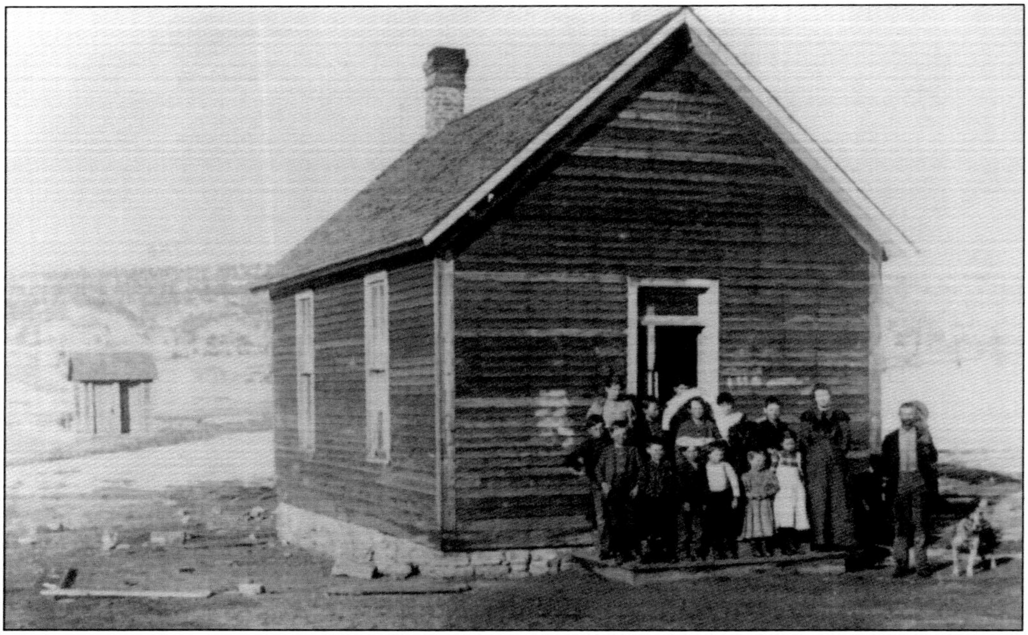

Weston County's First School. Hand in hand with work, home, and heaven, education helped make Weston County a community. The first school was built 14 miles north of Newcastle in 1888, and Frank Nefsy was the first teacher. He built desks and chairs from lumber left over from the school construction and had nine pupils. Pictured is the Beaver Creek School in the fall of 1898. (Courtesy of Dana Davis Tysdal and Mary Fawcett Kipping.)

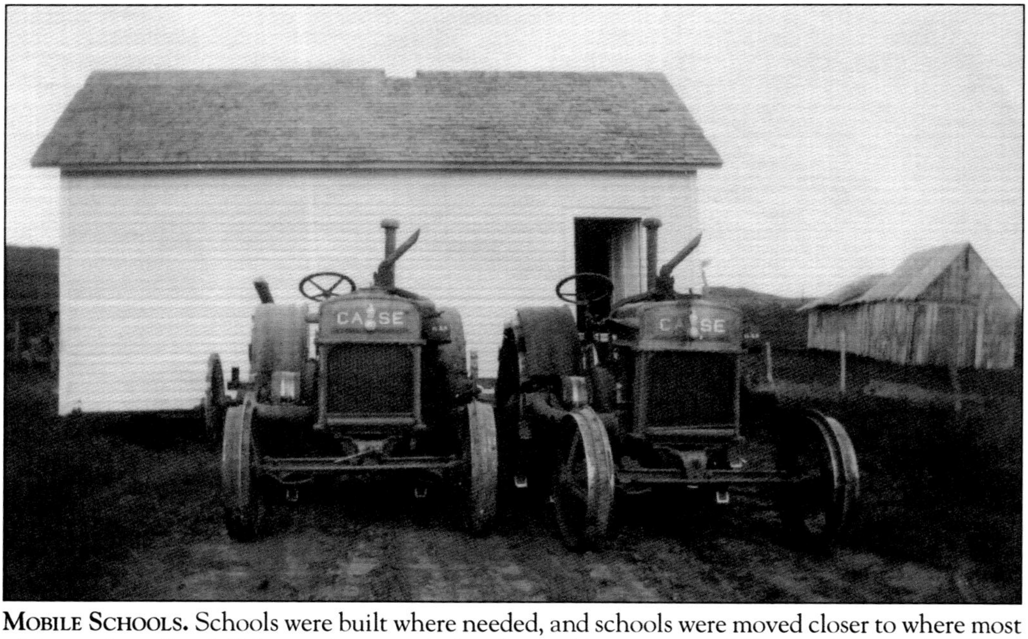

Mobile Schools. Schools were built where needed, and schools were moved closer to where most of the students lived. If the student population dropped in one area of Weston County, the school would be moved closer to students who would attend the school. Shown in the picture are steam tractors moving the Oelkers School. (Courtesy of Shelly Ritthaler.)

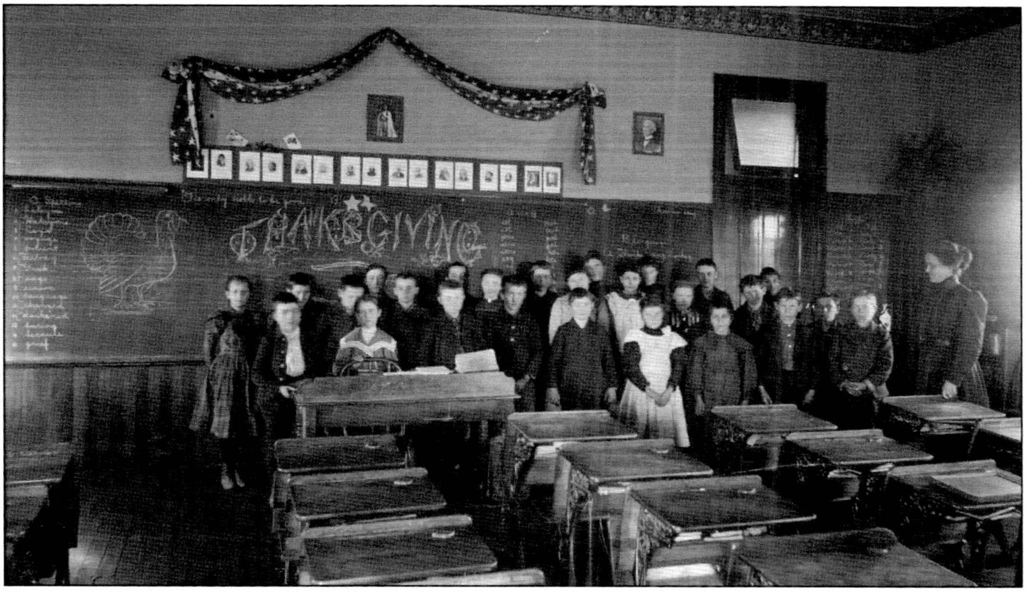

CAMBRIA SCHOOLS. Cambria had at least three schools during its 40-year existence. One school was situated in the center of town near the mining operations. Another was located in the residential area near the Catholic church. The third school was located on Antelope Table, 365 steps above the center of town. The Thanksgiving school picture is at Antelope Table School, and the picture below shows the school near the center of Cambria. (Both, AMM.)

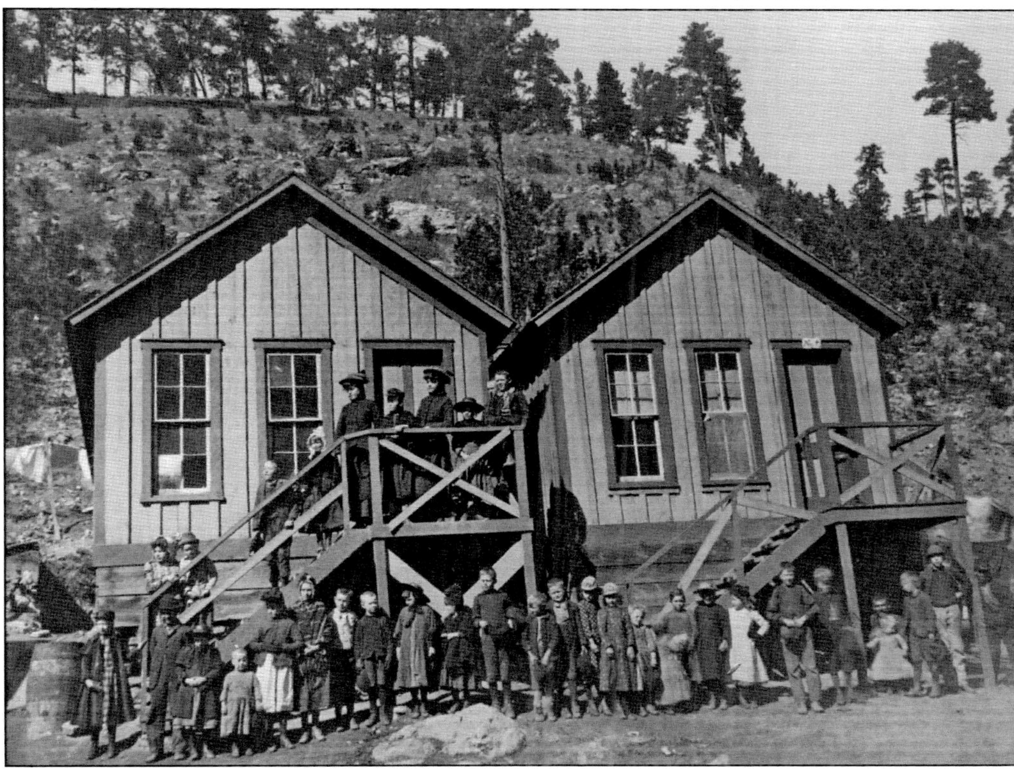

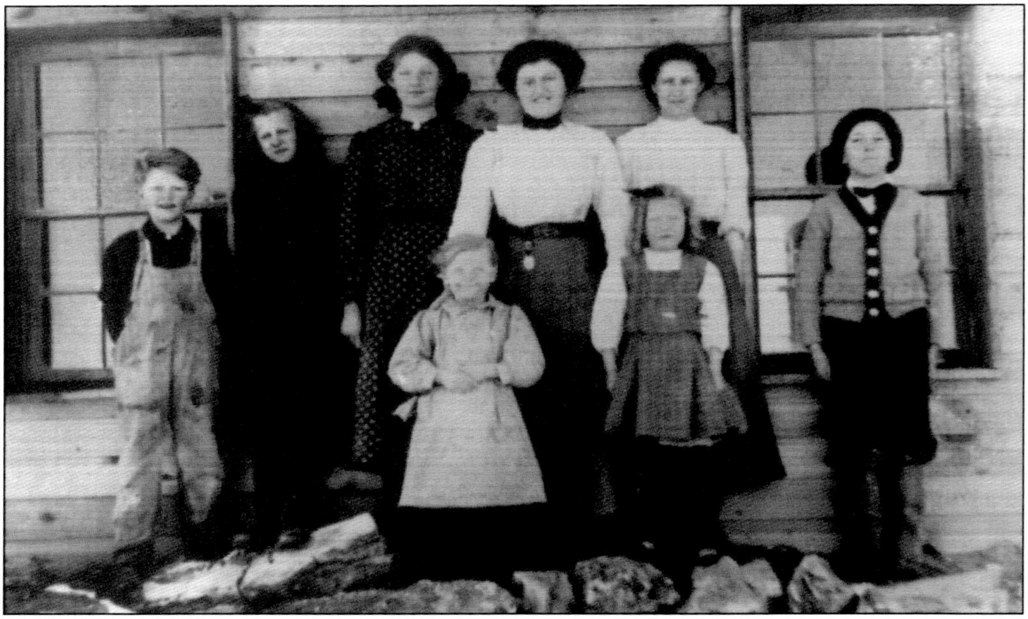

Howard School. West of Newcastle near Mush Creek and the Dunham Road was a community called Howard. Pictured is a class of the first school built in the Howard community. They are, from left to right, (first row) Fern Johnson and Ariel Humphreys; (second row) Glen Humphreys, Zella Johnson, possibly Bertha Johnson, Dorcas Cattles (teacher), Herma Bartholomew, and Howard Osborn.

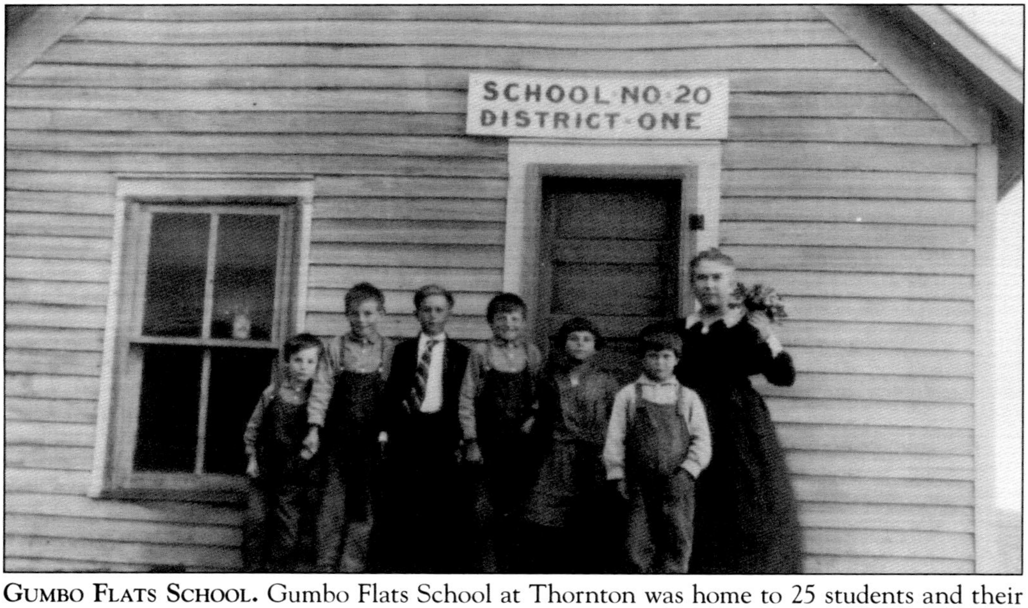

Gumbo Flats School. Gumbo Flats School at Thornton was home to 25 students and their teacher, Myra M. Lane, in 1922. Among those students were Dale Barritt, Tate Moore, Bernice and Orville Horn, Ester McCrady, Morse Mirich, and Lawrence, Paul, Homer, and Cecil Vinzant. When one of the homestead children, Bernice Horn, was asked what one did for entertainment, she replied, "We milked the cows and went to bed."

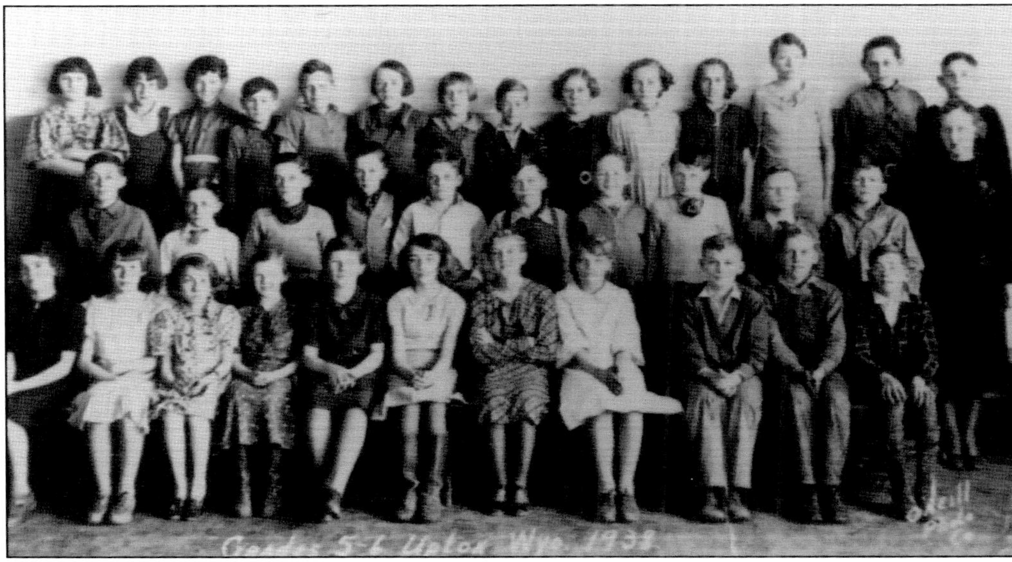

UPTON ELEMENTARY SCHOOL. Early school records from Upton were burned in a 1920 fire, but according to "History of the School" in a later school publication called *The Bobcat*, found at the Red Onion Museum in Upton, the "present school had its beginning in a two year course started back in 1910–11." In 1915, the first high school graduates from a three-year course were Mamie Darlington and Florence Ekwall. Upton graduated its first four-year class in 1919, graduating Sarah Minick and Albert Sheldon. After the fire, school was held in the telephone office, the harness shop, and the Acord pool hall. In 1920, commencement was held in the Methodist church, and graduates were Josie Roach, Mary Norris, Grace Norris, Laura May Norris, and Cecil Sweet. Upton High School teachers pictured below are, from left to right, Elizabeth Schneider, Clyde Johnson, Winnie Shacklett, and Edith Hilton. The 1935 Upton Elementary School grades five and six, pictured above, had 35 students, and it's obvious that graduating class sizes grew as the years passed.

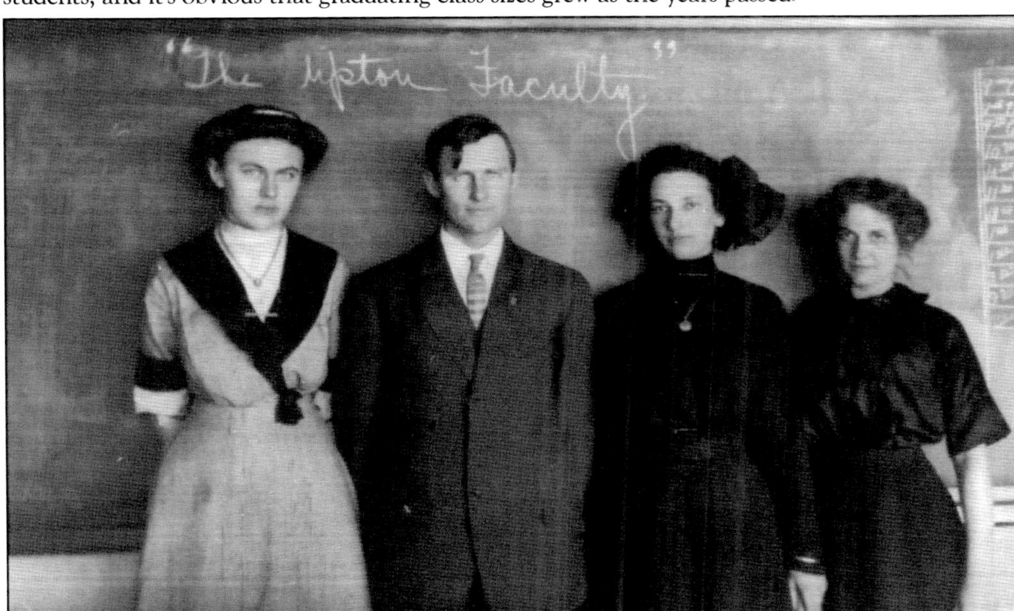

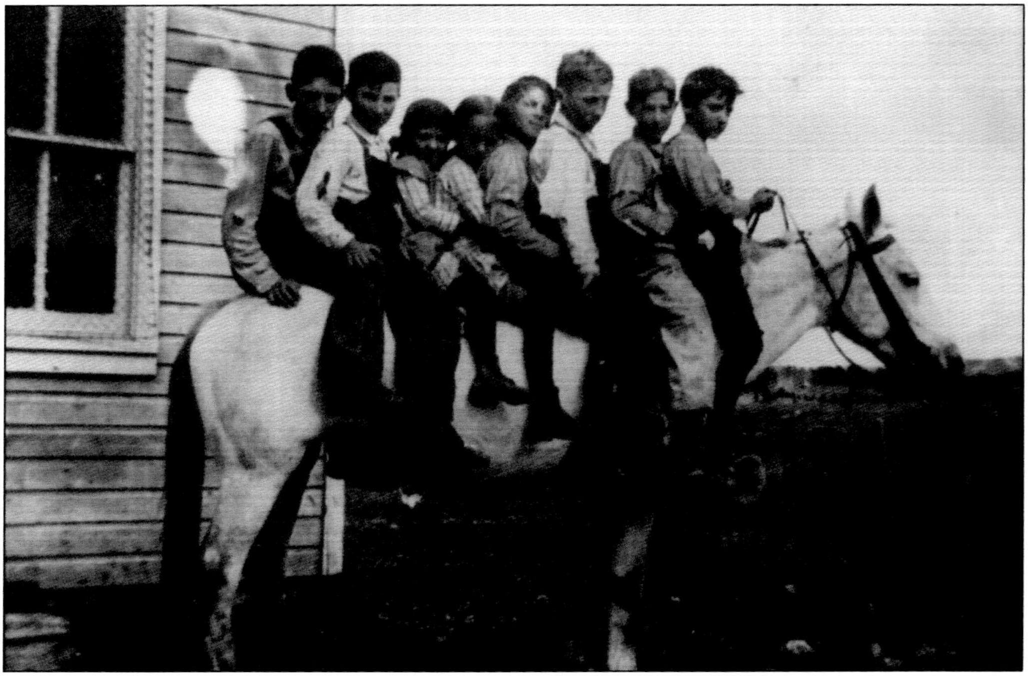

South Timber School. The ultimate and favorite class picture for homestead schools was to see how many kids could fit on a horse. South Timber School students pile on a good old favorite horse. From left to right are Eddie Schultze, Albert Hereford, Ina Schultze, Florence Bedell, Frank Schultze, Charles Hereford, Willie Petengill, and Clifford Schultze.

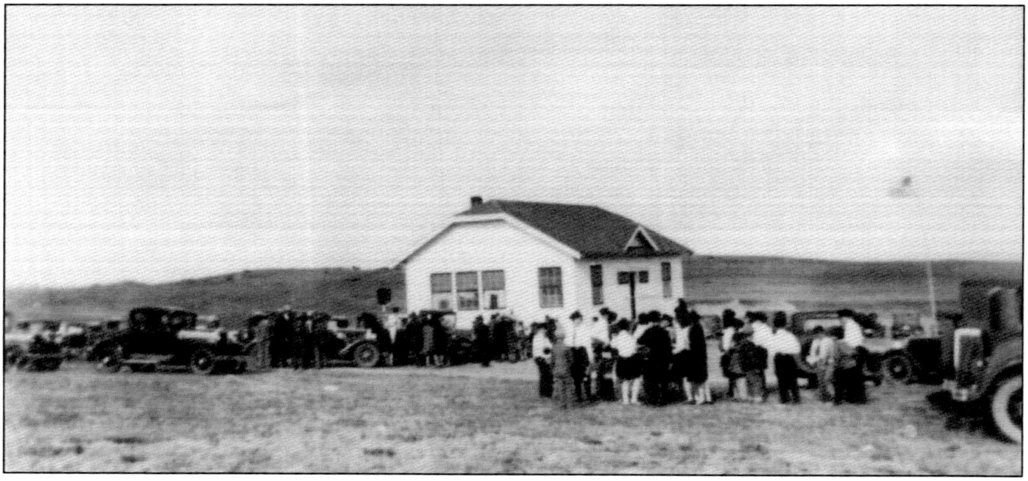

Morrissey School. The Morrissey Centralized School, 30 miles southwest of Newcastle, was established in 1928. A box social auctioneered by O.G. Fazine to raise money for a piano was part of the school dedication ceremony. At the time, it was a modern two-room building with a furnace and teacherage in the basement. According to the *News Letter Journal* in March 1930, the Morrissey School housed 40 schoolchildren and received the Wyoming Standard Shield for teaching accreditation.

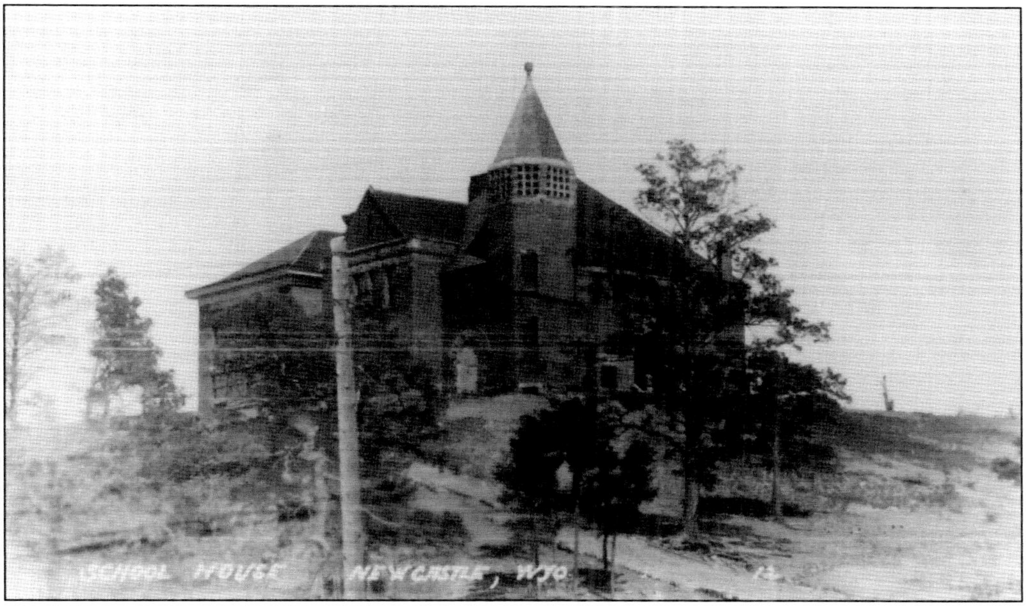

NEWCASTLE HIGH SCHOOL. In 1892, a new school opened in Newcastle. It cost $12,000. Bricks were made in Newcastle's own brick kilns. The school housed both elementary and secondary students. By 1922, Newcastle outgrew the school, and a new high school was built just below the old school. Both buildings are now gone—replaced by modern facilities. (Courtesy of Donna Fletcher.)

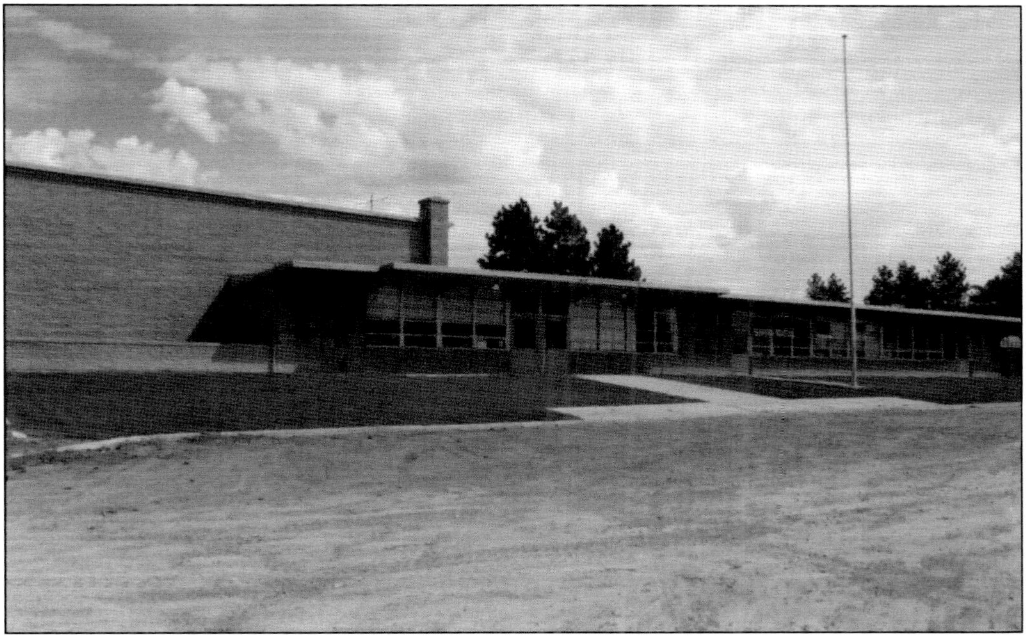

KITTY MOATS SCHOOL. The first school in Osage was built on land donated by the Nefsy brothers. A school building was constructed, but when the oil boom hit in 1922, two larger buildings were moved in next to the original one. In 1954, the old buildings were moved. A new one was built and named the Kitty Moats School. Pictured is the school, which was closed in 2009 after a decline in enrollment. Children in Osage are now bused to either Upton or Newcastle.

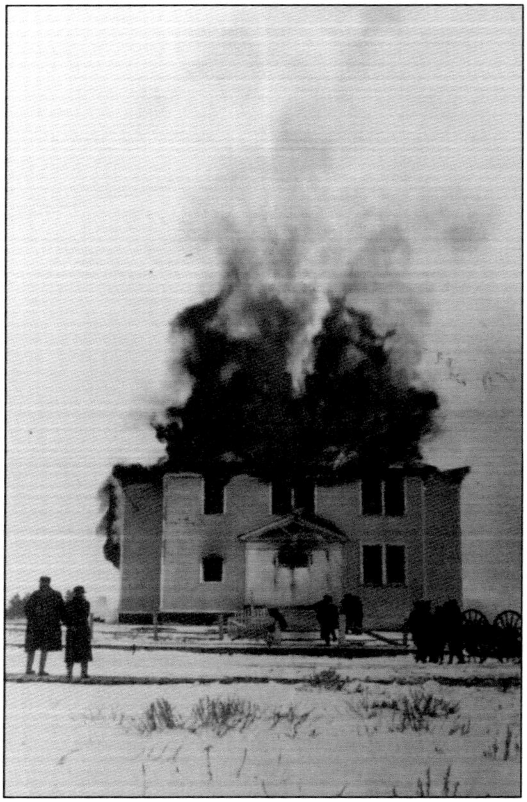

UPTON SCHOOL FIRE. School first began in 1909 in Upton in a new building. On November 5, 1920, a spectacular fire burned it to the ground. The students were taken out of the building, and two teachers escaped out of a window. No one was hurt, but the building was a total loss. In 1921, a new school was built.

MORGAN STORE. Fires were a recurring problem in early Weston County. Every home, business, or building usually had some sort of live fire for heating or cooking. Fuel came from small homesteader-run coal mines scattered around the county, the abundant timber on the northeast side of the county, or from heating oil that could be purchased from small, local petroleum refineries. Patrons at Noah Morgan's pool hall gather near the potbelly stove in 1927.

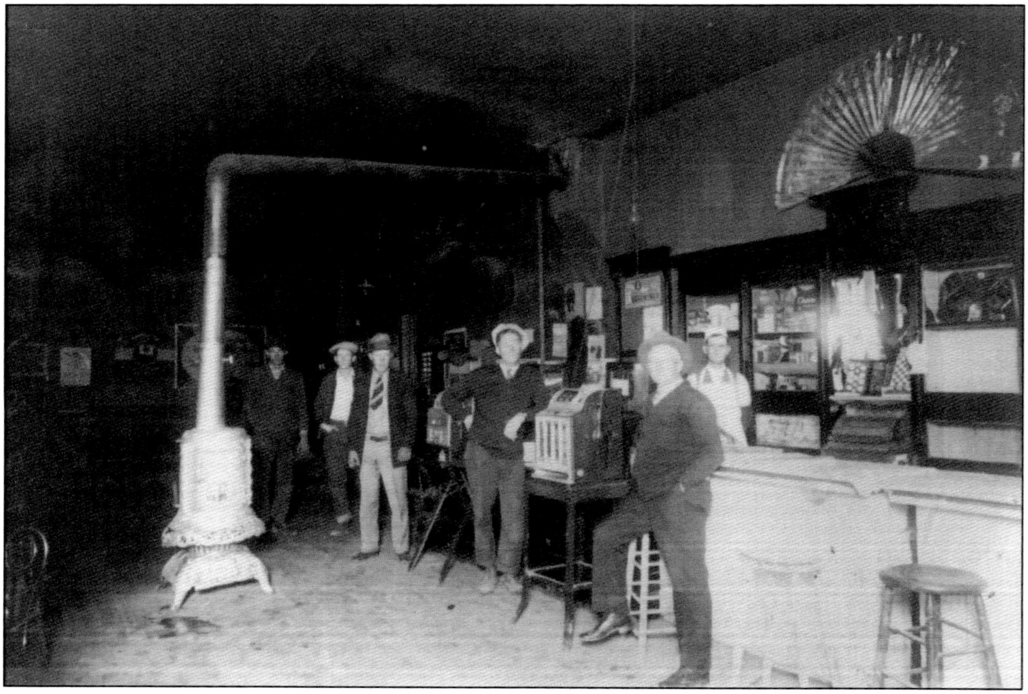

KEEPING WARM. For many Weston County children, keeping warm on the wind-blown and snowy high plains was a difficult reality and a way of life. Kenneth William Oelkers, a baby, snuggles near the family's heating stove in 1918. But snuggling near the fire was not enough. He, as was true with so very many homestead babies, did not survive infancy, according to Shelly Ritthaler. (OC.)

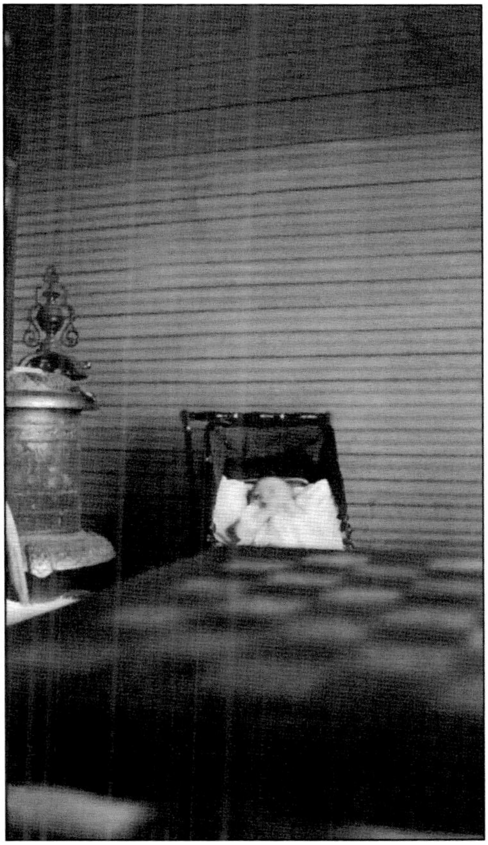

THE STAR HOTEL. Built about 1903, the Star Hotel was actually a house of ill repute. It operated until 1918 and was a profitable establishment in the little cow town. A barn on the back lot accommodated the horses of the guests. In 1941, the building became known as the Carlin Hospital when Dr. E.J. Carlin opened his practice of medicine. He left in the 1950s, and a fire consumed the building on January 31, 1980.

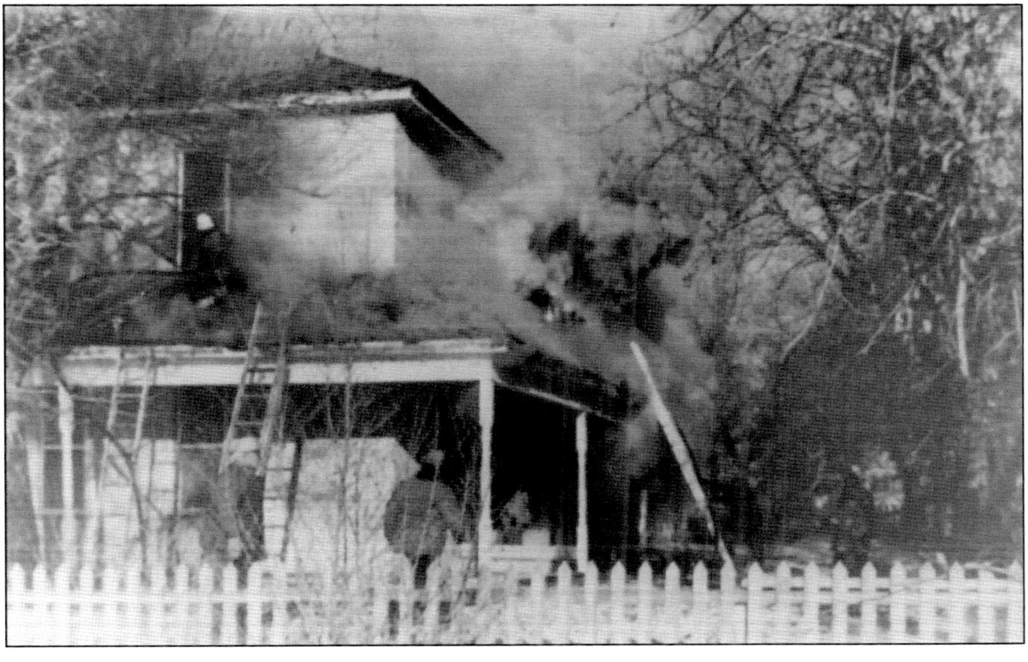

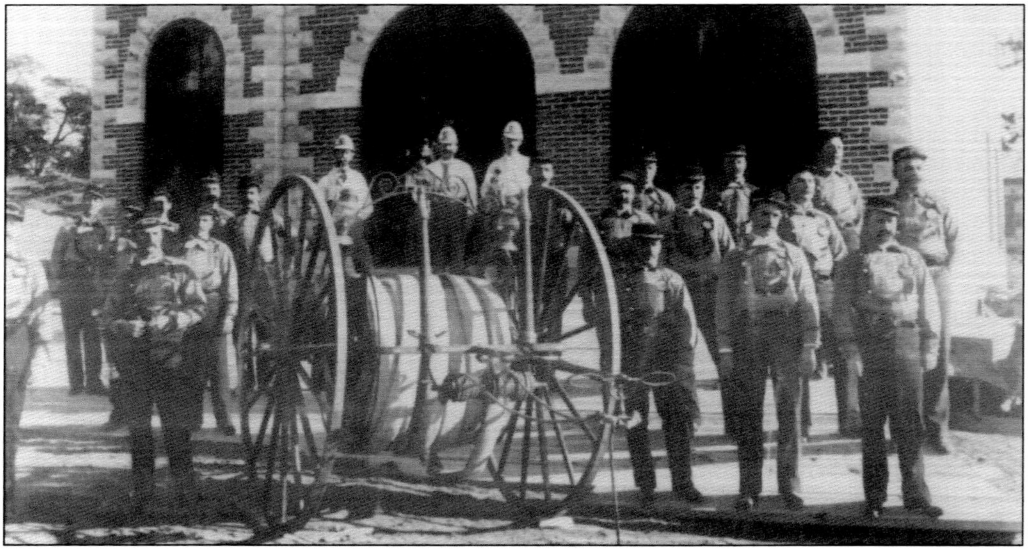

Newcastle Volunteer Fire Department. As soon as the town of Newcastle was organized in 1889, one of the first priorities was to organize a fire department. The volunteer department consisted of two divisions, the Mondell Hose Company and the Newcastle Hook and Ladder Company. Don Miller was foreman of the Mondell Hose Company, and Walter Schoonmaker, city mayor at that time, was assistant foreman. William H. Benns was foreman of the hook and ladder company, and John Handell was assistant foreman. In 1923, the fire department acquired its LaFrance fire truck, a 1921 Model T with a LaFrance fire apparatus mounted on it. However, it was not until 1933 that a city ordinance was passed establishing the Newcastle Volunteer Fire Department. The first fire chief was Clarence Brill, and his assistant chief was M.L. Hays.

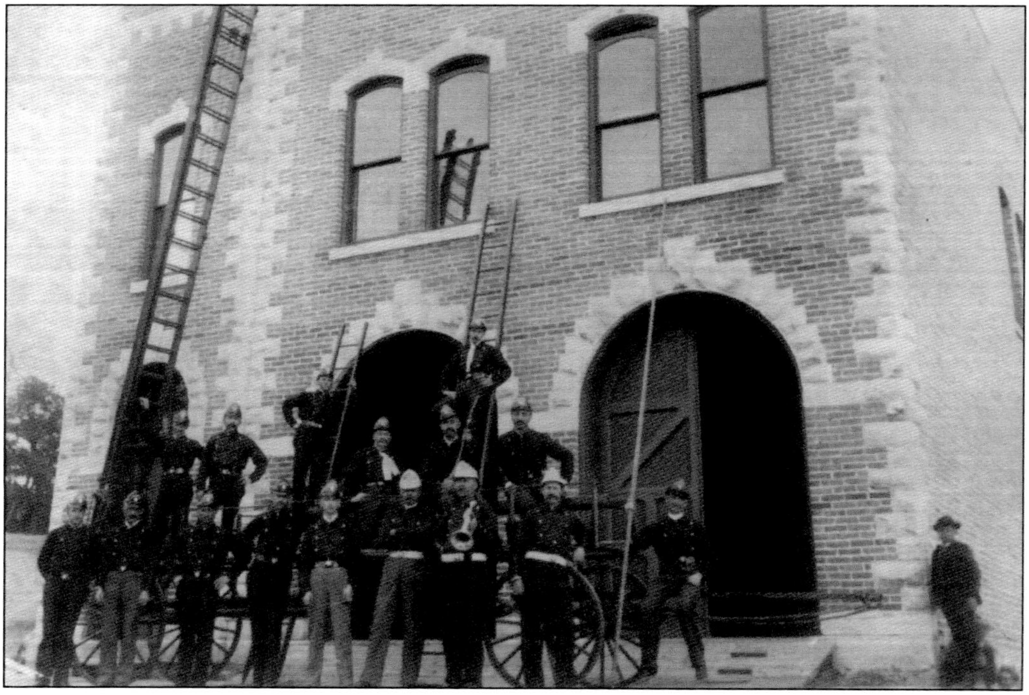

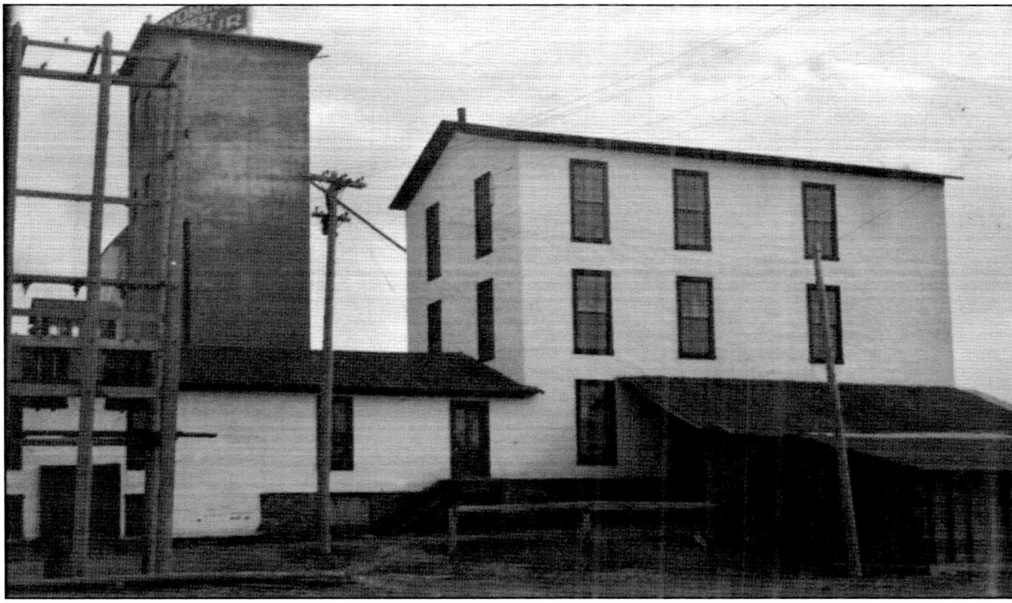

NEWCASTLE'S ELECTRIC PLANT. On September 4, 1905, the Newcastle Town Council granted George Getchell an electric light franchise. According to *Bridge to the Past*, the Western Electric Company of Omaha installed the equipment for the light plant in the new mill building under the supervision of Ralph B. Coleman. At night, the plant produced enough electricity to provide additional power for streetlights to supplement the city's power. (AMM.)

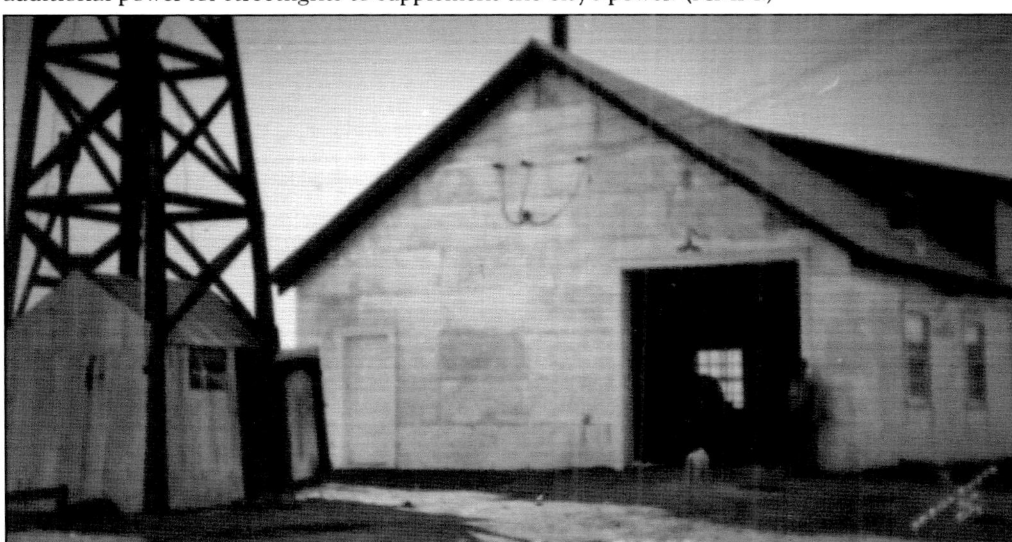

UPTON MUNICIPAL LIGHT PLANT. Because of frequent fire problems, people were anxious to reduce open-fire use in their homes and businesses. By 1911, Newcastle, Upton, and Osage acquired diesel-powered generating plants that ran low-voltage lights. An added advantage of Upton's light plant, according to Shelly Ritthaler, was that it had running water and showers. For 10¢, homesteaders could buy a shower and get ready for special occasions like church or the Saturday night dance.

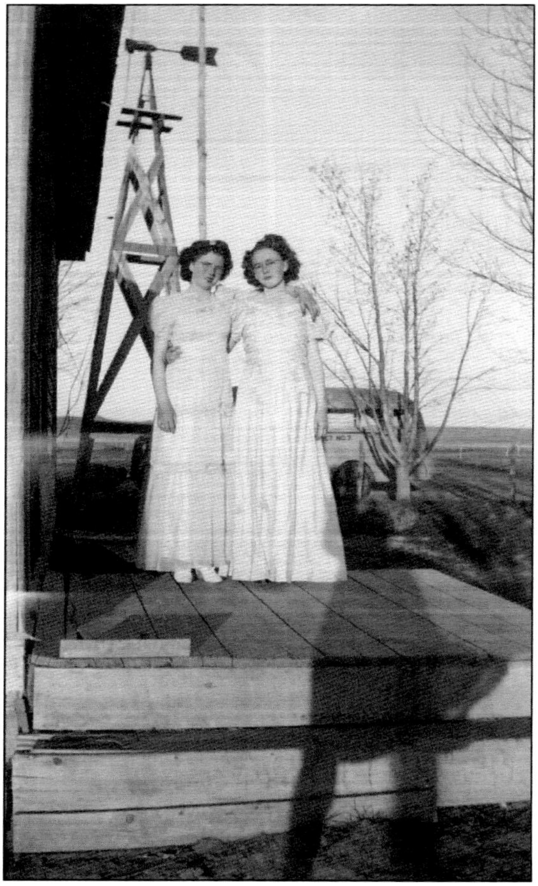

Wind Charger. Rural residents knew of electricity and desperately wanted to have it. Those who could afford it found different ways to generate their own low-voltage electricity. Some turned to wind power, as there was always a lot of wind. In the 1940s, as Doris (left) and Geraldine Oelkers pose in their formals, the wind charger tower can be seen in the background at their parents' ranch house. (Courtesy of Shelly Ritthaler.)

Rural Engineering. The Oelkers Ranch acquired running water and electricity from wind power. The windmill pumped water up into the water tank inside the tall building, which then gravity-fed water down into the house on the right and provided running water. The wind charger in the background charged a set of Delco batteries stored in a small house, so the family's house had low-voltage electricity when the wind blew enough. (Courtesy of Shelly Ritthaler.)

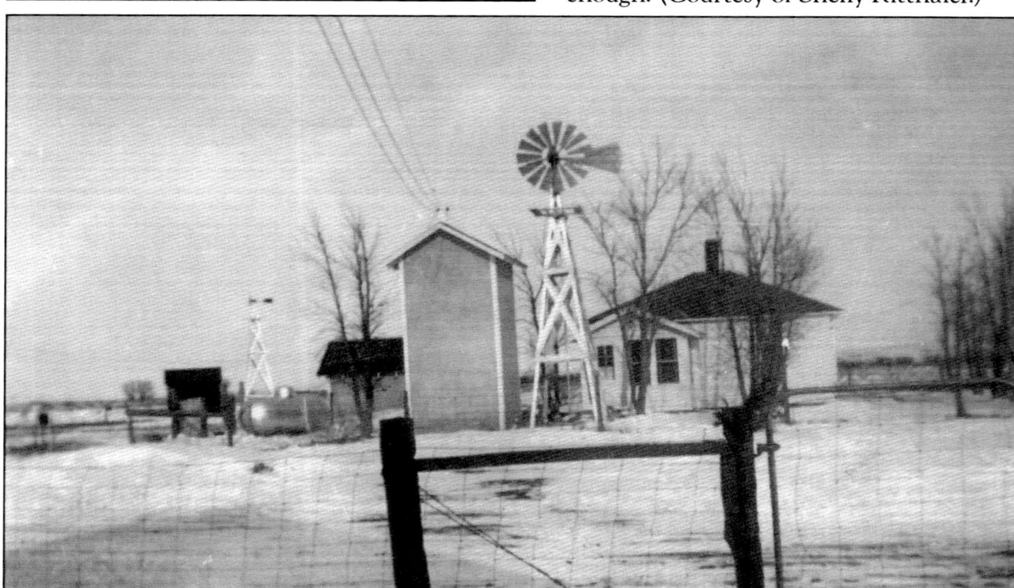

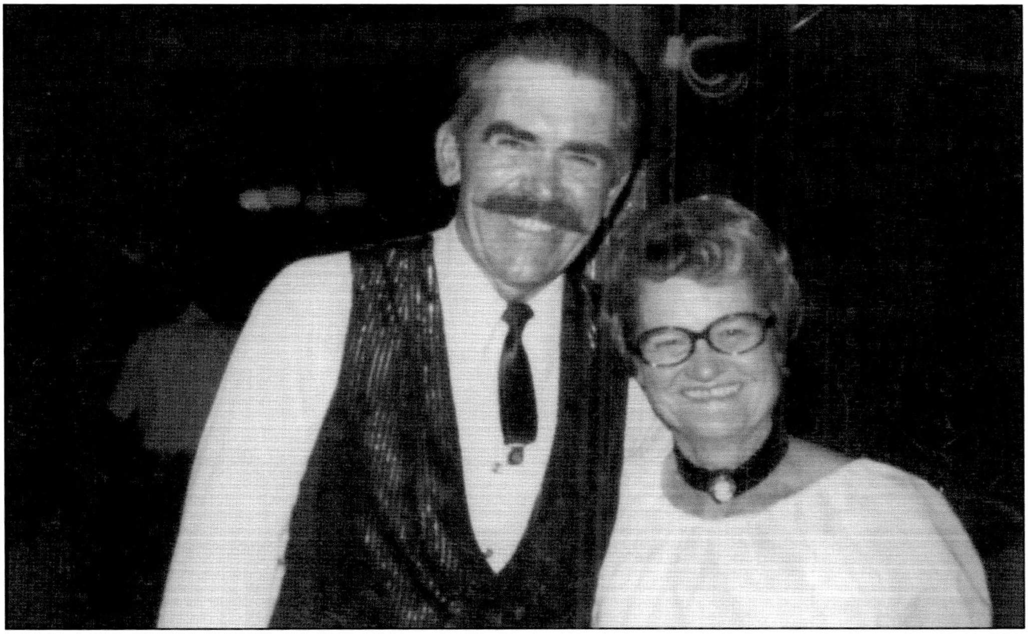

EARL CHRISTENSEN AND THE REA. In 1935, F.D. Roosevelt established the Rural Electrification Administration (REA) in order to provide affordable electricity to every rural home in America. Earl Christensen served on the local board working with the national REA program. His hardest job was to overcome skepticism of people who had endured the Depression and World War II and convince them of the benefits of REA electricity. Many did not have the $5 membership fee for the county's REA co-op. Shown are Earl and Mae Christensen. (EMC.)

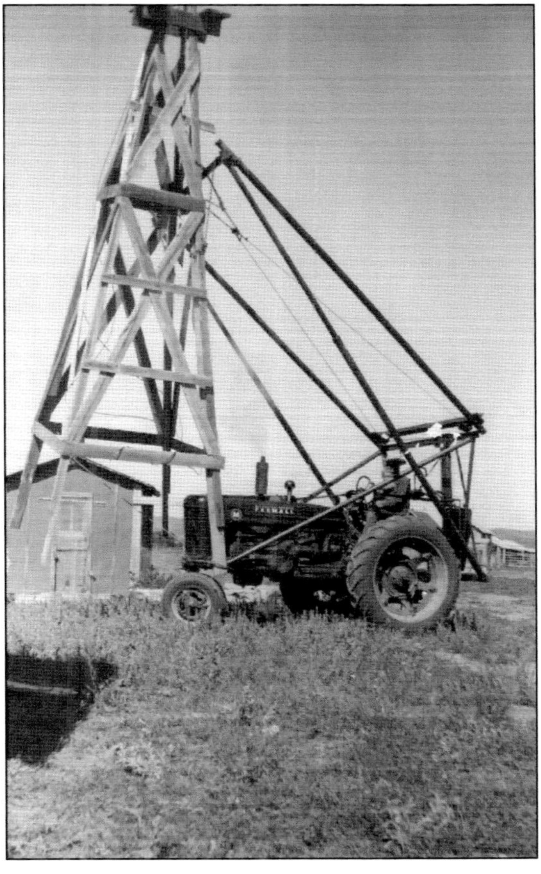

REA REPLACES WIND TOWERS. When the REA arrived, Walter Ritthaler removed his wind tower with his tractor. Soon, REA members found there was a downside of a steady and reliable source of electricity. They could continue working for longer hours. Normally, after the sun went down, they had to quit working, but electricity, which was supposed to make their lives easier, made it possible for them to work longer.

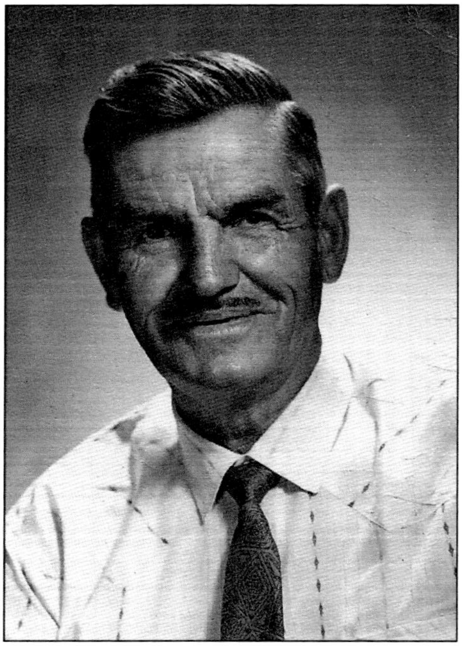

LeRoy Giffin and the Water Well Gusher. In 1943, Leroy Giffin was the driller on a rig drilling for oil near Osage. Drill hands and those who were there remember that the drill floor started to shake and rumble. Afraid of a gas explosion, every one dove off the rig and ran for cover. Suddenly, water burst from the well so hard that it blew the drill stem out of the hole. It caused a crater so big that the drilling rig almost fell into it. They had hit a massive underground artesian pool. Once tapped, water ran out of every surrounding rabbit and gopher hole. The resulting lake was later stocked for fishing. It made enough water that in 1948, Black Hills Power and Light built a water-cooled, coal-fired electrical power plant beside it. (Courtesy of Barbara Barritt.)

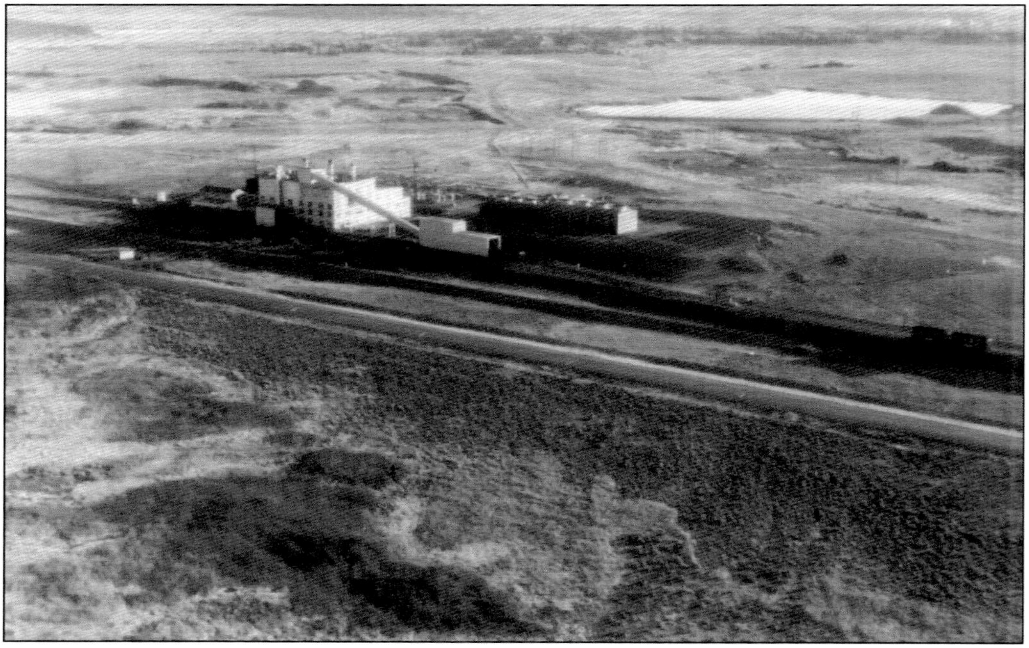

Osage Power Plant. Following the end of World War II, the increased use of electricity overtook the ability of the small diesel-powered generating plants in the small towns to keep up with the demand. People in rural areas hungered for more electricity. Power providers to both these groups got together and built a coal-powered, water-cooled electrical power plant near the lake accidently formed by a drilling rig that hit an artesian well. The Black Hills Power and Light Plant was built in 1948 and provided power as well as jobs for Weston County people for many years. It was replaced by cleaner, more efficient plants and closed down in 2011.

Eight

A Social Place

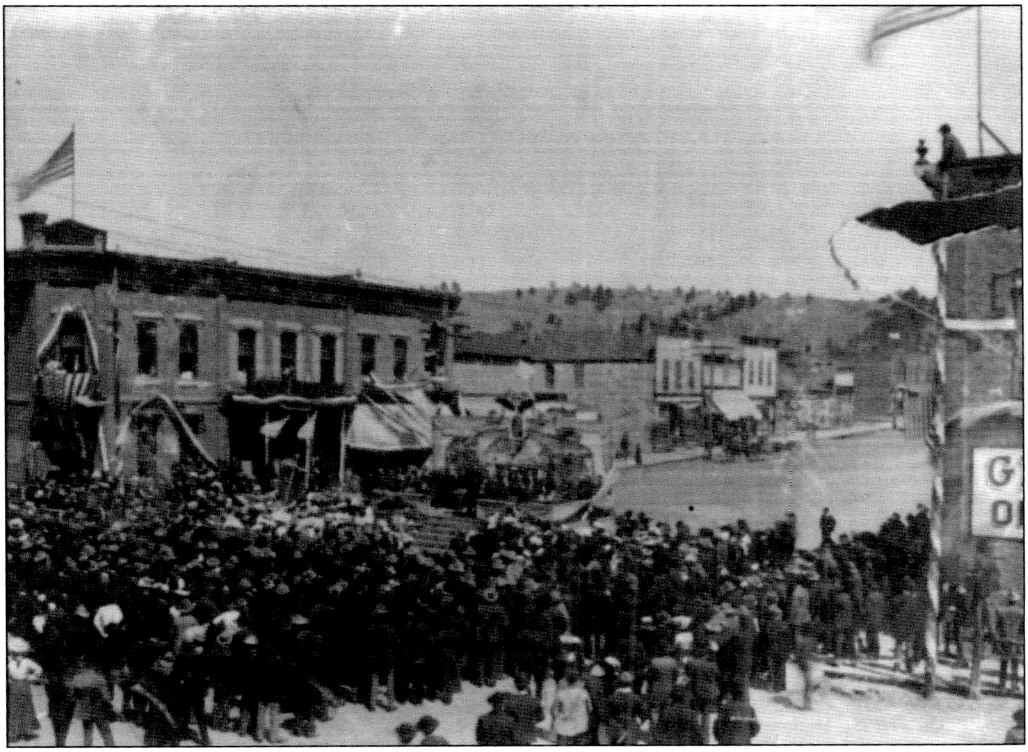

A Visit from the President. In 1903, Pres. Teddy Roosevelt, the 26th US president from 1901 to 1909, made a whistle-stop visit in Newcastle. Accompanied by Frank Mondell, who met the president's train in Sheridan, Roosevelt stopped at the depot, and Mayor Peter Kinney accompanied him to a platform at the crossing of Warren Avenue and Seneca Street. A crowd of 2,000 people dressed in their best and gathered to hear him speak.

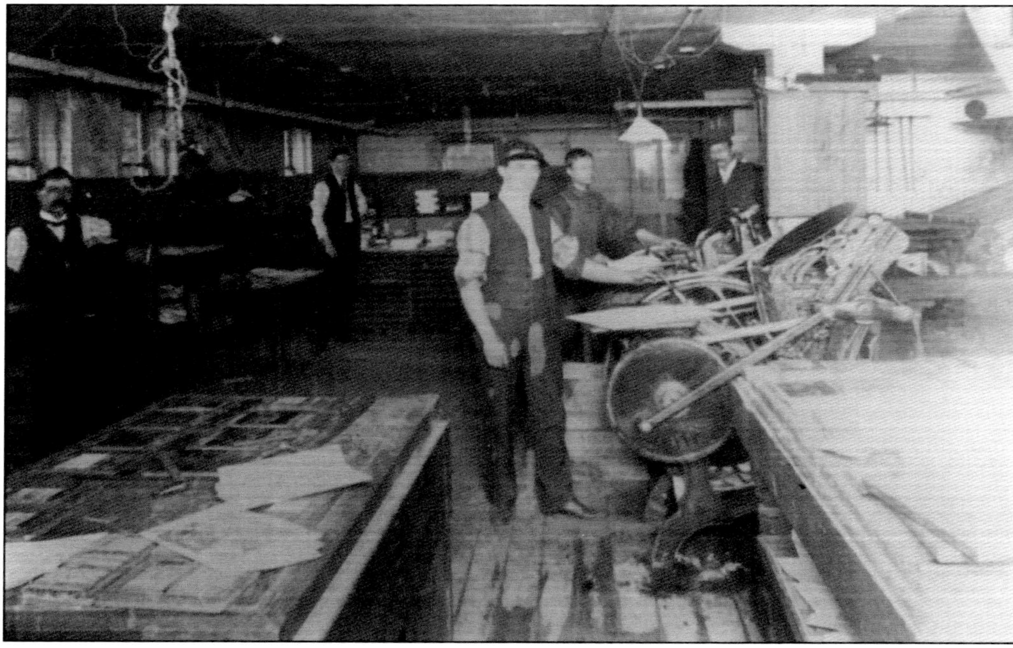

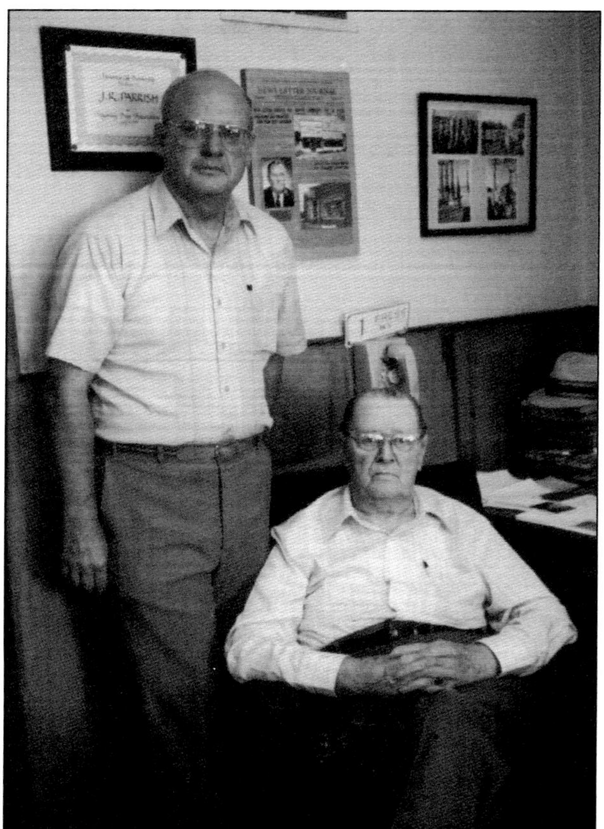

Newcastle's Early Newspapers. Weston County residents have been a social and communicative people. From the time lots were first sold in Newcastle in 1889, a newspaper called the *Newcastle Journal* was printed. In 1909, the *Upton News Letter* started printing. The papers changed names and ownership over the many years, but they still publish today under the names the *News Letter Journal* and the *Weston County Gazette*. Early-day workers are shown printing the Newcastle papers. (AMM.)

J.R. Parrish. In 1937, John R. Parrish purchased a part interest in the Newcastle *News Letter Journal*. In 1938, he became the sole owner of the paper. When Newcastle celebrated its golden anniversary in 1939, he published a commemorative issue of the paper, which is used today by many historians and interested people. In 1987, he retired and ended 50 years as publisher of the Newcastle paper. Shown is James Parrish standing next to his father, J.R. Parrish. (AMM.)

Peter Kinney. Born in Boston in 1861, Peter J. Kinney was one of the most progressive thinkers of his time. He made his way to the West and ended up in Tubb Town for its short life. He was among the first to buy lots in Newcastle, built the Palace Saloon, and later bought the Antlers Hotel. He built a light plant that provided the first electricity to Newcastle residents. He also installed a switchboard, which brought the first telephone service to the town. He served in many political leadership roles, including state senator.

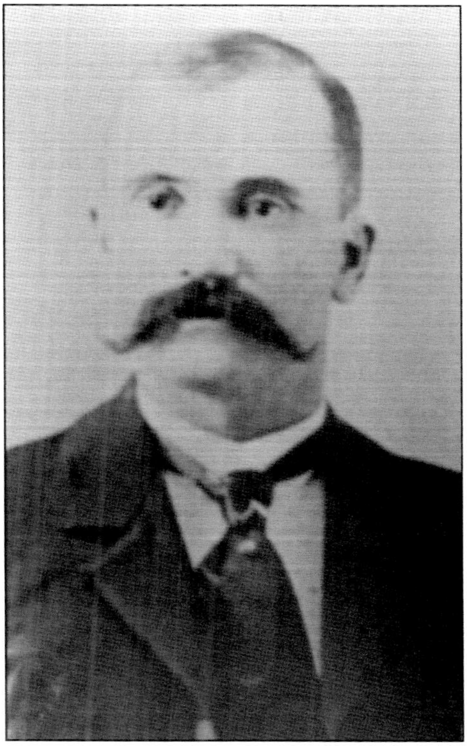

Telephone Switchboard Operator. In the early 1900s, the first telephone service in Upton was established, and in 1902, the Ranch and Home Telephone Company was organized to operate exchanges in Upton, Moorcroft, and Newcastle. In 1908, that company became Northern Wyoming Telephone Company and helped connect the three towns with long-distance service. The telephone companies employed many young women as switchboard operators. Pictured is Arlene Updike Jenkins operating the switchboard in Upton. (Courtesy of the Red Onion Museum.)

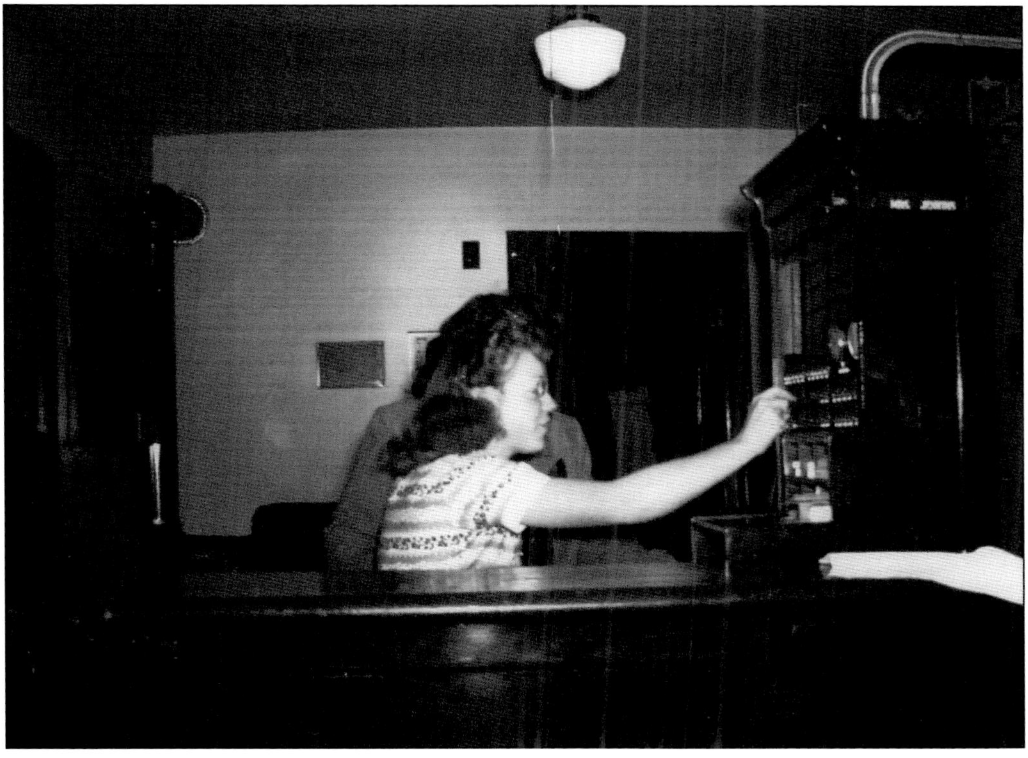

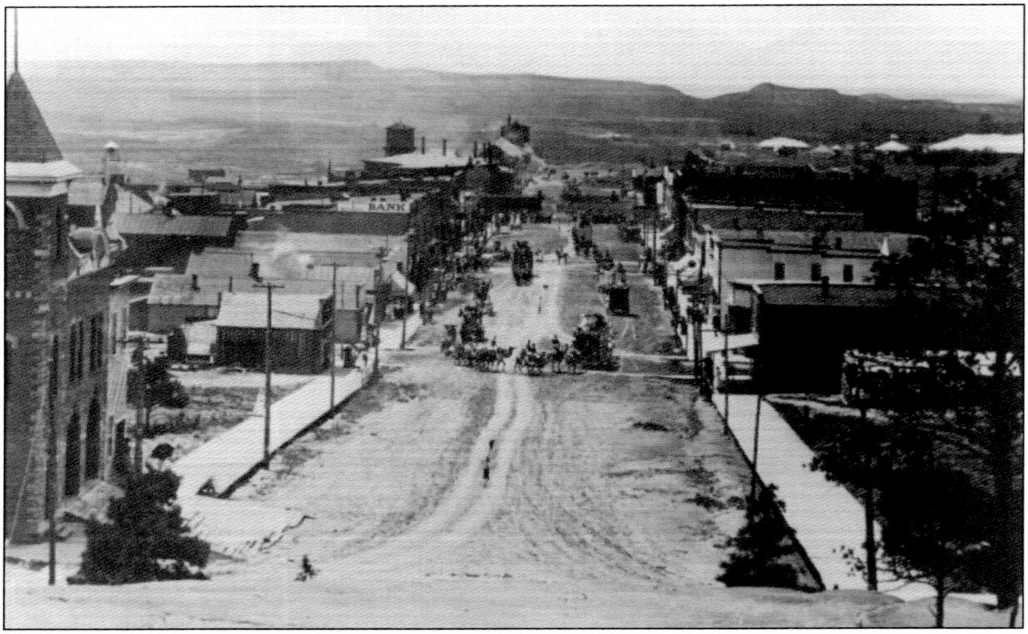

PARADE. Most early-day Weston County people lived in homes or homestead shacks smaller than an average-sized bedroom by today's standards. This, combined with the isolation of the communities and homes, made people eager for all kinds of social gatherings. Social gatherings could be dances, church socials, or parades from traveling shows. Pictured is an early-day Newcastle circus parade.

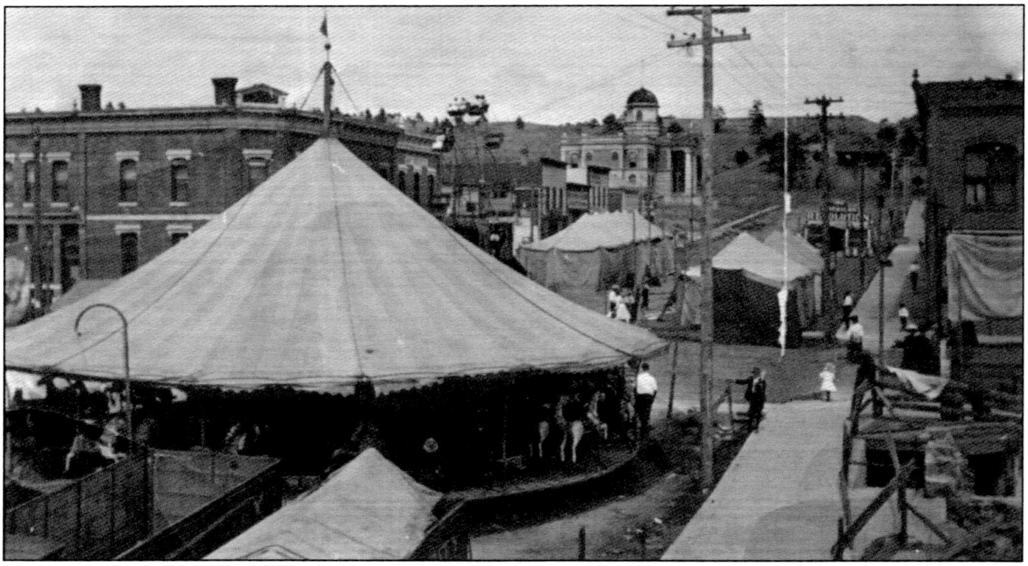

CARNIVAL. Newcastle residents gather and line up to ride the carousel at a visiting carnival. Note the man on the right with the shovel. He is keeping coal in the steamer that runs the engine that makes the carousel go around.

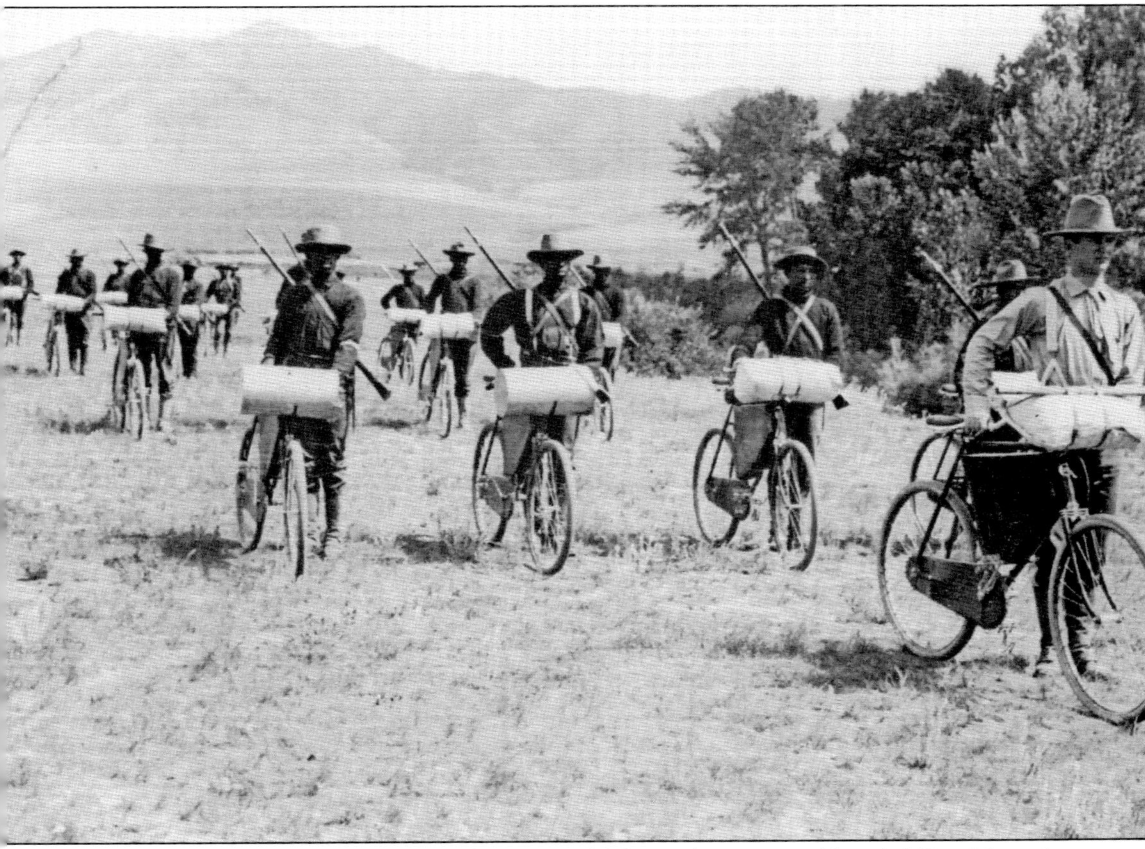

Buffalo Soldier Bicycle Corps. In 1897, a troop of African American soldiers left Fort Missoula in Montana on bicycles. They conducted drills and exercises on 100-pound iron bicycles to find out if the bicycle could be used as a viable piece of military equipment. They came to be called the Iron Riders. They rode from Montana to St. Louis, toured Yellowstone, and rode mountains and plains. Their diaries reported on June 30, "A good night's sleep was taken in Merino," which is now Upton. In Newcastle, on July 1, they spent "two hours swimming in the buoyant, salty water," which is assumed to be Salt Creek, before resuming their trip. They made the 1,900-mile trip to St. Louis, but the gumbo mud and lack of repairs along the way made it a difficult trip. For a brief moment, Weston County was a small part of their fame. (Courtesy of Wyoming State Archives, Department of State Parks and Cultural Resources.)

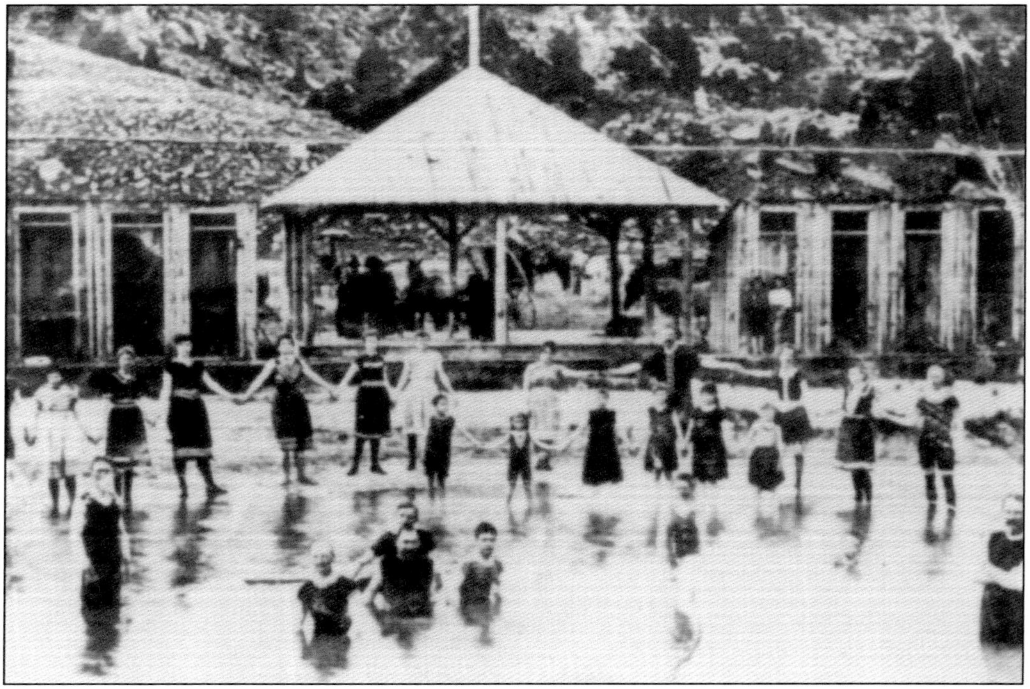

HUNYADI BEACH. Located on Salt Creek north of Tubb Town was a popular mineral springs and resort called Hunyadi Beach. People loved to swim in the salty water and take mineral baths for their health. There was a gazebo-styled pavilion for dances and dressing rooms for swimmers. When the resort was built at the Flying V Cambria Inn, the waters dried up at Hunyadi Beach, and the resort disappeared.

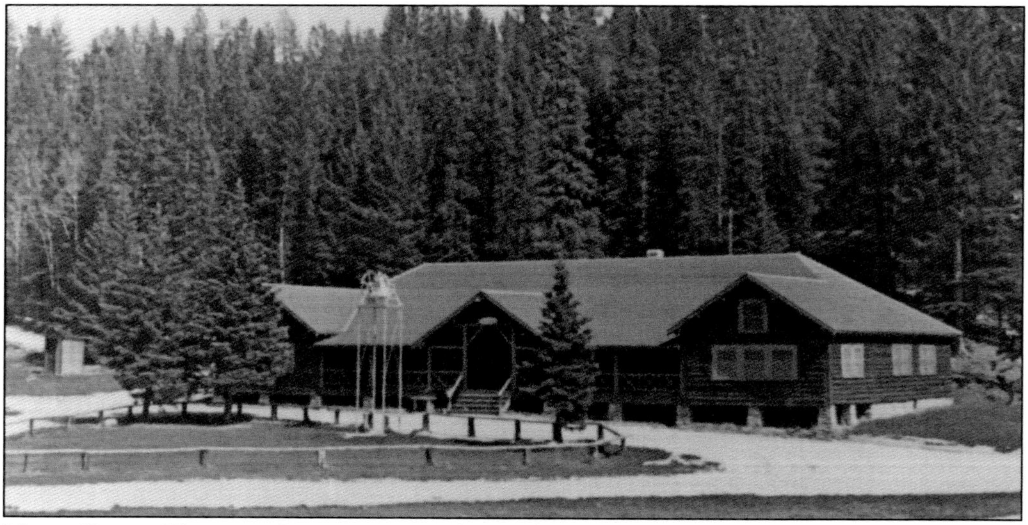

MALLO DANCE HALL AND LODGE. In 1913, the Mallo place, named after Henry and George Mallo, became the site for all kinds of dances, celebrations, and political rallies. In the 1930s, the property was purchased by Walter Schoonmaker, who donated the land to Weston County to be used as a recreational facility. With a WPA grant, the county built a large lodge and several cabins. In 1977, the original lodge burned and was rebuilt. It is pictured in 1933. (DH.)

MARTENS BAND. Residents gathered often for dances, weddings, and other social gatherings. Whatever the reason, the shared fun and company must have been a welcome relief from their hardworking lives. Many people played instruments, ranging from piano to accordion, banjo to guitar, and brass to woodwinds. Pictured from left to right are Lee, Henry, and Jack Martens posing with their instruments.

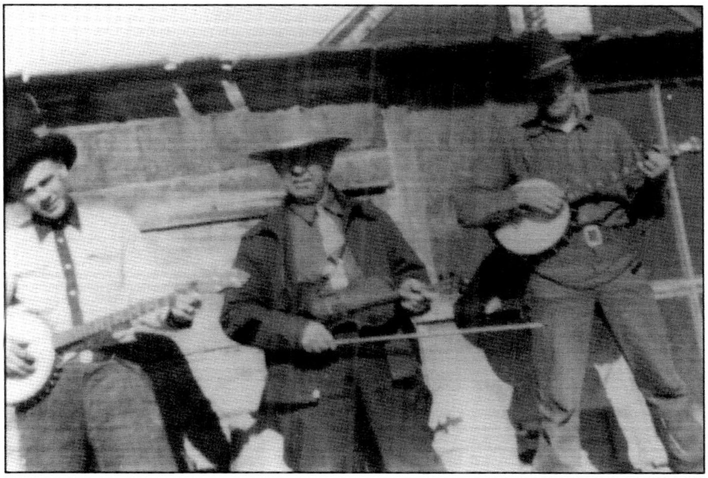

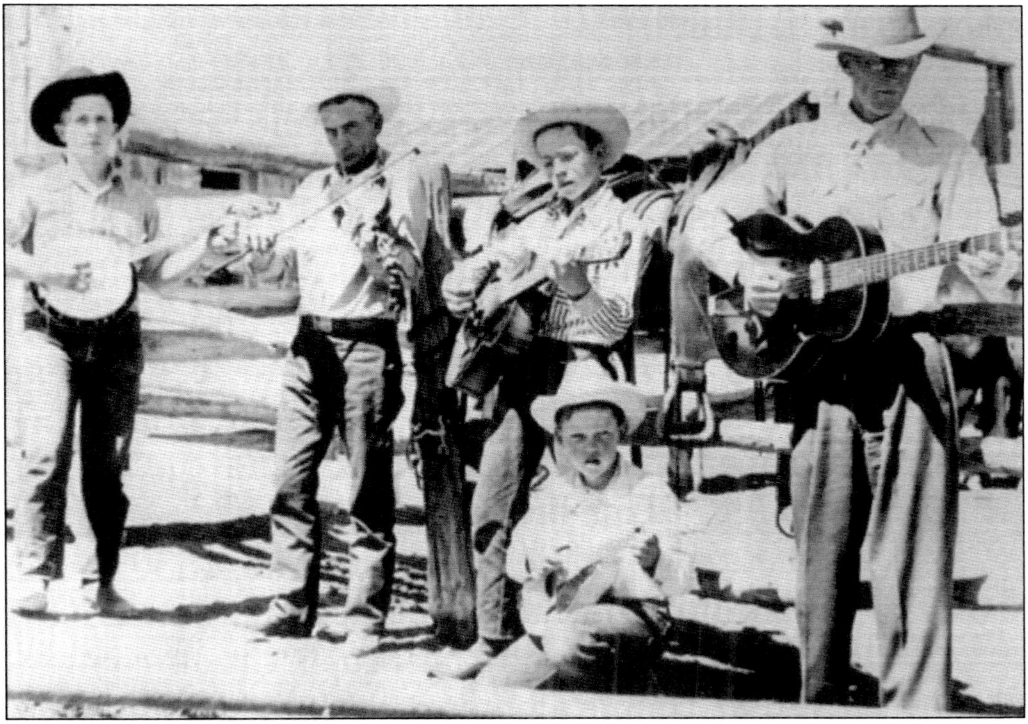

FORDYCE FAMILY BAND. In the 1930s, Joseph Stephen Fordyce started playing on a fiddle made by his grandfather. All of his children played together as the Fordyce Family Band. They played for benefit dances, weddings, and gatherings. In 1958, they finished playing together. Pictured are, from left to right, Johnny on banjo, Joe on fiddle, Buzz with guitar, Tommy on mandolin, and Johnny Martin with guitar. (DH.)

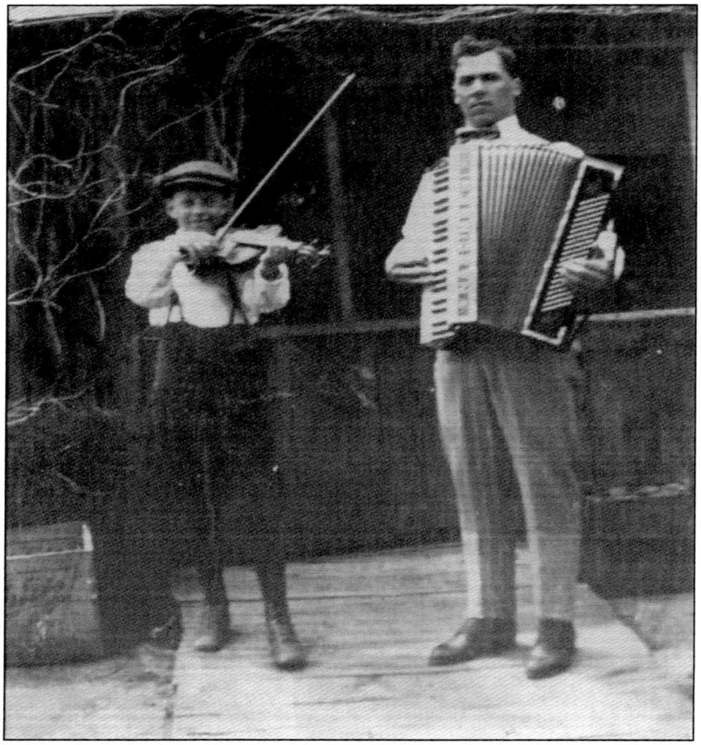

ESSENTIALS FOR DANCES. It did not take much to make a dance. Homes, dance halls, stores, community buildings, saloons, and schools played host to dances. Furniture was pushed back and floors were cleared. Fiddles, banjos, guitars, accordions, and pianos were readied. Often dances lasted all night long with a midnight supper break. Pictured are Johny Carnaghi playing his fiddle and Beppo Nascenbeni on the accordion. (AMM.)

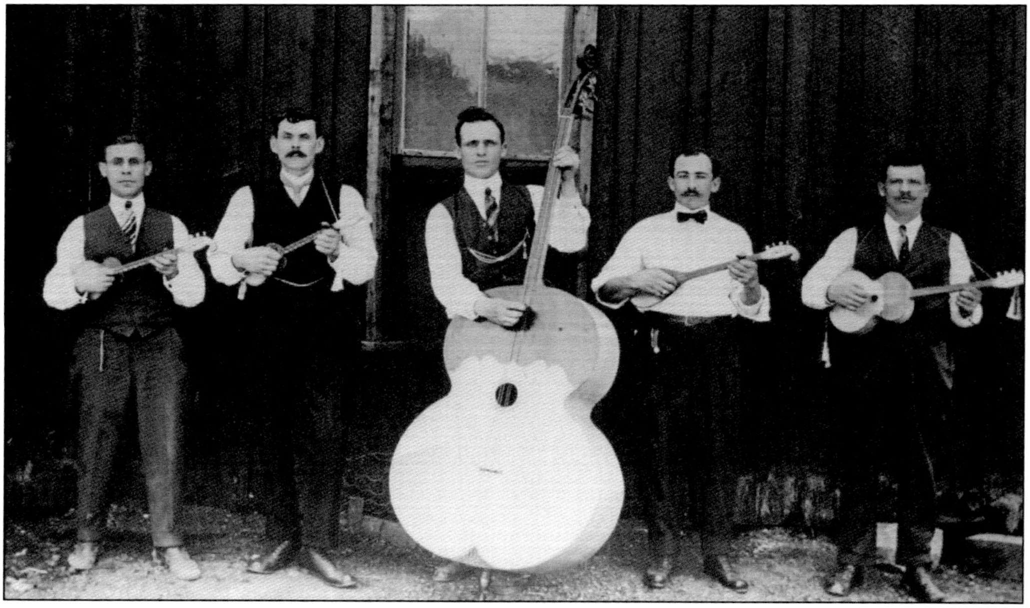

***TAMBURITZA* SERBIAN ORCHESTRA.** In 1917, Nick Mitich organized a Yugoslavian band, which was well known at the Cambria Opera House. The opera house had a fine waxed dance floor and was the cultural center of the coal-mining town. Pictured are, from left to right, George Vucich on the tamburitza, Radovan Bogucervitch with the harmony tamburitza, Nick Mitich with bull fiddle, Mike Gurcich on the mandolin, and Cvetko Velkovich with his tenor guitar. (AMM.)

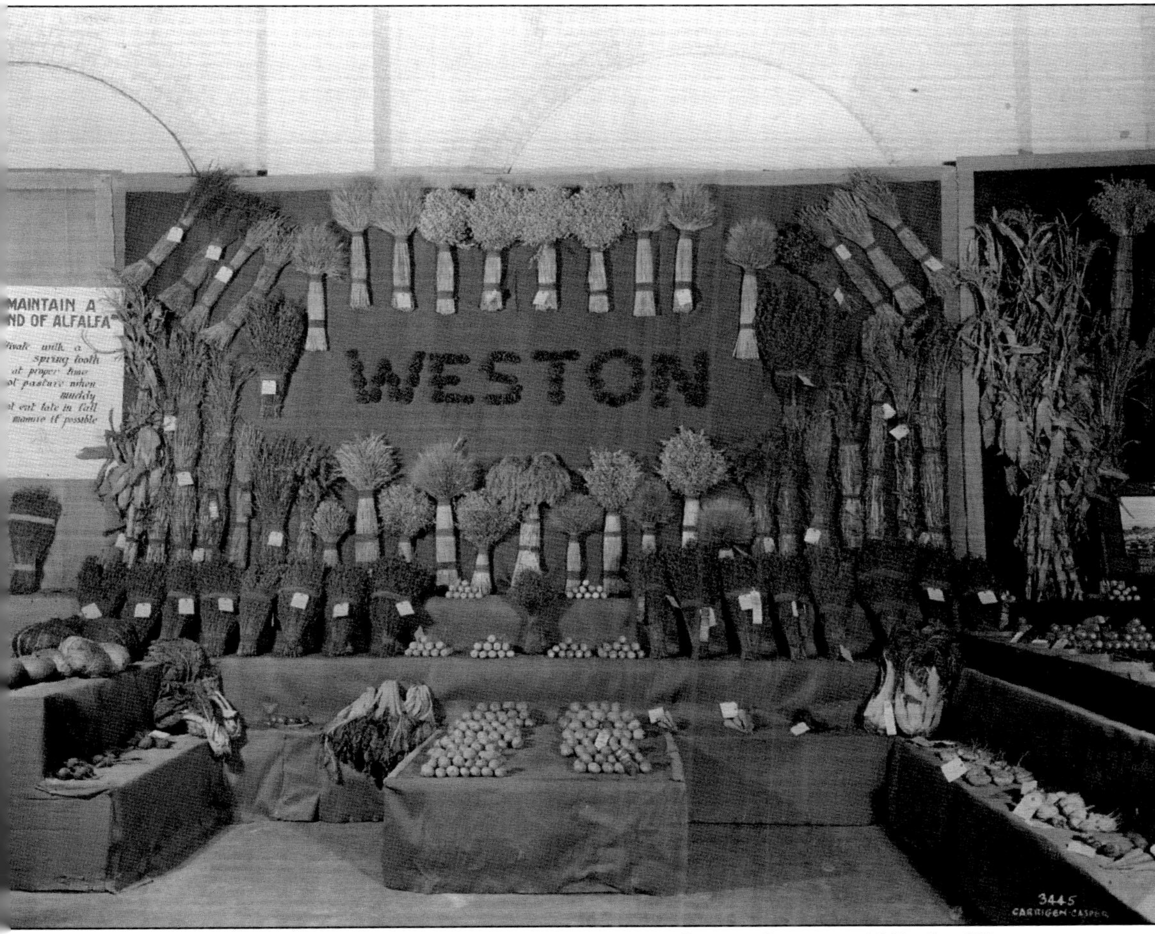

WESTON COUNTY EXHIBIT AT WYOMING STATE FAIR, 1931. Since it began in 1912, the Wyoming State Fair has offered a venue for counties to display their agricultural products. Weston County's 1931 display was a product of the Weston County Extension Service and received its support from farmers and ranchers who participated in the Weston County Fair. The Weston County Fair began in 1904, when local citizens wanted an event to display their agricultural successes as well as to have sporting contests. In 1935, the Kilpatrick brothers donated 36 acres to Weston County for use as a recreation facility and racetrack. This has been the home of the Weston County Fair since that time. (AMM.)

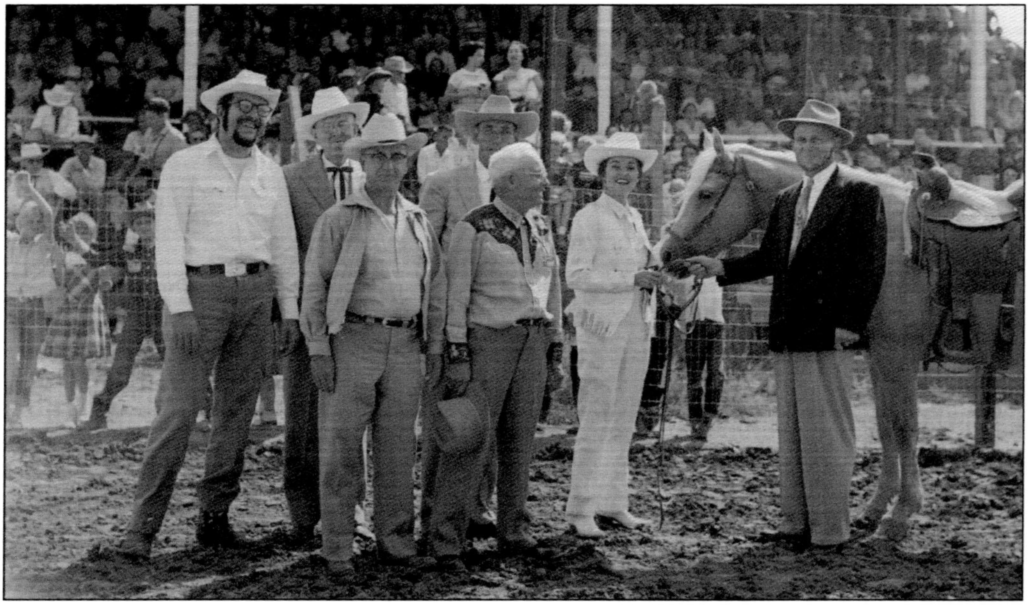

Miss America Visits Newcastle. In 1956, the granddaughter of Upton residents Bill and Helen Ritchie and the reigning Miss America, Sharon Kay Ritchie of Nebraska, was invited and attended the Weston County Fair and Rodeo. Violet Sedgwick, a Newcastle ranch woman, loaned Ritchie her favorite palomino horse to ride during the festivities, and Ritchie rode in the parade and opening ceremonies of the rodeo. (AMM.)

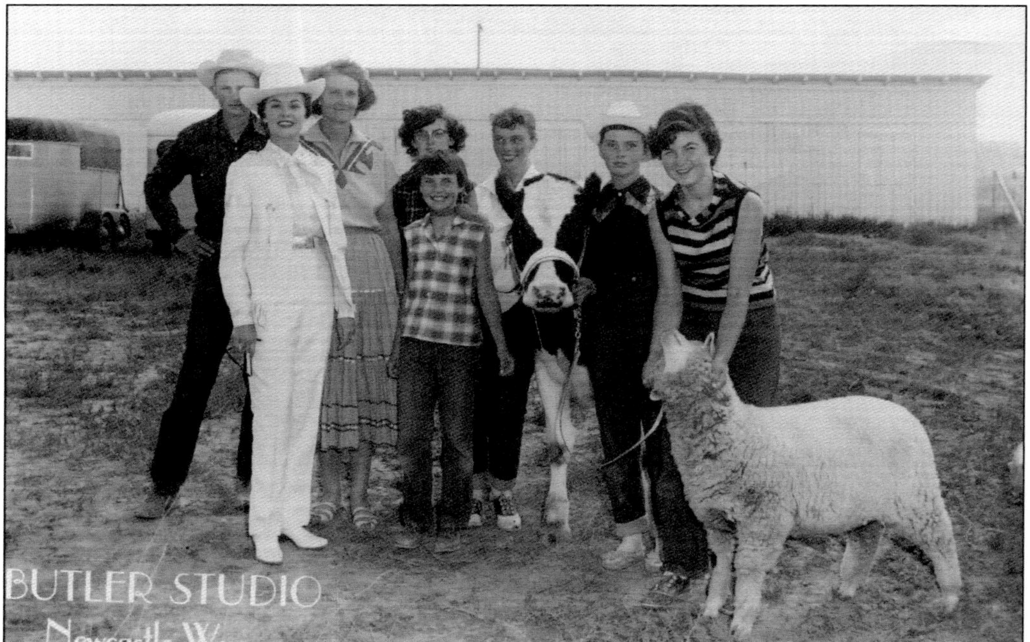

Happy Ranchers 4-H Club. Miss America Sharon Kay Ritchie poses with the Happy Ranchers 4-H Club. From left to right are Tony Marchant, Ritchie, Pauline Marchant, Joyce Bayne, Joyce Gaskill (in front of Joyce Bayne), Louise Hutt, Shirley Hutt, and Sue Gaskill. (AMM.)

Miss America 1956. Miss America spoke to a huge crowd of over 1,000 people. She thrilled the audience, who believed that, because she was the granddaughter of Weston County residents, she was one of Weston County's own as well. (AMM.)

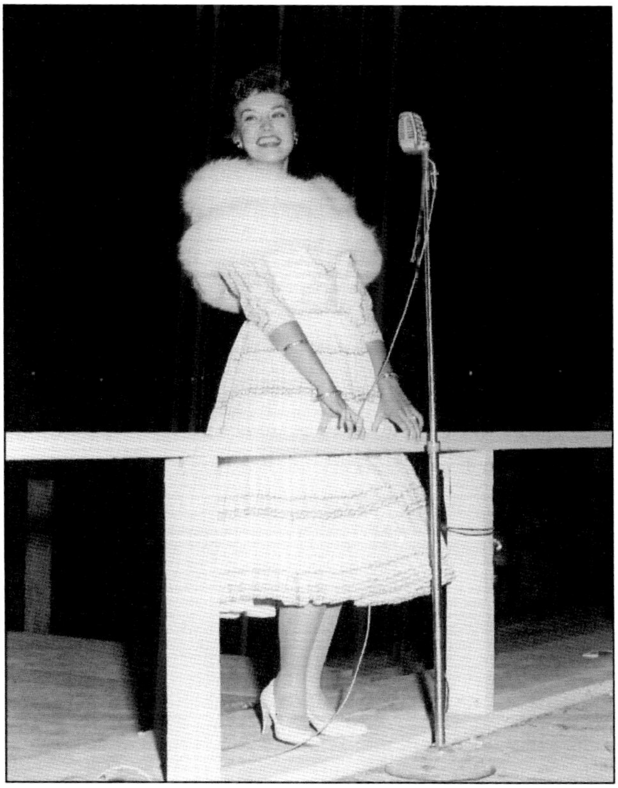

Soda Butte 4-H Club. When Sharon Kay Ritchie visited Weston County in 1956, she visited the county's 4-H clubs and was photographed by George Butler at many of the occasions. Soda Butte Club members are, from left to right, (first row) Mary Dale Mirich, Larry Dowdy, Robert Cranston, Carolyn Mirich, and Gene Cranston (leader); (second row) Jerri Mirich (leader), Tony Dowdy, Melvin Mirich, Roger Mellor, Sharon Kay Ritchie, and Carl Mirich. (Courtesy of Jerri Mirich.)

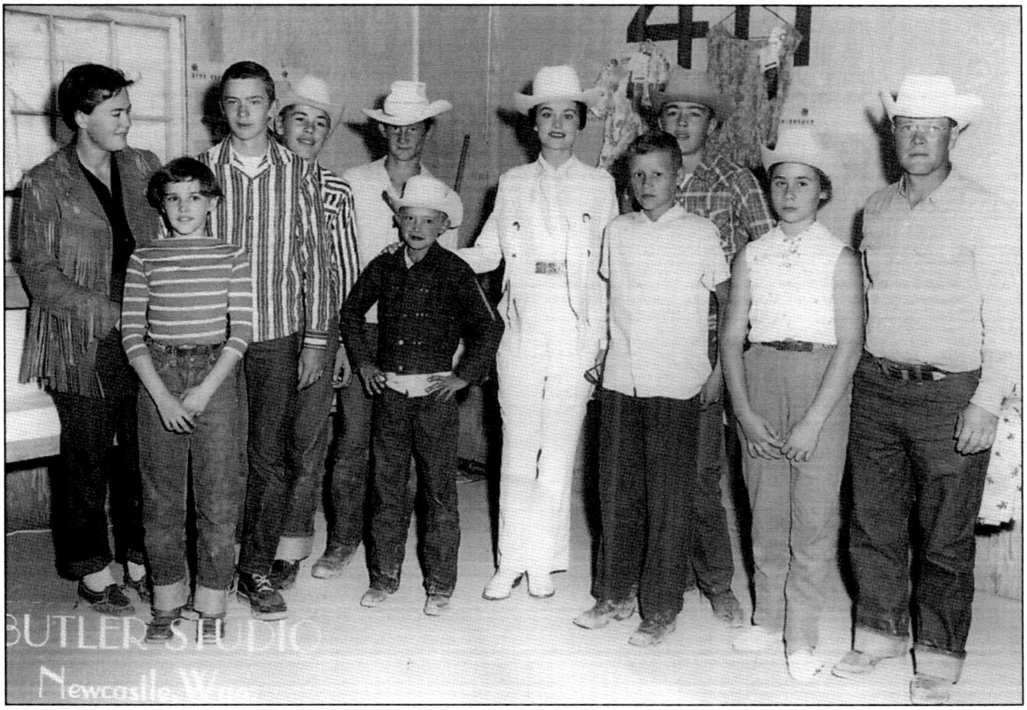

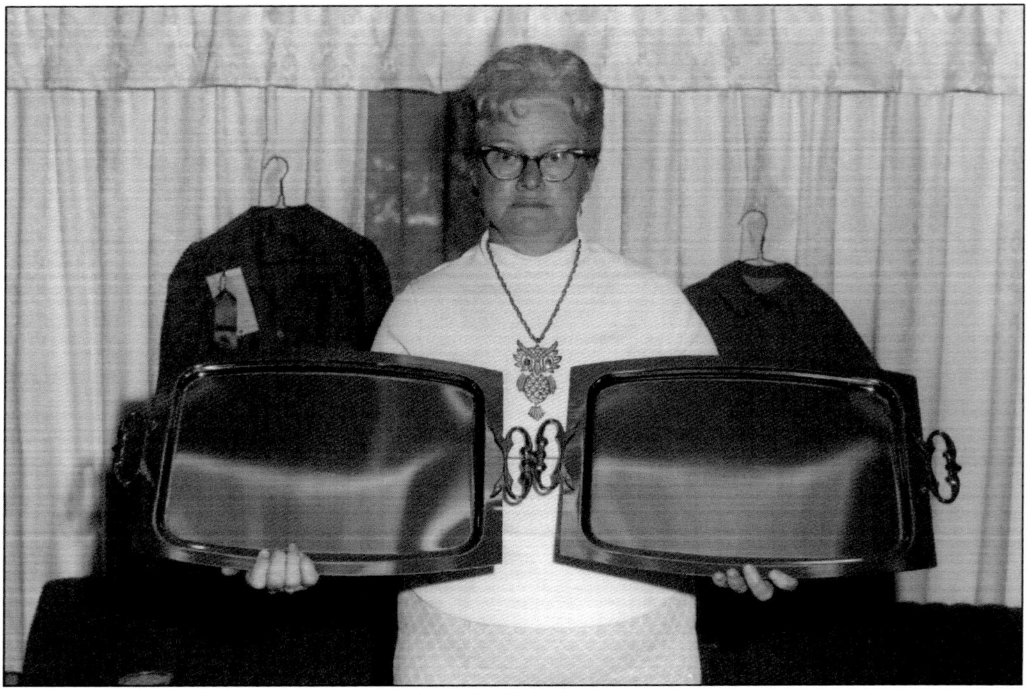

FLORENCE RAINBOLT. One of Weston County's most exuberant fair participants was Florence Rainbolt. Yearly, she prepared needlework, sewing, jams, jellies, and baked goods for the fair. She took top awards locally and at the Wyoming State Fair. She is pictured here with her state fair sweepstakes awards for needlework and culinary exhibits in 1973. (Courtesy of Bill Rainbolt.)

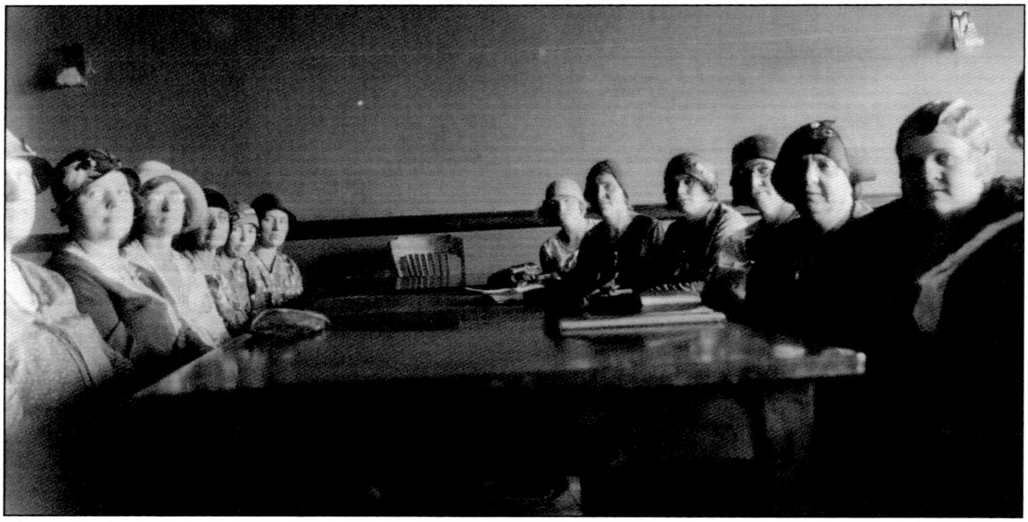

COUNTY COUNCIL OF HOMEMAKERS CLUBS. In 1914, Weston County's first agricultural extension agent was George Holmstead. Extension agents were sent to the counties as a service of the University of Wyoming. Most of Holmstead's work included working with the County Council of Defense for the World War I effort. They brought homemakers education and organized youth clubs. Pictured is the organization meeting of the Weston County Council of Homemakers Clubs. (WCEW.)

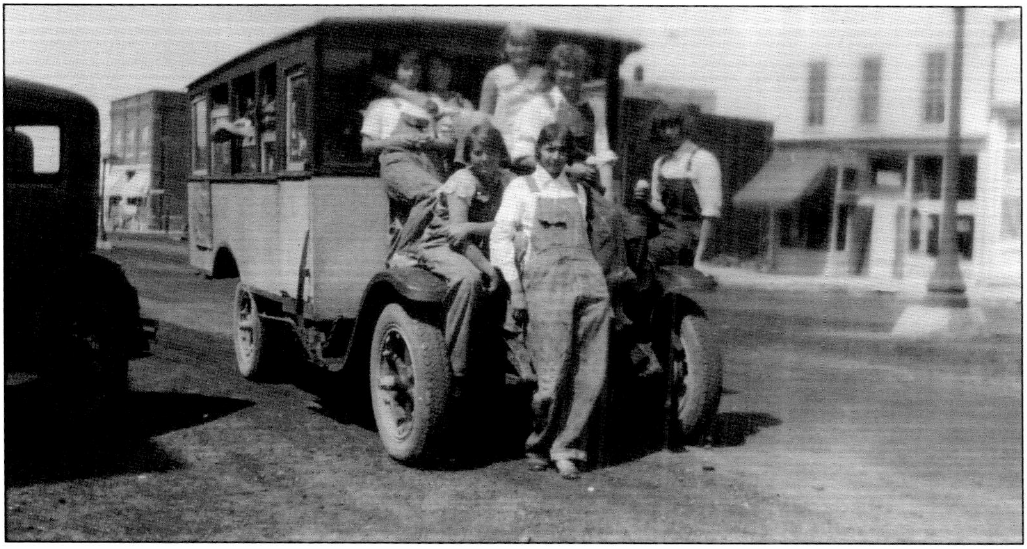

FAIRVIEW MOTHER'S HELPER CLUB. Part of the extension agent's job was to organize and help with youth social activities and club work. The 4-H program provided both a social outlet and a practical educational experience for Weston County's youth. Shown in this photograph is the Fairview Mother's Helpers Food Club leaving to go on a two-day camping trip in 1931. (WCEW.)

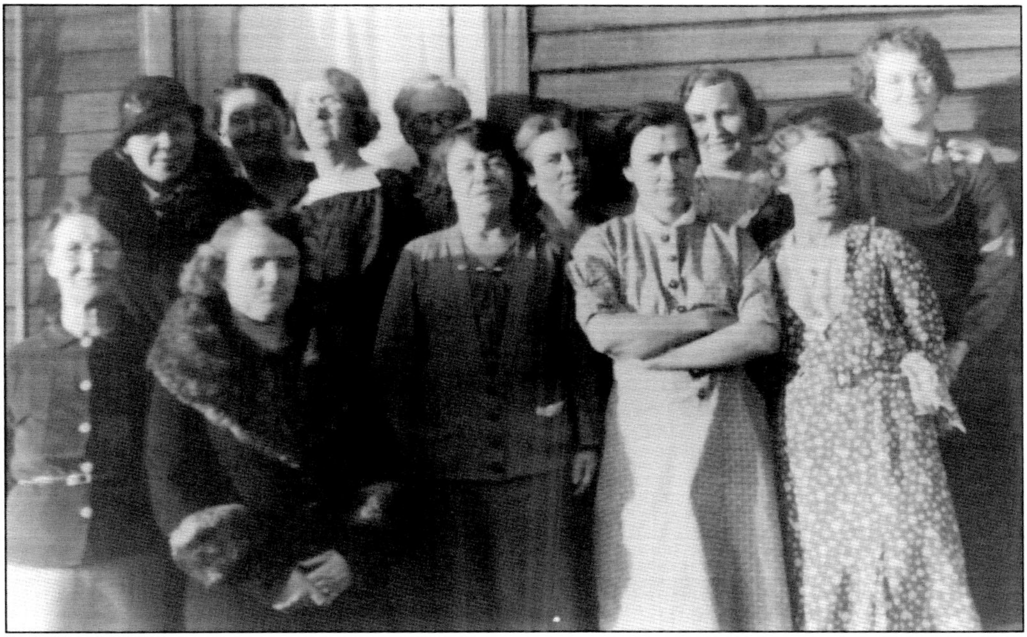

CHEERFUL WORKERS CLUB. The first Cheerful Workers Club was organized in 1931. Their slogan was "Day by day in every way, we are getting better and better." Pictured are the members in 1936. From left to right are (first row) Rachel McLaughlin, Mary Chapman, Willie Eaton, Bernice Thompson, and Vernice Dennis; (second row) Mame Gose, Laura Fulton, Lydia Rinehart, Cora Sheldon, Elinor Buell, Florence Teegarden, and Marion Buell. (WCEW.)

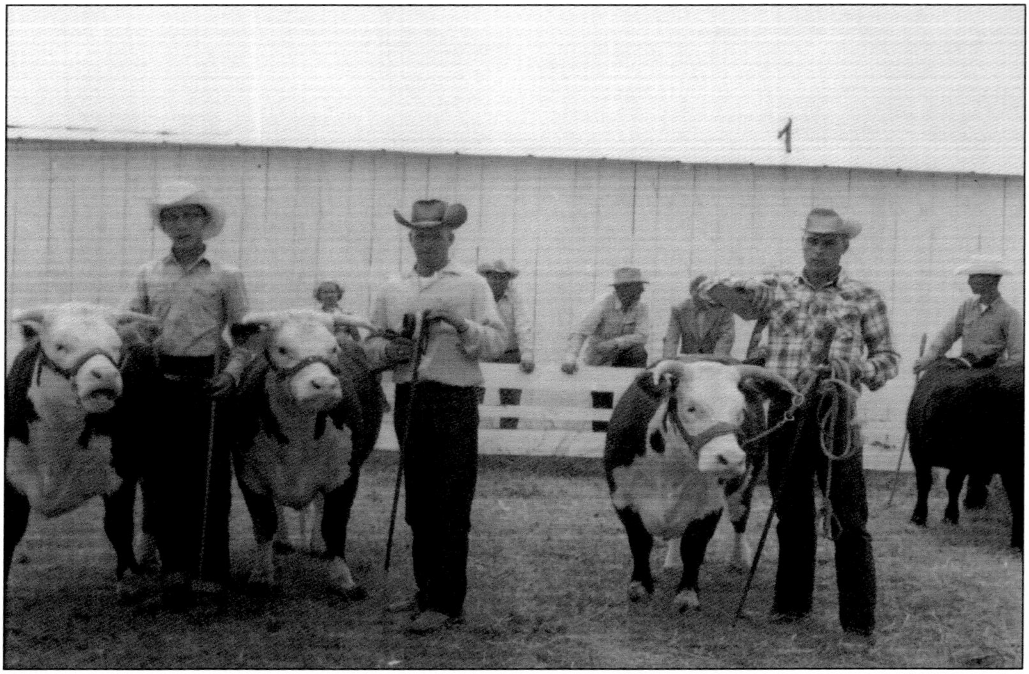

4-H LIVESTOCK SHOW. The first Weston County Fair beef show and auction was held in 1946. In 1948, at 43¢ a pound, 15 calves were sold at the sale. Over the years, the fair livestock sales have provided many youth with money for a first car and a healthy college fund. Pictured is the 1948 beef show at the Weston County Fair. Duane Kudlock from the Prairie 4-H Club won the show. (WCEW.)

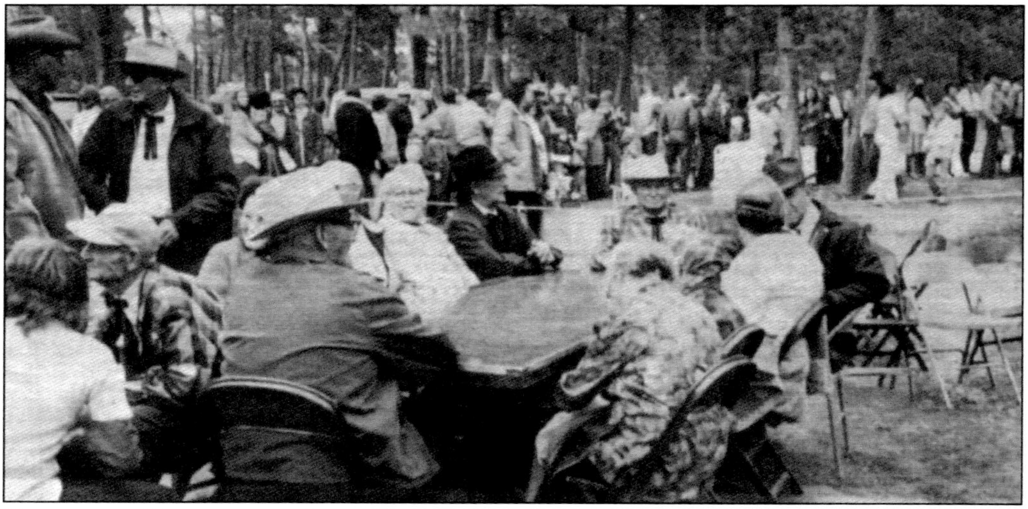

YEAR OF THE HOMESTEADER CELEBRATION, 1973. Each summer since about 1954, Upton has held an annual community celebration that includes a free barbecue, parade, and dance. Upton Fun Days is a big event. A town whose population is about 1,000 people usually serves free barbecue to 2,000 to 3,000 people. In 1973, the annual Fun Days Celebration theme was the Year of the Homesteader. Between 30 and 50 original homesteaders from Weston County were honored. (Courtesy of Red Onion Museum, *Weston County Gazette*, July 26, 1973.)

Nine

A Few Interested Residents

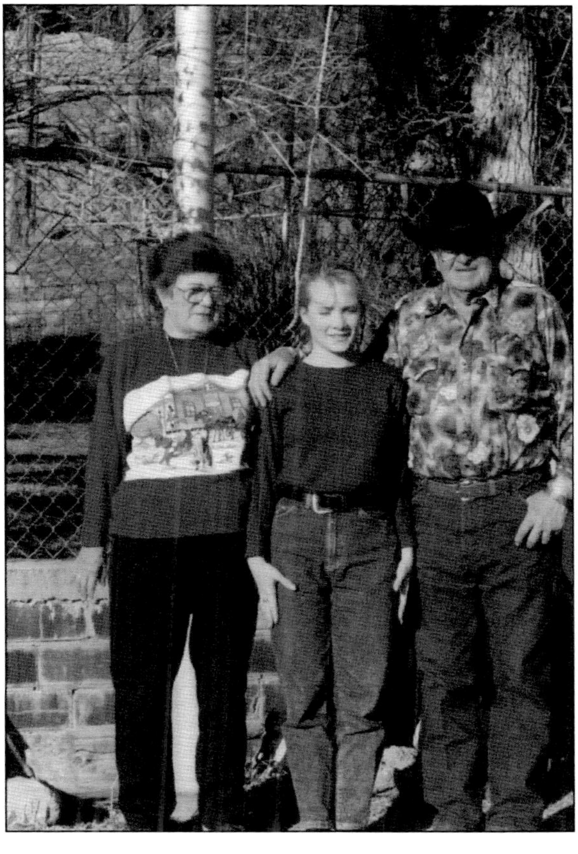

Leo Perino. Leo Perino began his horse sales in the late 1950s in Newcastle. Popular social gatherings for lovers of the old Western way of life, they were reminiscent of old weekend-long horse sales held in early-day Upton. The Perino sale grew into a two-day event that attracted people from several states and foreign countries. It ran consecutively for 52 years. Pictured is Leo; his wife, Vickie; and granddaughter Dana Perino. (Photograph by Matt Perino.)

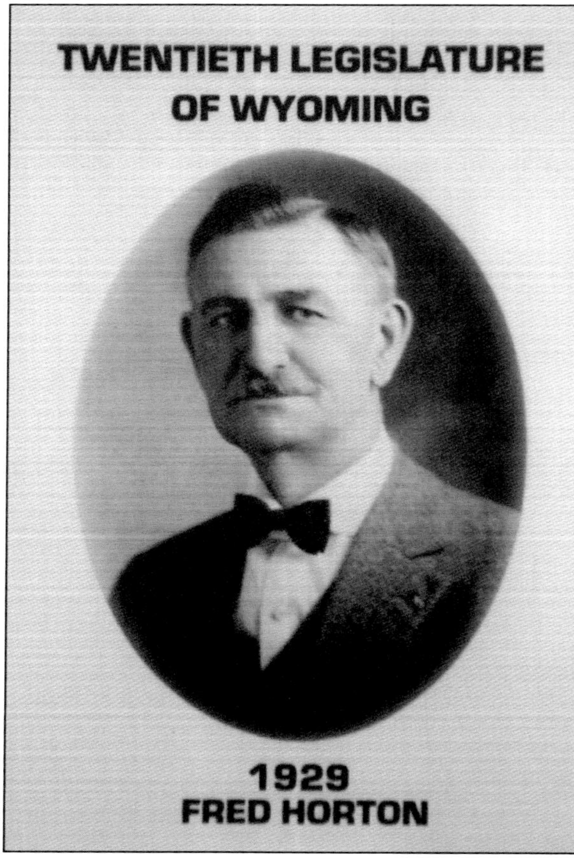

Dr. Fred Horton. In 1899, Dr. Fred Horton stepped off the train in Newcastle just as it was beginning to develop. He became the doctor for the booming towns in Weston County and served for 50 years as the active surgeon for the Burlington Railroad. In order to cover the large territory, trains were ordered to stop for him whenever he might flag them down. (AMM.)

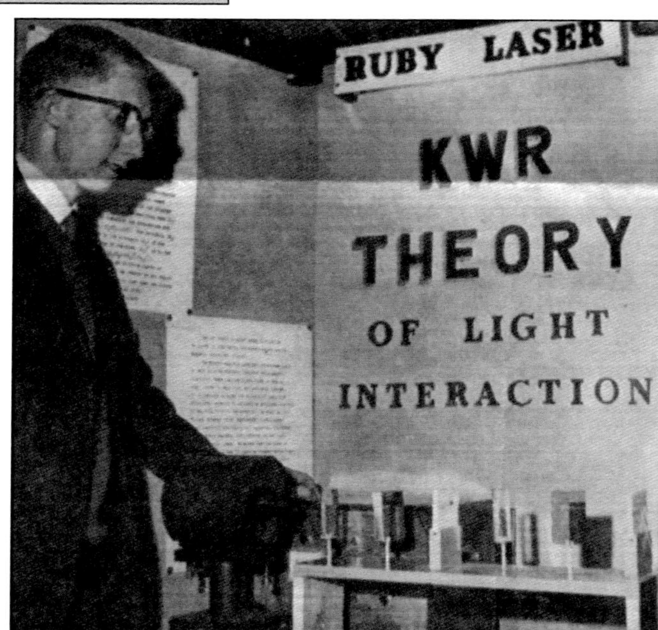

Kenneth Ritthaler. During high school, Kenneth Walter Ritthaler built a ruby laser for a science fair project. He won national attention and the National Science Conference Competition. He used a neon tube for a light source and passed it through a ruby crystal. His theory, called the KWR (his initials) Theory of Light, was used in the development of speed detection radar and laser technology and is taught in schools today. (Courtesy of Shelly Ritthaler.)

MABEL BROWN. Mabel Brown was probably Weston County's first serious historian. Realizing that many of the old-timers' stories were being lost, she collected as many oral histories as she could and published them in a magazine called *Bits and Pieces*. She served as editor, publisher, writer, and story collector. Often, she was the chief financier as well. The publication is considered one of the best regional history sources. (AMM.)

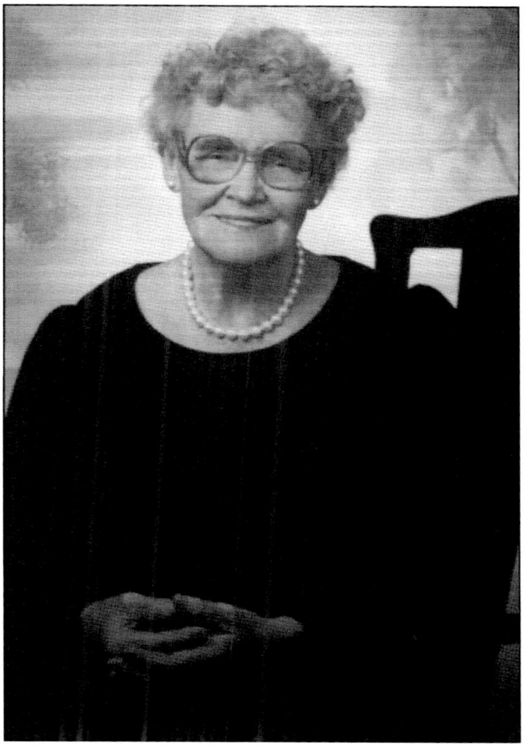

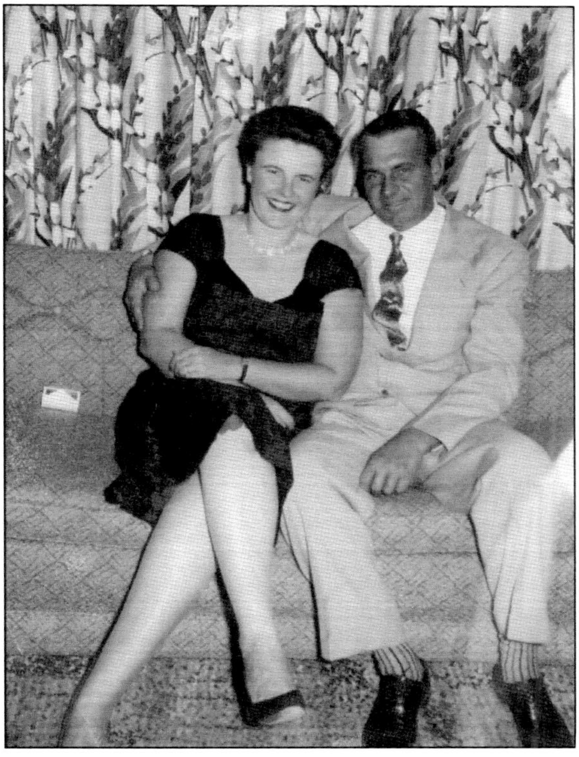

ALICE SCHUETTE. From the time Alice Schuette arrived in Weston County in 1946, she had an interest in Weston County's history. When Curtis Media Corporation approached her to compile a comprehensive history of the county, she enlisted the whole county on the collaborative project. Her work stands as an invaluable history of the county that includes 1,250 family stories. Alice and her husband, Charlie, pose for a picture in 1956. (AS.)

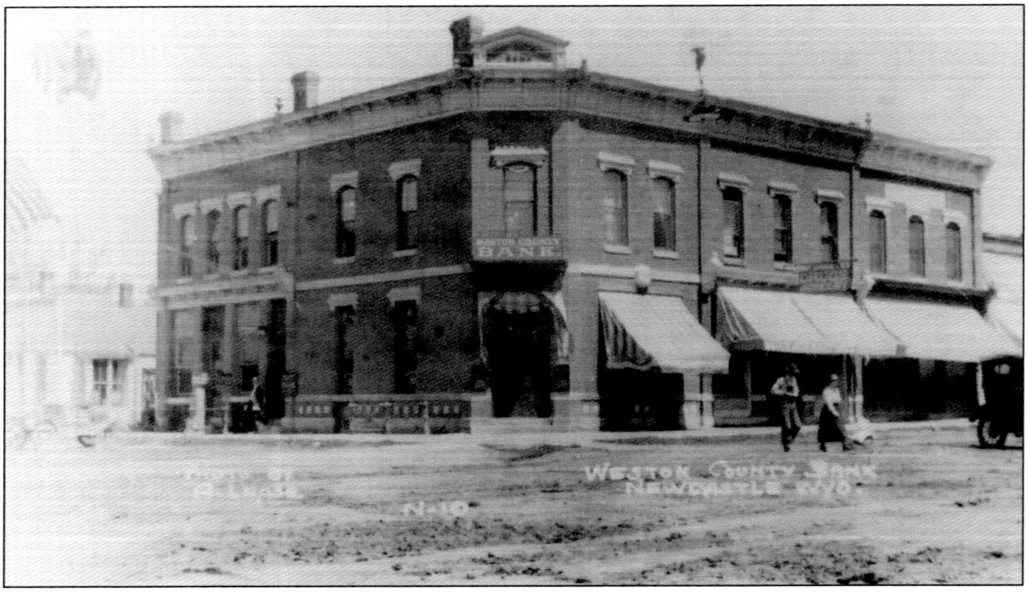

ANDY HANSEN. The First State Bank of Newcastle began serving Northeastern Wyoming in 1924. Andy Hansen started working there in 1926 as a bookkeeper and became bank president in 1967. During the Depression of 1930s, First State Bank was declared sound and was one of the first to qualify for the newly formed Federal Deposit Insurance Corporation depositor's insurance.

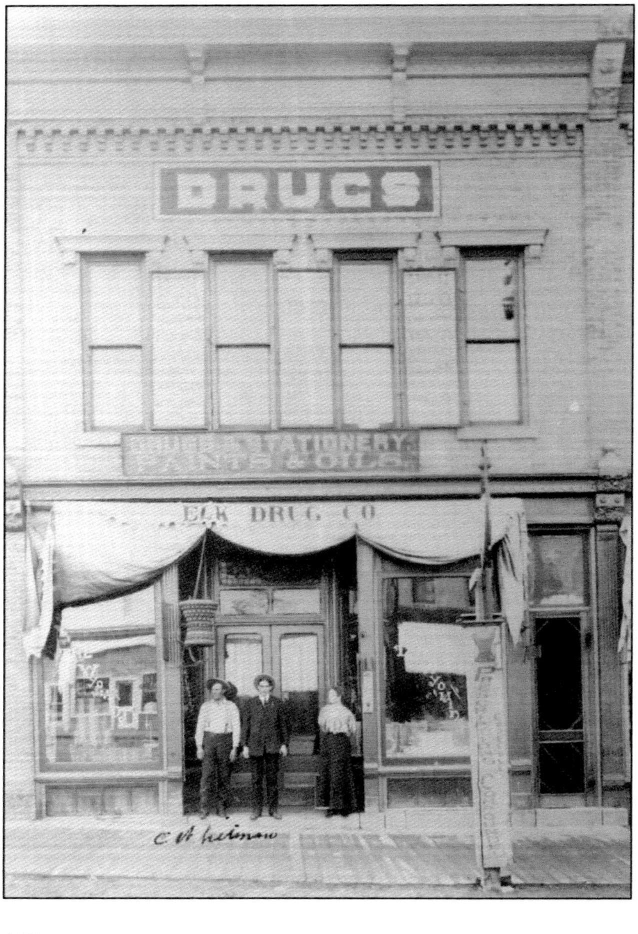

C.C. KIRKPATRICK. In front of the Elk Drugstore in 1907 is C.C. Kirkpatrick in the center with Mrs. Sam Musser, wife of the pharmacist. In 1910, C.C. Kirkpatrick and a group of local investors purchased the store and renamed it Newcastle Drug Company. Kirkpatrick's sons followed in the business with Jim as a pharmacist and Bill as a watchmaker and jeweler. In 1985, the store celebrated 75 years in business.

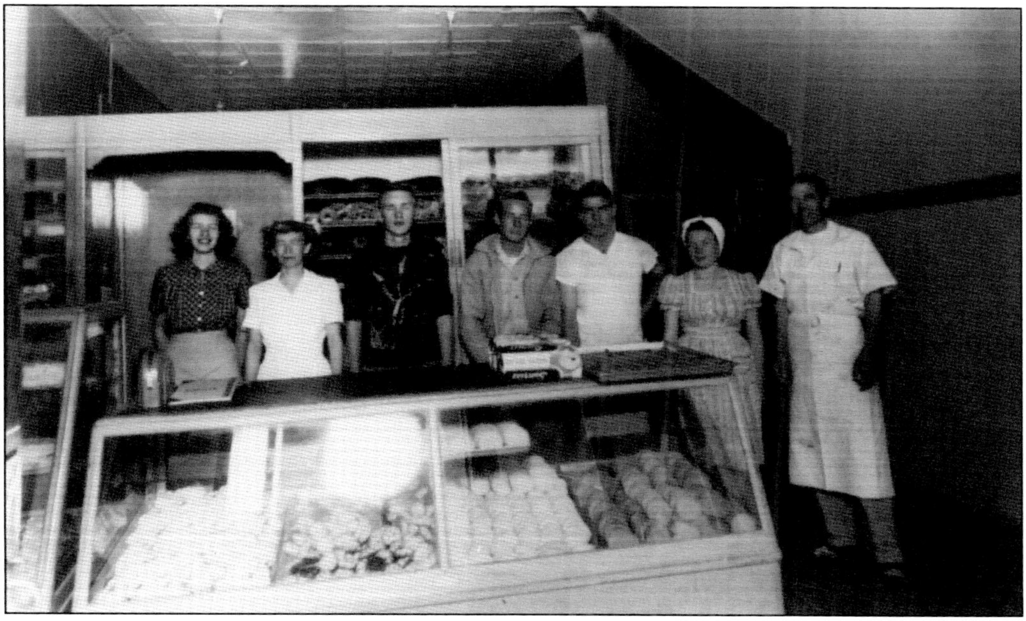

Steve Accola. Steve and Dorothy Accola purchased the Newcastle Bakery in 1948 from Bill and Mildred Fletcher. They operated the store, which was located in the Grieves Building, until they sold to John and Juanita Allen. Pictured are, from left to right, Donna Accola, Dorothy Accola, Myron Mason, "Squeek" Nelson, Jimmy Trenary, Charlotte (Kaiser) Nelson, and Steve Accola.

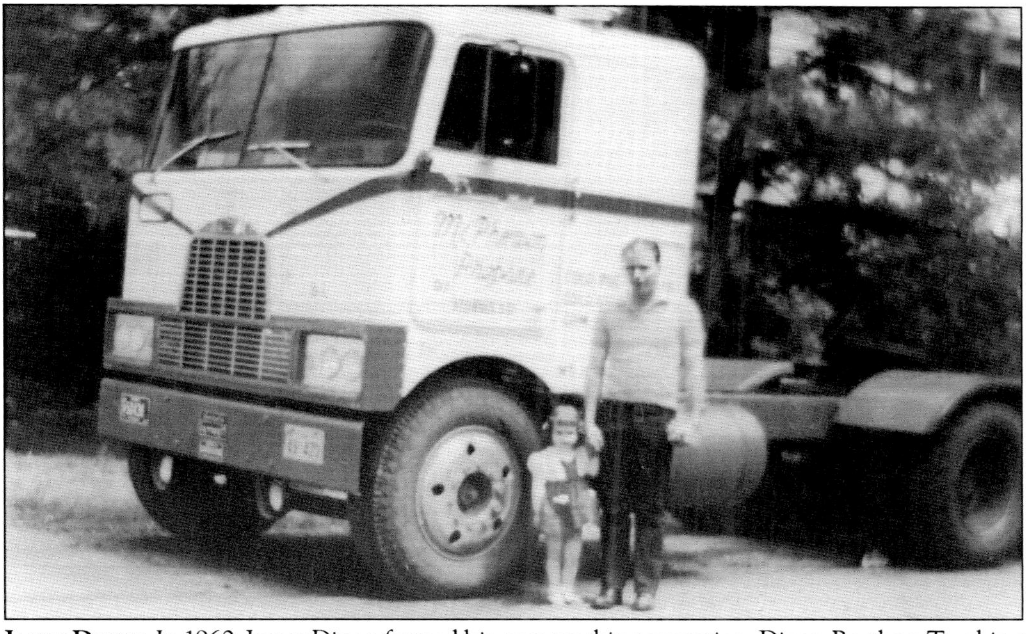

James Dixon. In 1960, James Dixon formed his own trucking operation. Dixon Brothers Trucking started when his brother joined him in the business. The company trucks lumber, steel, chemicals, cement, and petroleum products. It has trucked to all 48 contiguous states, but Weston County is home and headquarters. Jim served as president of the Wyoming Trucking Association. He is pictured with his daughter Sheila and the first truck. (Courtesy of Jim Dixon.)

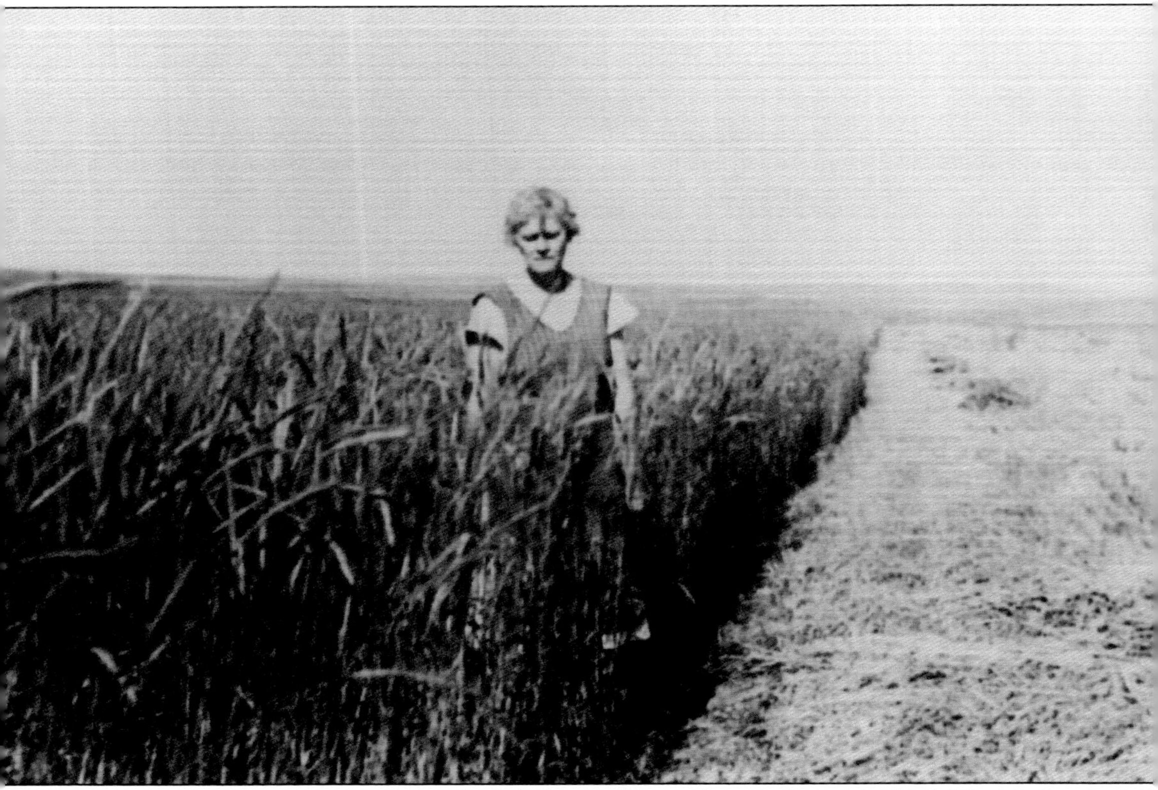

Mattie Middleton. Women washed clothes and hung them to dry in the brisk Weston County wind. Women had faith that they could plant seeds to grow food to sustain their families. Mattie Middleton moved with her family (John Martens) to Wyoming in the fall of 1912. Mattie is shown standing in a grain field about 1936. It was many women like her that built Weston County.

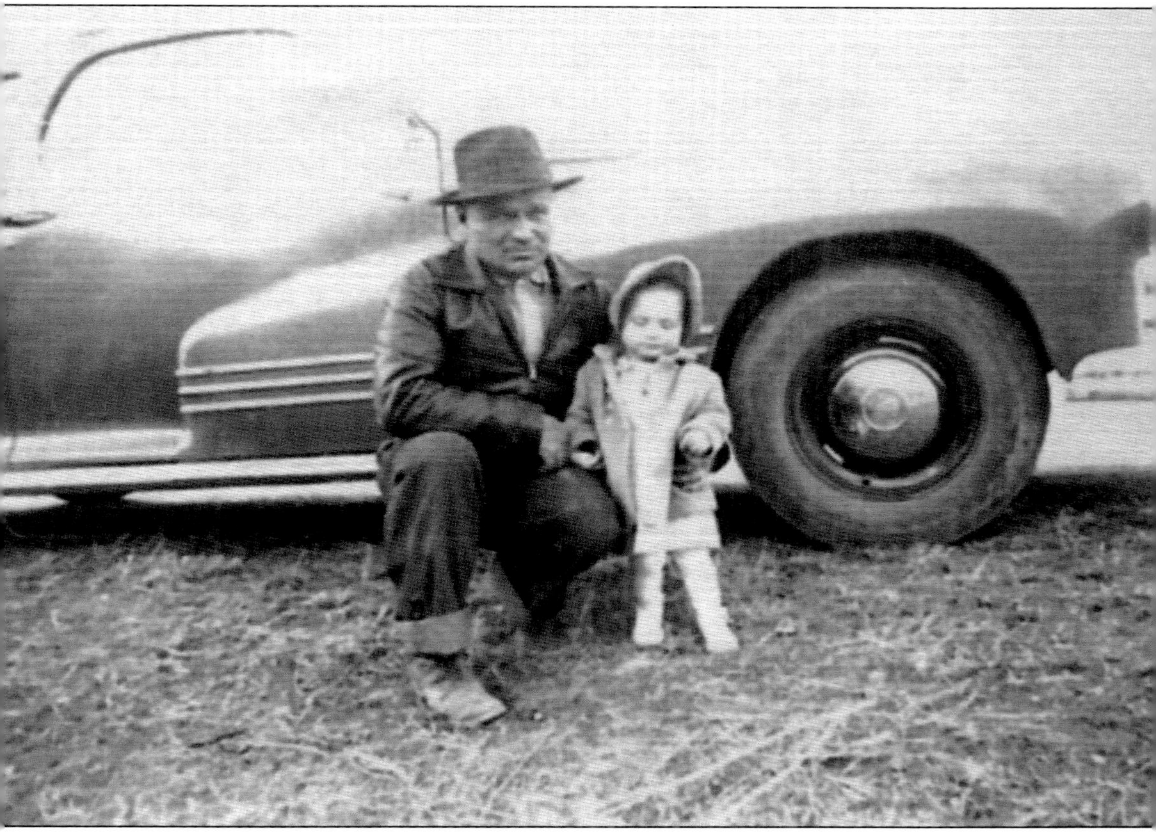

Howard Wheeler. It was men working on ranches, the oil patch, trucks, and refineries who built and made Weston County a place to live and raise families. Howard Wheeler worked in the oil field as a pumper, built houses and schools, and could fix anything. He poses by his 1947 Pontiac sedan with daughter Carol in 1949. A child of the Depression, he believed in hard work. (Courtesy of Shirley Demerrit.)

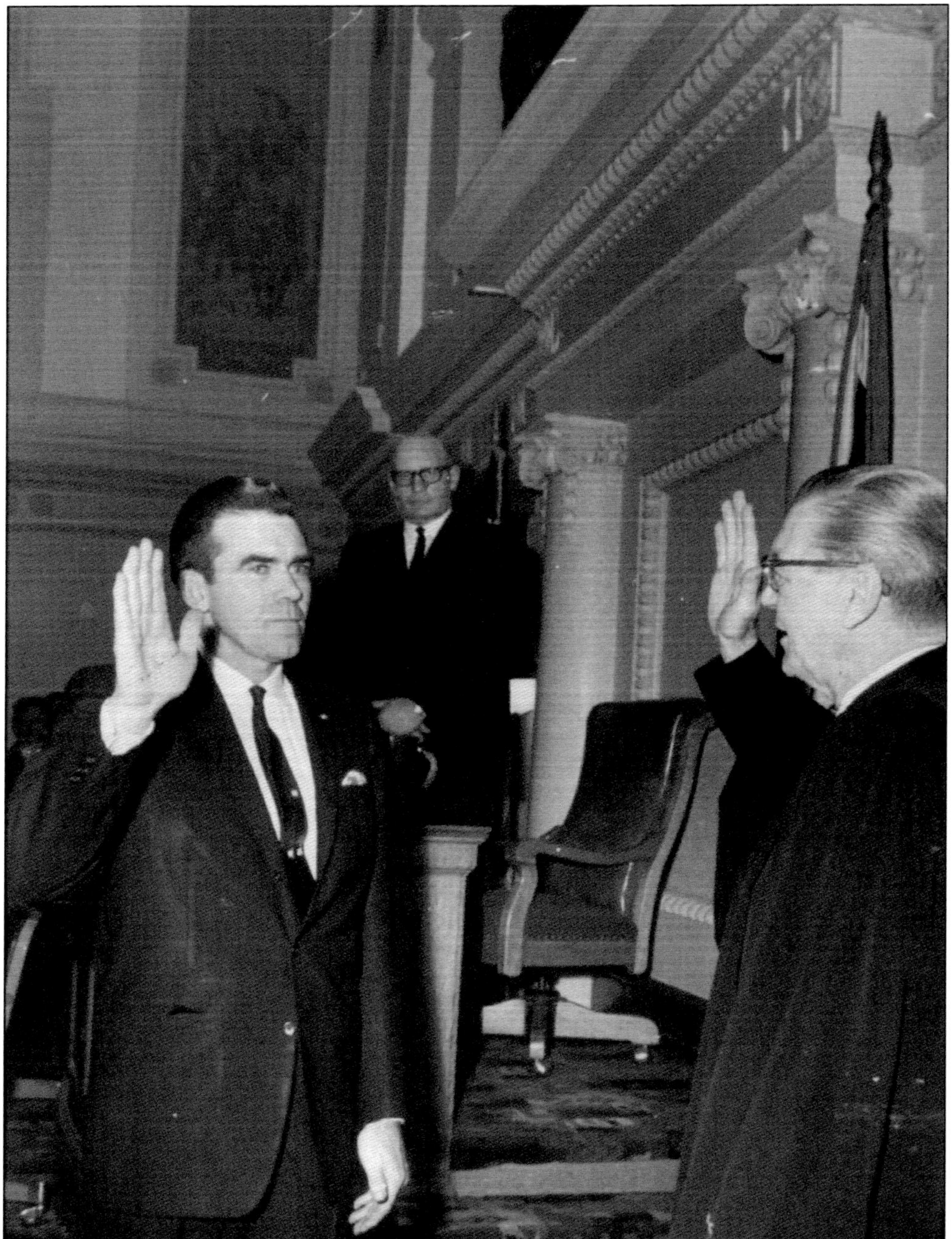

EARL CHRISTENSEN. Earl was born in 1919 in Sheridan, but he grew up and completed his education in Weston County. He graduated from the University of Wyoming in 1941 and has been busy serving Weston County or Wyoming since then. He was on the original REA board that brought electricity to Weston County's rural residents. He was elected to the Wyoming State Senate in 1958, serving as Senate president in 1969. He retired in 1982, ending a long and distinguished career of public service to Weston County and Wyoming. This picture shows him being sworn in as the Wyoming State Senate president. (EMC.)

INDEX